Medieval Iceland

Medieval Iceland

Society, Sagas, and Power

Jesse L. Byock

UNIVERSITY OF CALIFORNIA PRESS

Berkeley • Los Angeles • London

University of California Press
Berkeley and Los Angeles, California

University of California Press, Ltd.
London, England

Library of Congress Cataloging-in-Publication Data

Byock, Jesse L.
  Medieval Iceland.

  Bibliography: p.
  Includes index.
    1. Iceland—History—To 1262.   2. Sagas—History and criticism.
3. Ethnology—Iceland.   4. Iceland—Social conditions.   I. Title
DL352.B96   1988   949.1'2   87-38078

ISBN 978-0-520-06954-1 (alk. paper)

Printed in the United States of America

08

12   11   10   9   8   7

The paper used in this publication meets the minimum requirements
of ANSI / NISO Z39.48-1992 (R 1997) (*Permanence of Paper*). ∞

Cele and Lester Byock,
my parents, who first taught me to love history

In 1956 Jón Jóhannesson published a work on Iceland's
early history in which he . . . mentioned almost none of
the events recounted in the *Íslendinga sögur* [family sagas],
just as if they had never taken place. Yet, Jón Jóhannesson
was far from being extreme in his views. Shortly after his
History appeared, I asked him whether he believed that the
sagas were pure fiction. "No, not at all," he answered, "I
just don't know what to do with them." —And this is still
the situation today.

—Jónas Kristjánsson (1986)

Contents

Maps

Acknowledgments

This book touches many aspects of culture and society, and I deeply appreciate the assistance of those colleagues who have given freely of their expertise in a variety of specialized areas. I am thankful for the comments of Gunnar Karlsson, Helgi Thorláksson, Jakob Benediktsson, Peter Foote, Margaret Clunies Ross, Wendell Oswalt, Shaun Hughes, Andrew Dennis, Darryl Wieland, Per Sveaas Andersen, Daphne Davidson, Robert Benson, Björn Ellertsson, and Franz Bäuml, all of whom have been generous with their time. A Fulbright research fellowship and grants from the Academic Senate of the University of California, Los Angeles, enabled me to spend a significant amount of time in Iceland working with colleagues from the Árni Magnússon Manuscript Institute (Stofnun Árna Magnússonar) and from other departments of the University of Iceland. Thanks also to Magnús Stefánsson whose pioneering work on Staðir has been of great assistance.

Both my manuscript and I have benefited from the contagious lucidity of my editor and dear friend, Grace H. Stimson. I have learned much from our many enjoyable discussions about the art of writing. I also wish to thank my research assistants Jeffrey Mazo, a young scholar who shows unusual promise in the field, and Rebecca Ziegler, who is embarking on a career in library science. My acknowledgments would be incomplete without mentioning two old friends, Robert Guillemette, who used some of his many talents to draw the maps and Lori Gudmundson who helped. Tim Seymour prepared the maps for final publication.

All translations are my own except where noted. When it seemed appropriate I have translated the names of persons and places. Although I have not been entirely consistent, I hope that the information added will make the book easier for the nonspecialist to read.

Spelling and Pronunciation

A note for nonreaders of Old Icelandic: The letter þ ("thorn," upper case Þ) is pronounced like the *th* in thought; ð ("eth," upper case Ð) is pronounced like the *th* in breathe. For the convenience of readers unfamiliar with these characters, I have replaced þ by *th* in Old Icelandic technical terms and in proper names. I have retained the þ only in extensive quoted passages and in the bibliographic matter. My purpose is not to strive for pedantic consistency but to make both the book and the references more accessible. For similar reasons I have conformed to modern Icelandic practice in using the vowel æ for both Old Icelandic æ and œ, and ö for Old Icelandic ǫ.

Commonly Used Geographical Terms

á (pl. *ár*) = river
dalr = dale
ey (pl. gen. *eyja*) = island
eyrr (pl. *eyrar*) = gravelly riverbank or small tongue of land running into the sea
fell = hill
fjörðr (pl. *firðir*) = fjord
holt = a wood or a rough stony hill or ridge
hóll (pl. *hólar*) = a hill or a stone heap
jökull = glacier
nes = headland
tunga = tongue of land at the confluence of two rivers
vatn = lake
völlr (pl. *vellir*) = plain

Map 1. The North Atlantic world of the medieval Icelanders

1

Introduction

Wise men report that from Stad in Norway it is a voyage
of seven days west to Horn in eastern Iceland, and from
Snæfellsnes [in western Iceland] it is four days' sail west
to Greenland at the point where the sea is narrowest. It
is said that if one sails due west from Bergen to Cape Fare-
well in Greenland, one passes a half day's sail to the south
of Iceland. From Reykjanes in southern Iceland it is five
days south to Slyne Head in Ireland, and from Langanes
in northern Iceland it is four days northward to Svalbard
in the Arctic Sea.

—*The Book of Settlements*

Years ago the legal historian James Bryce wrote that medieval Iceland "is an almost unique instance of a community
whose culture and creative power flourished independently
of any favouring material conditions, and indeed under conditions in the highest degree unfavourable. Nor ought it to
be less interesting to the student of politics and laws as having produced a Constitution unlike any other whereof
records remain, and a body of law so elaborate and complex
that it is hard to believe that it existed among men whose
chief occupation was to kill one another."[1] Since Bryce's day
the study of Iceland has flourished and many writers have
explored different facets of the island's medieval culture. But
the essential contradictions that Bryce noted remain unre-

1. James Bryce, *Studies in History and Jurisprudence*, 2 vols. (1901; Freeport, N.Y.: Books for Libraries Press, 1968), 1:263.

solved. This book addresses these contradictions by examining the underlying structures and cultural codes that bound the different parts of Iceland's unusual society into a cohesive polity. It explores how Iceland's social order came into being and how it functioned.

The Norsemen who first settled Iceland in the late ninth century did not come as part of a planned national migration, a political movement, or an organized conquest. Called *landnámsmenn* (landtakers) by later generations, they were men and women who were asserting their self-interest. Shortly after the discovery of Iceland around 850 by Scandinavian seamen, reports of large tracts of free land on the island circulated throughout the Norse/viking cultural area, stretching from Norway to Ireland. The *landnámsmenn* (a term that includes women) seized the opportunity to bring their families 600 miles across the North Atlantic to the newly discovered land. In the sixty or so years of the *landnám* (literally the landtaking, ca. 870-930) at least 10,000 people, and perhaps as many as 20,000, emigrated to Iceland in small ships loaded with goods, implements, and domestic animals. The land they took was uncultivated and, except for a few Irish monks who quickly disappeared, uninhabited. The task facing the newcomers was to create a society on an empty island with a limited habitable area.

The settlement of Iceland was capitalized in part by viking depredations in Europe. These raids, which began in the late eighth century, brought plunder to Scandinavia and stimulated shipbuilding and trade. They made possible the convergence of the experience and technology necessary for a large transmarine colonization. In the years following Iceland's settlement, however, the descendants of the *landnámsmenn* saw their capital diminish in a remote place with a fragile subarctic ecology. Iceland, they found, allowed only limited agriculture. It also lacked the woodlands necessary to build and maintain oceangoing vessels, a factor that restricted the inhabitants' ability to exploit the almost inexhaustible fish stocks and sea mammal resources in the surrounding ocean. Inevitably the new society's development was dictated by competition among succeeding generations for the land's limited resources.

On the edge of the habitable world, and separated from their homelands by a dangerous ocean, the ninth- and tenth-century immigrants established a social order different from those they had left behind. Beyond the consensus that it was wise to be on friendly terms with the Norwegian king—most of the settlers came from southwest Norway—Iceland for centuries had no foreign policy, no defensive land or sea force, and no levy or regional military structures. Iceland was never invaded, nor was it a base for attacks against other countries.[2] The kings of Norway, Iceland's major potential enemy, were for centuries too weak or too absorbed in their own civil wars and domestic problems to play more than a sporadic role in Icelandic affairs. Until Norwegian royal power became formidable in the mid-thirteenth century, foreign monarchs and churchmen rarely had direct influence on events in Iceland. Politically, the island became an inward-looking country that was in contact with, but was largely independent of, the rest of Europe.

From the end of the settlement period in the 930s, Icelandic society operated without religious or political figures powerful enough to gain widespread authority. In the absence of national or regional leaders who might foster dissension with other countries over trade, wealth, dynastic claims, conquest, or territorial dominance, Iceland developed in response to its own circumscribed needs. The society that emerged was based on a system of decentralized self-government. This system regulated dispute and fostered a political stability that lasted from soon after the end of the settlement until the thirteenth century. The settlers began

2. The sagas do refer to many adventurous individuals who went abroad and joined viking or mercenary bands. *Hungrvaka*, a pious account of Iceland's first five bishops, says that during the episcopate of Iceland's first bishop, Ísleifr Gizurarson (1056-1080), some Icelanders became vikings: ". . . some men set out from Iceland on viking raids and harrying [*í víking ok á herskap*]." See *Byskupa sögur*, ed. Guðni Jónsson, vol. 1 ([Akureyri]: Íslendingasagnaútgáfan, 1953), ch. 2, p. 4.

by establishing local things, or assemblies, which had been the major forum for meetings of freemen in the Old Scandinavian (and Germanic) social order. The tenth-century Icelanders, by extending the mandate of such assemblies, transformed them into a self-contained governmental system without overlords. At its core was the Althing, a national assembly of freemen, established around 930.

The settlers in the tenth century developed economic and legal processes that institutionalized barter, the public brokerage of power, and the conduct of feud, all of which hindered the emergence of overlordship. These developments gave an individual free farmer (*bóndi*, pl. *bændr*) more self-determination than he would have had in a society dominated by lords. For several centuries the island enjoyed stability free of the type of dissension that was found among petty states in their Norse homelands, or other geographical units controlled by kings or by regional rulers. During this time, however, the population engaged in almost continuous petty feuding which, until the very end of the Free State, never reached the level of open warfare. Repeatedly, conflicts were contained by means of a legalistic system for regulating disputes. Although this system, with its intricate court procedure and its emphasis on resolution by compromise, did not always work smoothly, it did provide manageable solutions in disruptive situations.

Iceland's innovative social order may be attributed to the conditions of the settlement. The absence of an indigenous population on so large an island permitted the colonists to settle at any location of their choosing. As they did not need to cluster in communities in response to hostile threats, they enjoyed extraordinary freedom to adapt selectively to their new environment. In this frontier setting they established scattered settlements in accordance with the availability of resources. Individual farmsteads became largely self-sufficient economic units, and, partly as a consequence of this settlement pattern, feuds thrived. The immigrants became participants in a headless or stateless society, a type of social organization which anthropologists have identified in different parts of the world. The essential ingredient in such societies is the absence of institutionalized hierarchical structures associated with the centralizing political and economic functions of a state. Early Iceland fits loosely into this category since its leaders wielded little executive power and did not rule territorial units. Iceland did, however, have elements of statehood: a national legislature and a well-defined legal system that embraced the entire country.

Early Iceland is occasionally described as primitive, and it did have some features in common with so-called primitive societies. Among these are the role of feud, which served as a means of settling disputes, and the absence of cities or concentrated communities. Nevertheless, the term "primitive" is an unsatisfactory way to describe early Iceland, as its connotations are not easily reconciled with Iceland's situation as the major northern offshoot of Viking Age Scandinavia. Scandinavian culture was sufficiently sophisticated to allow its members routinely to cross the North Atlantic, set up trading towns in Ireland, establish the Danelaw and then conquer England, found the Norman state, rise to prominence in Old Russia, and trade with the Caliphate of Baghdad and the Byzantine Empire.

Some chieftains and farmers in Iceland were richer or more powerful than others. Dependent on these landowners were cotters, landless free laborers, and slaves. Chieftains (*goðar*, sing. *goði*) competed for status and for *thingmenn*, followers drawn from among the *bændr*.[3] *Goðar* were often recruited to participate in feuds among farmers or other chieftains. At times being called upon to advocate the position of others or to arbitrate solutions could be dangerous, for the

---

3. Hereafter the English term "chieftain" and the Icelandic term *goði* (pl. *goðar*) are used interchangeably. The terms "freeman" and "farmer" are used interchangeably with the Icelandic term for farmer, *bóndi* (pl. *bændr*). The terms 'thingman' and Icelandic *thingmaðr* (pl. *thingmenn*) are used similarly. In doing so I am following Icelandic usage, which rarely makes a distinction between thingman and farmer, although *thingmaðr* has a more specific meaning than *bóndi*. It denotes the relationship in which a freeman was required by law to be a follower of a *goði*, that is, to be "in thing." These relationships are discussed in more detail as the book progresses.

person intervening might even be killed. The *goðar* derived their official authority from owning all or part of a chieftaincy (*goðorð*, sing. and pl.). They regularly held feasts, made loans, presented gifts, and extended hospitality to farmers and to other chieftains. Through these activities and through their participation in feuds, the *goðar* were actively engaged in the transfer of wealth, including land.

It is difficult to determine the precise extent of ranking in medieval Iceland, for many free farmers, like chieftains, were prosperous landowners who were often called upon to act as advocates and arbitrators. Having emigrated from more hierarchical societies, the *landnámsmenn* brought with them elements of stratification which, from the start, were potentially destabilizing. That a chieftain might gain widespread territorial control and thus centralize political and governmental power in a region was always a threat. This hazard, however, was avoided until the late twelfth century and, in some regions, the early thirteenth by a system of checks and balances aimed at limiting the power of individual chieftains. These mechanisms are examined in this book. We see that farmers openly granted authority to chieftains, and that during much of Iceland's early history dissatisfied farmers could retract authority from one leader and give it to another. For the chieftains, permanent coercive power remained unobtainable until the very end of the Free State.

From the tenth into the twelfth century, social differentiation in Iceland was relatively fluid, with few rigid barriers. Aggressive farmers could become chieftains, and the degree of ranking throughout the society was limited by convention, law, and economics. In the late twelfth and early thirteenth centuries, however, the situation began to change, and one can perceive a movement toward incipient statehood. Yet even in this late period, stratification in Iceland did not approach the degree of differential ranking or limit the access to strategic resources as it did in other Norse societies, where kings, jarls, and regional military leaders wielded executive authority.

When comparing early Iceland with other societies, one

must keep in mind certain essential factors. Medieval Iceland was not a tribal society, nor was the authority of its leaders based on ownership or rule of defined territorial units. What, then, was Iceland? Briefly, it was a society whose development was determined by the dynamics of its immigrant experience. From this experience there emerged an innovative social order marked by aspects of statelessness as well as elements of incipient statehood. Features of both ranked and stratified societies were present.

Cultural focus, a long-established anthropological concept, is the tendency of every culture to exhibit more complexity and wider scope in some of its aspects and institutions than in others.[4] When a society focuses on a particular dimension of culture, that dimension is more likely to develop in new ways and to generate new ideas because more activity and closer scrutiny are directed to it than to other aspects. In Iceland the cultural focus was on law, which became the catalyst in the organization of extrafamilial life and served as an element of continuity throughout Iceland's medieval history.

The social order that evolved in Iceland avoided the establishment of official hierarchies without going so far as to create egalitarianism. Consensus played a prominent role in decision making. Iceland's governmental features evolved from issues that specifically concerned the political and legal rights of free farmers. A freeman's place in Iceland was defined not by hierarchical ranking but rather by alliances with individual chieftains. The relationship between a *goði* and his followers was set by law. Law in medieval Iceland touched virtually all aspects of social intercourse. It was implemented by a process I define as advocacy, a core dynamic in the society.

Concentrating on the society's cultural focus, this book explores the course of legal and political decision making,

---

4. For the classic formulation of cultural focus see Melville J. Herskovits, *Man and His Works: The Science of Cultural Anthropology*, 12th ptg. (New York: Alfred A. Knopf, 1970), pp. 542-560.

especially from the tenth through the twelfth century, the formative period of the Old Icelandic Free State. Founded with the establishment of the Althing, the Free State lasted until 1262-1264 when, after more than 300 years of independence, the Icelanders agreed to pay tribute to the Norwegian Crown. It was internal disorders that brought about the end of the Free State. The turmoil, especially from 1230 to 1260, was caused by the unprecedented accumulation of power and wealth in the hands of a small number of chieftains. The troubles were exacerbated, especially after 1240, by the consistent intervention in Iceland of the newly strengthened Norwegian Crown with the support of the Norwegian archbishop.

For most of the more than 300 years of independence prior to the Norwegian takeover, however, Icelandic society functioned effectively, based on the dynamics of the relationship between *goðar* and *bændr*. By examining the socioeconomic system that regulated the flow of wealth and the use of power, I seek to integrate historical information with inferences about the functioning society and its chieftains. These inferences can be drawn from the economic and legal patterns discernible in the family and the early Sturlunga sagas.[5] This study, then, complements literary analyses of the sagas and augments them with what we know or can learn about medieval Icelandic society. The sagas, the most comprehensive extant portrayal of a Western medieval society, had both a literary and a sociological function, but this dual nature has not been sufficiently examined.

Historians, even those interested in social history, have tended to avoid using the family sagas. These vernacular prose narratives about the tenth and early eleventh centuries are relatively late sources, the first of them having been writ-

---

5. The current standard editions of the family sagas are found in *Íslenzk fornrit*, vols. 2-14 (Reykjavik: Hið íslenzka fornritafélag, 1933-1968). The standard edition of the Sturlung compilation is *Sturlunga saga*, ed. Jón Jóhannesson, Magnús Finnbogason, and Kristján Eldjárn, 2 vols. (Reykjavik: Sturlunguútgáfan, 1946). In this book I refer to each saga by *ÍF* or *Sturl.* volume and chapter.

ten down, as far as can be determined, at the end of the twelfth century, though most of them date from the thirteenth century. At times the storytellers invented characters and occurrences. When Icelanders are portrayed traveling abroad, as in the instance of the warrior Egill Skallagrímsson, the stories have an air of fantasy, but when the action is set in Iceland, even the supernatural episodes are usually placed in a formal social setting. Saga stories reveal the normative codes of the society and indicate to the reader basic rules of conduct.

The family sagas are an anomalous medieval European literature. They are not folktales, epics, romances, or chronicles, but mostly realistic stories about everyday issues confronting Icelandic farmers and their chieftains. The tales center on disputes and feuds over insults, land, chieftaincies, seductions, inheritance, bodily injuries, missing livestock, claims to chattels, love, accusations of witchcraft, hauntings, beached whales, scurrilous or erotic verses, cheating and stealing, harboring of outlaws, and struggles for local status. The stories are multifaceted; we find virtue and deceit as well as the banality and humor of everyday life. Often we see a chilling picture of the hardships resulting from limited resources. The literature describes in detail the machinations of those aspiring to power and the responses of their weaker prey, who were often unable to undertake lawsuits in their own defense or to protect their lands from encroachment.

The family and Sturlunga sagas are the product of an insular rural society that from the tenth to the thirteenth century showed continuity in its cultural focus on law. They mostly portray events surrounding crises occurring within the context of local affairs. The social patterns embedded in these texts display the complementary nature of wealth acquisition and power politics in the medieval community. Like so many features of Icelandic culture, honor also is tied to competition, particularly competition at law. Loss of honor was a public matter signaling that the individual was capable of defending neither himself nor his property.

The issue of the sagas as sources is later treated in detail (chapter 3), but here it is sufficient to point out that continued adherence to the older view, stressing the literary value of the family sagas and playing down their relevance as social documents, is self-defeating. History is more than the compilation of facts, and the sagas are far from fantasy. The medieval Icelanders wrote the sagas about themselves and for themselves, thus opening an extraordinary window through which we can observe the operation of a medieval society. By considering saga literature in conjunction with medieval Icelanders' histories and laws, we enhance our understanding of social processes and finally abandon arguments about the historicity of specific events. We learn how chieftains and their thingmen functioned in their communities and maintained power and status within a decentralized society. We come a step closer to perceiving the essence of medieval Iceland.

The issues illustrated in the family and Sturlunga sagas arise naturally from the concerns that confronted medieval Icelanders. Although Iceland is a fifth larger than Ireland it cannot support a large population. Most of the interior is uninhabitable because of its distance from the surrounding ocean, warmed by a northern branch of the Gulf Stream, and almost all the settlers lived in the coastal regions, where fish, seals, stranded whales, and abundant bird life and eggs augmented the food produced by sheep and cattle raising. There were no dangerous predatory animals; the arctic fox was probably the only land mammal in Iceland when the settlers arrived. From the beginning, the Icelanders lived on often isolated farmsteads surrounded by the hayfields and pastures necessary to maintain their herds;[6] they were a pastoral society based on fixed farmsteads.

Chieftains were essential to the functioning of the Icelandic Free State. To all appearances they peacefully assumed leadership, with the consent of the free farmers, in the early tenth century. A chieftaincy was treated as a private possession that normally passed to a family member, though not

6. This settlement pattern continued until the nineteenth century.

necessarily a first son. In some instances family possession of a *goðorð* became so strong a tradition that the chieftaincy was named after a certain family, as, for example, the Reyknesingagoðorð and the Dalverjagoðorð. Possession of a *goðorð* was, however, not confined to a specific group and until the twelfth century membership in a lineage was not a necessary requirement. In addition to being inherited, a *goðorð* could be and was purchased, shared, or received as a gift.

As class distinctions and bloodlines did not constitute formal barriers, an ambitious, successful individual could set his sights on acquiring a *goðorð* and thus seek his reward within Icelandic political life. The availability of such positions of authority contributed to the stability of the Free State in the early centuries.

Although we cannot be precise about numbers, there is no doubt that many *goðar* exchanged their previous pagan religious function for that of Christian priest when Iceland converted to Christianity in the year 1000.[7] Having survived so dramatic a religious change, they retained their traditional authority and solidified their political control in the eleventh and twelfth centuries. By the thirteenth century a small group of the more powerful chieftains, called in modern studies *stórgoðar* or *stórhöfðingjar*, literally "large *goðar*" or "large leaders," emerged from among the most wealthy and powerful chieftain families.

The chieftains dominated government and law as advocates, legislators, nominators of judges, arbitrators, and enforcers. Among the attendant privileges the most important was leadership of a legally constituted following of thingmen. To some extent the value of possessing a *goðorð* was

7. Because of uncertainty as to what calendars the medieval Icelanders used at different times, a controversy exists as to whether the conversion should be dated by our modern calendar to 999 or 1000. Ólafía Einarsdóttir argues for the year 999 in *Studier i kronologisk metode i tidlig islandsk historieskrivning*, Bibliotheca historica Lundensis 13 (Stockholm: Natur och kultur, 1964), pp. 72-90. Jakob Benediktsson in his introduction to *Íslendingabók*, ÍF 1, reviews in detail the question of dating, including the views of Ólafía Einarsdóttir (pp. xxix-xxxv). Because the precise date is in doubt, and probably will remain so, I have chosen the traditional year of 1000.

enhanced because so few chieftaincies existed. Around 965, as part of a series of constitutional reforms, the number of *goðorð* was limited to thirty-nine, with an additional nine men being given the title of *goði*.[8] The duties of these new chieftains, however, were mostly limited to participation in the legislative and political functions of the Althing. The actual number of chieftains at any particular time was perhaps as much as double or more the number of chieftaincies, since each of the several persons who might share a single *goðorð* could call himself a *goði*.

APPROACH AND ORGANIZATION

Icelandic sources speak of many chieftains in the early centuries. Just how these leaders acquired their wealth during this formative period has never been explained. Yet the answer to this question holds the key to understanding how the different elements in Iceland's complex medieval society operated as a cohesive body politic. In this book I seek to fill this gap. Icelandic society acknowledged the legal rights of the free farmers but provided no formal executive institutions to enforce those rights. Farmers, involved in conflict and unable to enforce their own claims, turned to advocates, especially *goðar*, who had power at their disposal and superior opportunities to manipulate the legal system. *Goðar*, for their support of farmers and other chieftains in lawsuits and feuds, expected to be paid in the wealth that was in limited supply in Iceland.

Chapter 2 of this book examines the extant Icelandic historical and legal sources and considers their relevance to the study of social processes, especially the relationship between chieftains and farmers. Chapter 3 addresses the related question of the historical validity of the sagas. In chapter 4 I turn to the formation of the island's governmental institutions and outline the configurations of the assemblies and courts. Chapter 5 questions how best to define Iceland's system of

8. Chieftaincies are discussed in more detail in chapters 4 and 6.

wealth exchange and examines the different sources of income which the chieftains, as private individuals, had at their disposal. Chapter 6 explores the development of Iceland's consensual system of governance with its complex processes of collaboration and reciprocity. The chapter concentrates on the two main types of third-party intervention which made government in Iceland workable. In Chapter 7 I consider the place of the Icelandic church in light of social traditions established in the early centuries. The first half of chapter 8 analyzes a series of family saga incidents relating to a major source of the chieftains' wealth: the exploitation of farmers who, beset by difficulties, required assistance from men of influence. This analysis leads to a discussion of the ties of mutual interdependence between the *goðar* and the *bændr*, including the potential for profit inherent in such ties. The second part of chapter 8 uses examples from *Sturlunga saga* to explain the use and abuse of power as well as the acquisition of wealth.

In chapters 9 and 10 I expand the inquiry by considering how these relationships functioned in the context of local conflict and by distinguishing the checks and balances that are an integral part of the Icelandic system of nonterritorial authority. Two extended conflicts arising from the greed for wealth and power are analyzed: one is found in *Eyrbyggja saga* from the western part of the country, the other in *Vápnfirðinga saga* from the East Fjords. These two saga stories of feud from opposite ends of the island illuminate the success of a particular type of hero in Icelandic literature: the leader who not only destroys an overbearing rival but also survives the legal consequences of such an act with his power intact. My conclusions are presented in chapter 11.

2

Historical and Legal Sources

Many men say that writing about the settlement is un-
necessary. But it seems to me that we would be better able
to answer foreigners who upbraid us for our descent from
scoundrels or thralls if we knew our true origins for certain. Similarly, for those men who want to know old lore
or to reckon genealogies, it is better to begin at the beginning rather than to jump right into the middle. And of
course all wise peoples want to know about the beginnings
of their settlement and of their own families.
—*The Book of Settlements*

Iceland is the first "new nation" to have come into being
in the full light of history, and it is the only European
society whose origins are known.
—Richard F. Tomasson

Anyone engaging in the study of medieval Iceland soon
faces the problem of sources. The difficulty looms larger if
the emphasis, as in this study, is on the centuries immediately following the colonization in the 870s. Only a few texts
contain useful information about this early period.

The historical sources relevant to the study of early Iceland fall into several categories: histories and genealogies,
legal compilations, annals, diplomatic collections, and
church writings. The sagas and these historical texts, including most of the church writings, are written in West
Norse, the vernacular language shared by Iceland and Norway from the twelfth to the mid-fourteenth century. This
dialect was an outgrowth, with minor changes, of what in

medieval times was called the Danish tongue, *dönsk tunga,* the common language spoken by all Scandinavians at the time of Iceland's settlement.

The chief historical writings are *Landnámabók (The Book of Settlements)* and *Íslendingabók (The Book of the Icelanders).*[1] These texts, which include genealogies as well as historical sections, together offer considerable information about the island's settlement. *Íslendingabók,* the smaller of the two, is a concise overview (ten or so pages in a printed edition) of Iceland's history from 870 to 1120. It was probably written between 1122 and 1132 by the Christian priest and *goði* Ari Thorgilsson, who was called inn fróði (the Learned). Two versions—the "older" and the "younger"—were extant in the medieval period, but only the younger has survived, in two seventeenth-century copies.

Íslendingabók is an invaluable source. It touches on a wide variety of subjects, albeit on many of them only briefly. Among the ninth- and tenth-century events it records are Iceland's settlement, the adoption of Iceland's first oral laws, the founding of the Althing, the subsequent reform of the constitution and courts, and the adjustment of the calendar. *Íslendingabók* is also an early source for the settlement of Greenland and the discovery of Vínland (ch. 6):

> The country that is called Greenland was discovered and set-
> tled from Iceland. A man called Eiríkr inn rauði [the Red]
> from Breiðafjörðr [Broad Fjord] went there from here and
> claimed the land later called Eiríksfjörðr. He called the coun-
> try Greenland, saying men would be encouraged to go there
> if it had a good name. They found human settlements, frag-
> ments of boats, and stone artifacts. From these remains it
> could be concluded that the same type of people had lived
> there as had settled in Vínland—the ones whom the Green-
> landers call Skrælings. Eiríkr began the settlement fourteen
> or fifteen winters before Christianity came here to Iceland,

1. The standard editions of *Íslendingabók* and *Landnámabók* were edited by Jakob Benediktsson in volume 1 (in 2 parts) of *Íslenzk fornrit* (Reykjavik: Hið íslenzka fornritafélag, 1968) (hereafter abbreviated *ÍF*). Chapters of *Landnámabók* cited in this book are from either the *Sturlubók* (S), *Hauksbók* (H), or *Melabók* (M) manuscripts.

according to what a man, who himself followed Eiríkr inn rauði on the voyage, told Thorkell Gellisson in Greenland.

The above entry is symptomatic of the strengths and limitations of Ari's work. On the one hand we sense that the statement is based on verified information, which includes dating the Greenland settlement to about 985. Ari tells us at the beginning of *Íslendingabók* that Thorkell Gellisson was his paternal uncle and a man "who remembered far back." On the other hand we learn nothing from Ari's account about the social, economic, or political reasons behind the decision of some Icelanders in 985—only fifty-five years after establishment of the Althing—to emigrate to a place that to them must have seemed to be at the very end of the world.

Almost three-fourths of *Íslendingabók* is devoted to selected events occurring between 996 and 1120. This period included the life span of the author and of the older men and women who served as his oral informants. Ari covers Iceland's conversion to Christianity, the presence of foreign missionary bishops, the establishment of Iceland's two bishoprics, the introduction of the Fifth Court (for appeals), the first tithe law, the census of farmers paying the thing tax before introduction of the tithe, and the first writing down of the laws.

There is no doubt that Ari was a careful historian. At times, however, his objectivity and his choice of subject matter were influenced by his interest in strengthening the church, his predilection for stressing the Norwegian ancestry of the settlers, and his desire to record events of special significance from his local region of Breiðafjörðr in western Iceland.[2] Most of the people Ari mentions are individuals with whom he has some link of kinship. In genealogies he traces his own descent through the kings of Norway and Sweden to the gods Njörðr and Freyr—a respectable lineage for an Icelander.

Landnámabók is much larger than *Íslendingabók*, the extant versions filling several hundred pages in a modern printed

2. Björn Sigfússon, *Um Íslendingabók* (Reykjavik: Víkingsprent, 1944).

volume. It was written as a record of the settlement and a genealogy of the Icelanders. Through a welter of predominantly terse entries, *The Book of Settlements* accounts for approximately 400 *landnámsmenn*. Sometimes it tells where these colonists came from and who their forefathers were in Scandinavia. We learn where the *landnámsmenn* settled and some details about their land claims. At times the kinship lines of *landnámsmenn* are traced through succeeding generations of Icelanders. The first *Landnámabók*, now lost, was written in the early decades of the twelfth century. Ari the Learned may have been one of the authors, or at least he may have had a hand in the work. The major extant versions of *Landnámabók*—*Sturlubók, Hauksbók,* and *Melabók* (the latter a fragment of only two vellum leaves)—date from the thirteenth to the fifteenth century.[3] These mention 1,500 farm and place names as well as more than 3,500 people. The material, arranged geographically, gives a seemingly complete picture of the whole country.

Although *Íslendingabók* and *Landnámabók* report specific information, the entries are often so concise that they merely hint at a picture of the functioning society. For example, the following passage from *Landnámabók* (S86, H74) names major characters but leaves us in the dark as to the nature of what appears to have been, in the late tenth century, a serious dispute in a small fjord in western Iceland called Álptafjörðr (Swans' Fjord): "Thórólfr bægifótr [Lamefoot] was the father of Arnkell goði and of Geirríðr who married Thórólfr from Mávahlíð. The sons of Thorbrandr from Álptafjörðr were named Thorleifr Kimbi, and Thóroddr, Snorri, Thorfinnr, Illugi, and Thormóðr. They quarreled with Arnkell over the inheritance of their freedmen and they, together with Snorri goði, killed him at Örlygsstaðir." *Eyrbyggja saga* gives a more

---

3. For the textual history of *Landnámabók* see Jakob Benediktsson's introduction to *Landnámabók, ÍF* 1, pp. l-cxxiv; Jón Jóhannesson, *Gerðir Landnámabókar* (Reykjavik: Félagsprentsmiðjan, 1941); Sveinbjörn Rafnsson, *Studier i Landnámabók: Kritiska bidrag till den isländska fristatstidens historia,* Bibliotheca Historica Lundensis 31 (Lund: C. W. K. Gleerup, 1974), pp. 13-67.

detailed account of the actions leading to Arnkell's death (see chapter 9).[4] The historical reliability of many entries in *Landnámabók* is questionable. The thirteenth- and fourteenth-century redactors of the *Sturlubók* and *Hauksbók* versions extensively altered the older texts.[5] Guided by their tastes and interests, these medieval historians frequently used the family sagas to augment or to replace what appeared in earlier, now lost, versions of *Landnámabók*. At times genealogies are traced to what seems to be the redactors' own families.

Icelandic annals, diplomatic texts, and church writings offer only limited information about the early society. The earliest extant annals are relatively late sources, written at the end of the thirteenth century.[6] Their secondhand informa-

4. There is little doubt that Sturla Þórðarson, the thirteenth-century author of the *Sturlubók* version of *The Book of Settlements*, knew *Eyrbyggja saga*.

5. The reliability of *Landnámabók* and *Íslendingabók* has been questioned by numerous scholars. Olaf Olsen, *Hørg, hov og kirke: Historiske og arkæologiske vikingetidsstudier* (Copenhagen: Gad, 1966), has concluded that much of the information concerning heathen practices and sanctuaries in *Landnámabók* is of late origin, probably culled from the sagas. Other aspects of the story of Iceland's settlement and state building given in these books have been questioned by Sigurður Líndal, "Sendiför Úlfljóts: Ásamt nokkrum athugasemdum um landnám Ingólfs Arnarsonar," *Skírnir* 143(1969):5-26; and by Preben Meulengracht Sørensen, "Sagan um Ingólf og Hjörleif: Athugasemdir um söguskoðun Íslendinga á seinni hluta þjóðveldisaldar," *Skírnir* 148(1974):20-40. Hans Bekker-Nielsen, "Frode mænd og tradition," in *Norrøn fortællekunst: kapitler af den norsk-islandske middelalderlitteraturs historie*, ed. Hans Bekker-Nielsen, Thorkil Damsgaard Olsen, and Ole Widding (Copenhagen: Akademisk forlag, 1965), pp. 35-41, emphasizes, perhaps too strongly, the continental influences on those twelfth- and thirteenth-century sources that tell of Iceland's earlier periods. Sveinbjörn Rafnsson, *Studier i Landnámabók*, has reconsidered the purpose of *Landnámabók*. He argues that the information was altered to support twelfth- and thirteenth-century claims to landownership. For a discussion of Sveinbjörn Rafnsson's views see Jakob Benediktsson, "Markmið Landnámabókar: Nýjar rannsóknir," *Skírnir* 148(1974):207-215. See also Jakob Benediktsson's introductions to *Íslendingabók* and *Landnámabók*, ÍF 1, and his "Landnámabók: Some Remarks on Its Value as a Historical Source," *Saga-Book of the Viking Society for Northern Research* 17(1969):275-292.

6. Jónas Kristjánsson, "Annálar og Íslendingasögur," *Gripla* 4(1980):295-319; Gustav Storm, ed., *Islandske annaler indtil 1578* (Kristiania: Udgivne for det norske historiske kildeskriftfond, 1888).

tion about the first two centuries is sparse and inaccurate. *Diplomatarium Islandicum*, the scholarly collection of documents, judgments, contracts, church inventories, and other writings, is only slightly more helpful for the early period.[7] This magnificent assemblage of sources is, however, an invaluable tool for the study of medieval Iceland after the twelfth century. Around 1200 the first bishops' sagas (*byskupa sögur*) were written about Iceland's two saintly bishops, Thorlákr Thórhallsson and Jón Ögmundarson.[8] Probably the lives of these men were originally written in Latin, but all that remains is a number of fragments from an early saga about Thorlákr. The lives of the first five bishops are treated in *Hungrvaka* (literally "hunger waker"),[9] a brief church history written in the very early 1200s which reports events from the first half of the eleventh century until 1176. The lives of nine of the Skálholt bishops and three of the Hólar bishops were written down in the thirteenth and early fourteenth centuries. Some of them, such as Páll Jónsson, bishop of Skálholt at the turn of the thirteenth century, merited separate sagas. Almost all these writings were in the vernacular. The bishops' sagas and other church writings focus on

7. *Diplomatarium Islandicum: Íslenzkt fornbréfasafn*, 16 vols. (Copenhagen and Reykjavik: S. L. Möller and Hið íslenzka bókmentafélag, 1857-1952), hereafter abbreviated as *Dl*.
8. *Jóns saga* was most probably written between 1201 and 1210. The bishops' sagas are contained in three major editions: (1) *Biskupa sögur*, ed. Hið íslenzka bókmentafélag, 2 vols. (Copenhagen: S. L. Möllers, 1858-1878); (2) *Byskupa sögur*, ed. Jón Helgason (Copenhagen: Det kongelige nordiske oldskriftselskap, 1938), the first volume of an uncompleted series subsequently considered as Editiones Arnamagnæanæ, ser. A, 13, pt. 1, and followed by *Byskupa sögur*, Editiones Arnamagnæanæ, ser. A, 13, pt. 2 (Copenhagen: Reitzel, 1978), published without an introduction; (3) *Byskupa sögur*, ed. Guðni Jónsson, 3 vols. ([Akureyri]: Íslendingasagnaútgáfan, Haukadalsútgáfan, 1953). The Guðni Jónsson edition, although more popular in presentation, remains a highly serviceable text. Because it is more readily available than any of the other editions, I have cited it where possible.
9. The unknown author tells us at the start of *Hungrvaka* that his intention is to awaken the readers' hunger for more learning about his subject. See *Byskupa sögur*, ed. Guðni Jónsson, vol. 1 ([Akureyri]: Íslendingasagnaútgáfan, 1953), pp. 1-31.

the lives, turmoils, and joys of Iceland's prominent churchmen and saints. They provide a wealth of information about
selected topics such as the conversion, the establishment of
Iceland's two bishoprics, the manner of choosing Iceland's
bishops, and the role of priests in the society. Church texts
touch on the functioning of the early secular society only in
passing. For the later period, beginning in the twelfth century but especially in the thirteenth century and in the first
half of the fourteenth, the bishops' sagas and other church
documents offer information on a wide variety of subjects,
including church finances.

Iceland has a rare treasure in its lawbooks. Collectively
the extant Free State laws are called *Grágás*, meaning "gray
goose," a name whose origin is unknown.[10] Unlike other
Scandinavian law, *Grágás* was compiled without concern for
royal justice or prerogatives. Its resolutions and rulings illustrate the limits and precedents of a legal system that operated without an executive authority. Knowledge of the law
is often essential to understanding medieval Iceland, especially events portrayed in its sagas. *Grágás* was the law of a
society in which order was maintained principally through
negotiation and compromise and in which the upholding of
an individual's rights through legal proceedings, such as
prosecution and the exaction of penalties, was a private responsibility. Together the sagas and the laws reflect the medieval Icelanders' conception of how their society worked.
The law was not a set code that everyone was expected to

10. The name *Grágás* first appears in an inventory taken in 1548 at the
bishop's seat at Skálholt. The standard edition of *Grágás* (hereafter abbreviated as GG) was edited by Vilhjálmur Finsen and published in three volumes. Ia and Ib: *Grágás: Islændernes Lovbog i Fristatens Tid, udgivet efter det
Kongelige Bibliotheks Haandskrift* (Copenhagen: Brødrene Berlings Bogtrykkeri, 1852); II: *Grágás efter det Arnamagnæanske Haandskrift Nr. 334 fol., Staðarhólsbók* (Copenhagen: Gyldendalske Boghandel, 1879); III: *Grágás: Stykker,
som findes i det Arnamagnæanske Haandskrift Nr. 351 fol. Skálholtsbók og en Række
andre Haandskrifter* (Copenhagen: Gyldendalske Boghandel, 1883). An
English translation of sections 1-117 of vol. I appeared in 1980: *Laws of Early
Iceland: Grágás I*, trans. Andrew Dennis, Peter Foote, and Richard Perkins,
University of Manitoba Icelandic Studies 3 (Winnipeg: University of Manitoba Press, 1980).

obey, but a group of rules that individuals could use to their advantage or turn to the disadvantage of others. The sagas show characters routinely breaking the law when they thought they could get away with it, and it may well be that people acted in precisely this way.[11]

The heart of *Grágás* is two large manuscripts. One is called *Konungsbók*, the king's book, so named because in later years it was owned by the Danish Crown and kept in the Old Royal Library in Copenhagen. The other, *Staðarhólsbók*, is named for the farm in western Iceland where it was found in the sixteenth century. The leaves of these manuscript volumes are, like most other medieval Icelandic books, made of calfskin. Dating from the mid-thirteenth century, they are well-preserved large folios, skillfully written and ornamented with polychrome initials.[12] Their production must have been extremely expensive, but we do not know for whom the work was done. Neither *Konungsbók* nor *Staðarhólsbók* is an official codex. Rather, they are private lawbooks that cover, even if somewhat haphazardly, the breadth and depth of Iceland's constitutional and judicial systems.

In addition to the two main components of *Grágás*, a number of diverse vellum fragments have survived from early volumes, one of them dating perhaps from as early as 1150. A few otherwise unknown entries, as well as many sections of the law which repeat provisions recorded earlier, are found in various fourteenth- and fifteenth-century manuscripts.

Grágás preserves many laws that far predate the extant thirteenth-century manuscripts. The writing down of var-

---

11. As Kirsten Hastrup, *Culture and History in Medieval Iceland: An Anthropological Analysis of Structure and Change* (Oxford: Clarendon Press, 1985), notes (p. 208), "The very existence of the law as a written text tends to obscure its true status as a 'text' within a larger context. The *Grágás* was not an external expression of the Freestate (although metaphorically related to it)—it was an integral part of the definition of the social reality."

12. *Konungsbók* (*Codex Regius*, gl. kgl. Saml. 1157 fol.) is usually dated to around 1250 and *Staðarhólsbók* (A.M. 334 fol.) to the years between 1260 and 1270. The two lawbooks are now found in the Stofnun Árna Magnússonar (Árni Magnússon Manuscript Institute) in Reykjavik.

ious legal provisions probably began as early as the late eleventh century, and scholars often assume that the tithe laws of 1096, as well as an earlier treaty (see chapter 6) between the Icelanders and Norway's King Óláfr the Saint, were among Iceland's first written legal documents. The process of transcribing and codifying the laws was formalized in the winter of 1117-18, when a commission headed by the chieftain Hafliði Másson was, according to Ari's *Íslendingabók* (ch. 10), empowered by the *lögrétta*, the legislative council at the Althing, to undertake the work:

> The first summer that Bergthórr [Hrafnsson, lawspeaker 1117-1122] recited the law, a new law [*nýmæli*, sing. and pl.] was passed that the laws should be written out in a book at Hafliði Másson's farm during the following winter according to the speech and consultation of Hafliði, Bergthórr, and other wise men who were selected for the task. They were to put into the laws all the new provisions [*nýmæli*] that seemed to them better than the old laws. The laws were to be said aloud the following summer in the *lögrétta* and would all take effect if a majority did not oppose them. And that was how *Vígslóði* [the Manslaughter Section] and much else in the law came to be written down and read aloud in the *lögrétta* by clerics the following summer.

This first writing of *Vígslóði* is now lost, although a later version is found in *Grágás*.

The *lögrétta* was the central legislative institution of the Free State. According to *Grágás*,[13] its function was to amend old laws (*rétta lög sín*) and to initiate new legislation (*gera nýmæli*). Although there is no doubt that the *lögrétta* enacted new laws, *Grágás* says nothing as to the procedure by which they were to be adopted. We know that only chieftains had the right to vote in the *lögrétta*, but did a simple majority suffice to pass legislation or was a unanimous vote required? This question has been debated for a century.[14] The initiative to formulate new laws, however, was not limited to the *lög-*

---

13. GG Ia, p. 212 (ch. 117). The precise meaning of this entry has stirred much debate; see Sigurður Líndal, "Lög og lagasetning í íslenzka þjóðveldinu," *Skírnir* 158(1984):124, esp. nn. 3 and 4.

14. Ibid., pp. 139-141. Líndal argues for a unanimous vote.

rétta. According to *Íslendingabók* (chs. 4 and 5) private individuals could also introduce legislation at the Law Rock (*lögberg*) at the Althing. Further, a disputant who questioned the interpretation of a law, or who believed that no existing ruling applied to a specific situation, could initiate legislation by bringing a case before the *lögretta* for clarification by vote. The legislative council's determination might reinterpret or supersede old law, thereby establishing new legislation. The *lögrétta* was thus able to adapt Icelandic law to meet prevailing needs. It is probable that in the course of time the rules of voting and procedure in the *lögrétta* and at the courts were altered to some extent.

Public access to lawmaking in the *lögrétta* and at the *lögberg* may have brought innovations to Icelandic law. It may also have been responsible for proliferation of enactments on matters of minor significance, a notable feature of *Grágás*. *Nýmæli* has long been a troublesome aspect of *Grágás*. To be valid in all or part of the country, new law required ratification, principally by acceptance over a period of time.[15] Unfortunately, the lawbooks seldom specify whether ratification had or had not occurred.

The writing down of the laws ensured the transmission into the thirteenth century of many older legal provisions. For example, although slavery had almost certainly died out by 1117, the thirteenth-century texts record many rules concerning slavery. Legal scholars such as Lúðvík Ingvarsson have argued with good reason that provisions regarding the underlying structure of the Icelandic government—for example, those specifying the composition of the quarter courts, the springtime assemblies, and the Fifth Court—closely approximate the provisions of the original tenth- and

---

15. *GG* Ia, p. 37 (ch. 8), and III, p. 443 (A.M. 58 8ᵛᵒ). These two entries are not in agreement. *GG* I requires that a new law will not be in force for more than three years, after which time it will lose its validity if it is not publicly recited every third summer thereafter. *GG* III calls for *nýmæli* to be recited publicly at the Law Rock every summer for three years following the initial enactment. If this regulation is observed the law is thereafter fully established. The two entries probably stem from different periods.

eleventh-century laws.[16] In a number of areas, landownership for instance, there seems little reason to doubt that the
burden of the entries is conservative and old.[17]

Laws pertaining to the Christian faith and institutions,
including those concerned with the offices of bishops and
priests, baptism, burial, witchcraft, feast and holy days, fast-
ing, and sorcery, are principally contained in the Christian
Law Section (*Kristinna laga þáttr*) of *Grágás*.[18] This special
group of laws, which governed relations between the church
and temporal society, was written sometime between 1122
and 1133. Often called the "Old Christian Laws" (*Kristinn réttr
forni*), these laws contain provisions that may go back as far
as the conversion to Christianity at the beginning of the eleventh century. They also include revisions of later eleventh-
century enactments as well as new laws from the twelfth
century pertaining to religion.

The Christian Law Section was adopted at a time when
the secular legal system had matured. In matters touching
lay society, no separate ecclesiastical jurisdiction was permitted, and there are few provisions for an independent
church. Christian enactments accepted hereditary private
control of churches and, for the most part, were adapted to
the already centuries-old Icelandic traditions of law and legal
procedure. In general, throughout the history of the Free
State and beyond, the Old Christian Laws defined the rights
and prerogatives of the Icelandic church. Their provisions
remained in force in the southern diocese of Skálholt until
1275, when the "New Christian Laws" (*Kristinn réttr nýi*) were

16. Lúðvík Ingvarsson, *Refsingar á Íslandi á þjóðveldistímanum* (Reykjavik:
Bókaútgáfa Menningarsjóðs, 1970), p. 18.

17. Andrew Dennis, "*Grágás*: An Examination of the Content and Technique of the Old Icelandic Law Books, Focused on Þingskapaþáttr (the 'Assembly Section')," Ph.D. dissertation, Cambridge University, 1973, p. 3,
notes that in addition to rules of constitution and procedure the original
laws "would have dealt with such matters as: homicide, assault, theft, were-
gild, family law, inheritance, land, drift, negotiable currency, and commerce."

18. *GG* Ia, pp. 3-37 (chs. 1-19); II, pp. 1-62 (chs. 1-55); III, pp. 1-376,
502-507.

introduced.[19] This new code of Christian law, which established the principle that the Icelandic church had the right
to control its property and to govern itself, was not accepted
in the northern diocese of Hólar until 1354. Even at this late
date not all the new provisions were enforced.

Although *Konungsbok* and *Staðurhólsbók* are basically similar, they differ from each other in order, word choice, and
to some extent in content. Of the two, *Konungsbók* is the more
important. It contains several sections missing from *Staðarhólsbók*, among them the Assembly Procedures Section (*Þingskapaþáttr*), the Wergild Ring List (*Baugatal*), the Lawspeaker's Section (*Lögsögumannsþáttr*), and the Law Council Section
(*Lögréttuþáttr*). For its part, *Staðarhólsbók* preserves a number
of provisions that are not in *Konungsbók*, and it is generally
more detailed in the sections that appear in both manuscripts. It is not unusual to find in *Konungsbók* only the beginning or, occasionally, the beginning and the ending of an
entry. The missing part may sometimes be found elsewhere,
especially in *Staðarhólsbók*, which also has a number of similarly abridged entries. This peculiar method of entry may
have arisen because, when the books were written or copied,
their owners possessed other manuscripts in which the provisions in question were written out in full. Truncating the
entries thus would have saved the cost of labor and parch-
ment.

Grágás differs from other Scandinavian collections of laws
in significant respects. There are no provisions for defense
or other military arrangements, and the constitution that it
proposes is without parallel elsewhere in Scandinavia. Even
basic matters like the rules of court procedure, including
rules of proof and strictures governing presentation of cases
before the court, show an independent development. The
penal code also has its peculiarities. The laws, when treating
offenses committed by freemen, contain no provisions for

19. *Norges gamle love indtil 1387*, vol. 5, ed. Gustav Storm and Ebbe Hertz-
berg (Christiania: Grøndahl & Søn, 1895), pp. 16-56.

governmental officers to carry out corporal punishment or to enact a death penalty. In keeping with the cultural focus, vengeance killings, a central aspect of private feud, were incorporated into the law, and thus violent redress became privileged. This incorporation, as well as the general proliferation of legal sanctions, compensated for the absence of executive institutions. If private parties were sanctioned to undertake privileged vengeance, such actions were, nevertheless, restricted. *Vígslóði* specifies both on whom and when vengeance may be taken: "It is the law that a man who has been injured is entitled, if he wishes, to avenge himself up to the time of the Althing where he is required to pursue the case for the wounds; it is the same for all those who have the right to avenge a killing. Those who have the right to avenge a killing are the principals of a manslaughter case. The man who inflicted the injury can be killed, having forfeited immunity [hence compensation] if killed by the principal or any of his followers, and it is also lawful for other men to avenge him [the person killed] within 24 hours if they want to."[20] Private parties were also responsible for restraining violent individuals in their midst: "If a man goes berserk, the penalty is lesser outlawry. The same penalty applies to those men who are present except if they restrain him. But if they succeed in restraining him then the penalty falls on none of them. If it happens again, lesser outlawry applies."[21]

Bulk is another distinctive feature of *Grágás. Konungsbók* alone is three and a half times the size of the Danish East Sjælland Laws, the largest of the Scandinavian provincial lawbooks.[22] Furthermore, the Icelandic provisions have a

20. *GG* Ia, p. 147 (ch. 86); *GG* II, pp. 303-304 (ch. 275). Men had the right to kill for certain offenses against women (*GG* Ia, pp. 164-166 [ch. 90]). Aspects of vengeance in the sagas and *Grágás* are considered by Ólafur Lárusson, "Hefndir," in *Lög og saga* (Reykjavik: Hlaðbúð, 1958), pp. 146-178; Lúðvík Ingvarsson, *Refsingar*, pp. 62-93; William Ian Miller, "Choosing the Avenger: Some Aspects of the Bloodfeud in Medieval Iceland and England," *Law and History Review* 1(1983):159-204.

21. *GG* Ia, p. 23 (ch. 7).

22. Ólafur Lárusson, "On Grágás—the Oldest Icelandic Code of Law,"

sober and straightforward style, in contrast with the alliterative, formulaic diction of other Scandinavian laws. The direct, almost literary, style of *Grágás* may result from the manner in which the oral laws were revised when first written down, although, as Peter Foote has suggested, *Grágás's* diction may simply reflect the original oral character of the laws.[23]

Grágás provides a wealth of detail about Old Icelandic society. For example, the legal entries often give a precise picture of the formal rights and duties of freemen and outline the composition and arrangement of assemblies and courts. Nevertheless, reliance on written law has its limitations. Although *Grágás* gives much information about Icelandic governmental and social institutions, it rarely specifies how these elements fit together. It is one thing to know the proposed composition of a court or an assembly; it is quite another to understand how bodies and gatherings actually worked when they met in open fields in medieval Iceland. Alongside the provisions in *Grágás* there surely existed a body of customary rule and law whose operation we at times witness in the sagas.

Konungsbók and *Staðarhólsbók* are compendia of the law, not treatises on legal procedure and application. The individuals who used these extensive compilations understood the ways in which their society functioned. They did not require their lawbooks to give instructions in the essential arts of posturing, negotiating, and arbitrating; instead, they reserved the detailing of such social behavior to the sagas. In entries concerned with situations from everyday life, *Grágás* often makes minute distinctions. It provides a mass of frequently lengthy rulings on a wide variety of issues in daily

---

Proceedings of the Third Viking Congress, Reykjavik, 1956. *Árbók hins Íslenzka Fornleifafélags*, 1958, p. 86.

23. Peter Foote, "Oral and Literary Tradition in Early Scandinavian Law: Aspects of a Problem," in *Oral Tradition—Literary Tradition: A Symposium*, ed. Hans Bekker-Nielsen, Peter Foote, Andreas Haarder, and Hans Frede Nielsen (Odense: Odense University Press, 1977), pp. 54-55.

life, often specifying penalties of fines or outlawry. For example, in a section concerning horse riding, entitled *Vm hross reiðir*, the following provisions form only a small portion of the complete entry on this subject (GG Ib, pp. 61-65 [ch. 164]):

> If a man climbs on the back of a man's horse without permission, he incurs a fine of six ounces.[24] Now if he rides away, then he incurs a payment of three marks. There are three ways of riding a horse which constitute outlawry. One is if a man rides so that three farms are on one side and he rides past them. The second is if a man rides past those mountains that divide the watersheds between districts. The third is if a man rides between quarters. There is an option to summon for a lesser offense even if a larger distance be ridden. If a man summons another man for horse riding, charging that he has ridden his horse past three farms, then he causes fines to be incurred along with outlawry. A jury of twelve shall preside when outlawry is to be determined. Now if the verdict is against him, it is up to him to ask for acquittal based on whether he had ridden so near to those three farms all lying on one side that a man with good eyesight could see him riding in daylight from all those farms if one were to check and there must not be hills or ridges blocking the line of sight. If a man lends a man a horse . . .

Outlawry and fines were the primary penalties under the laws of the Free State. A large part of *Grágás* is devoted to cataloging the fines that could be levied for different infractions. The imposition of fines clearly was intended as an

24. The precise value of this fine is not clear, as standards and values varied considerably during the Free State period. The medieval Icelanders never minted their own coins, but the early settlers brought with them silver and foreign coins, as well as the Norwegian units of currency: the mörk (mark)—nearly half a pound—equaling 8 aurar (ounces, sing. eyrir). The ounce and mark began as units of weight but over the course of the eleventh century evolved into units of value. Pure silver was replaced by alloys, and *vaðmál*, homespun cloth, became the basis of the currency. Although there was little gold in Iceland, as a unit of value a mark of gold equaled eight marks of silver. The fine of six ounces would be equivalent to 36 ells of homespun; its value in silver would depend on the current rate of exchange. The medieval Icelandic standards and values are discussed at greater length in chapter 5.

important method of restraining violence, insult, and aggression. Fines were levied in settlements made in and out of court, but private settlements remained subject to approval at the *lögrétta*. Such settlements, often mentioned in the family and Sturlunga sagas, seem to have been common elements of dispute resolution. The sagas consistently imply that an individual could not expect to settle more cases than he could pay for.

Outlawry, which provided the island society with an efficient means of removing troublemakers, is mentioned frequently in the laws. Dependence on outlawry exempted Iceland from the need to maintain a policing body to oversee the imposition of corporal punishment, execution, or incarceration. *Grágás* names two types of outlawry: *fjörbaugsgarðr*, lesser outlawry, and *skóggangr*, full outlawry.[25] Both punishments included confiscation of property. Lesser outlawry brought a sentence of three years' exile abroad. If a *fjörbaugsmaðr*, a lesser outlaw, failed to leave the country within three years, he became a full outlaw, a *skógarmaðr*. A full outlaw was denied all assistance in Iceland; he was not to be harbored by anyone, nor could he be helped out of the country. In effect, this punishment was tantamount to a death sentence, for a *skógarmaðr* could be killed with impunity.

The *lögrétta* could mitigate the sentence of full outlawry, allowing a *skógarmaðr* to leave Iceland for life. In such instances the outlaw traveled abroad without the rights of an Icelander. Removal of these rights jeopardized the safety and the status of an individual, especially one who wished to stay in Norway, because Iceland and Norway maintained from the early eleventh century a treaty (see chapter 6) guaranteeing the rights of each other's citizens. A third type of

25. Lúðvík Ingvarsson, *Refsingar*, pp. 94-173, 339-348; Magnús Már Lárusson, "Fredløshed: Island," *KLNM* 4, cols. 603-608; Dennis, Foote, and Perkins, *Laws of Early Iceland*, pp. 7-8; and Jesse L. Byock, *Feud in the Icelandic Saga* (Berkeley, Los Angeles, London: University of California Press, 1982), pp. 219-220.

outlawry, not mentioned in the laws, was district outlawry. Named *héraðssekt*, this form of outlawry was a judgment limited to a *hérað*, a local district.

3

The Family and Sturlunga Sagas

Each society's social drama could be expected to have its own "style," too, its aesthetic of conflict and redress, and one might also expect that the principal actors would give verbal or behavioral expression to the values composing or embellishing that style.

—Victor W. Turner

The Sagas differ from all other "heroic" literatures in the larger proportion that they give to the meanness of reality.

—W. P. Ker

The family sagas, dealing with the tenth and early eleventh centuries, and the Sturlunga sagas, covering the years from approximately 1120 to 1264, are the most important, as well as the most extensive, source for a study of social and economic forces in medieval Iceland. These two related groups of vernacular prose narratives are rich mines of information about the normative codes in Iceland's medieval community.

THE STURLUNGA COMPILATION

Sturlunga saga is a large compilation of sagas named for the Sturlungs, an influential family in the last century of the Free State.[1] Along with the bishops' sagas, the sagas in the

1. The name *Sturlunga saga* first appears in an extant seventeenth-century source, although the collection may have borne this title earlier. The

Sturlunga compilation are often called contemporary sagas (*samtíðarsögur*) because the twelfth- and thirteenth-century events they describe took place about the same time as the sagas were written. *Sturlunga saga* provides a wealth of information about this later period. The individual sagas included in the compilation were written by many authors, all but one of whom remain unknown. The one identified author, Sturla Thórðarson (d. 1284), nephew of the chieftain and writer Snorri Sturluson, was an active chieftain at the end of the Free State.

The different texts contained in *Sturlunga saga* were first gathered into a single large book around 1300, a time when many such compilations were being assembled.[2] The initial Sturlunga compilation had been copied several times before it was lost. Two of these transcriptions, vellum manuscripts from the second half of the fourteenth century, fortunately survived intact as late as the seventeenth century, when many of the sagas were copied into books made from relatively inexpensive imported paper. Once their contents had been transferred to a more easily read format, the vellum books lost almost all value to the contemporary population.

---

sagas and tales included in the standard edition (see chapter 1, note 5) are as follows: *Sturl.* 1 contains *Geirmundar þáttr heljarskinns, Þorgils saga ok Haf-liða, Haukdæla þáttr, Sturlu saga, Prestssaga Guðmundar góða, Guðmundar saga dýra, Hrafns saga Sveinbjarnarsonar,* and *Íslendinga saga. Sturl.* 2 includes *Þórðar saga kakala, Svínfellinga saga, Þorgils saga skarða, Sturlu þáttr,* and *Arons saga.*

2. These costly vellum books, often impressively illustrated, preserved many texts that otherwise would have been lost. Compilations might be mainly a gathering of sagas of one kind, such as the extant *Flateyjarbók* (ca. 1390), consisting of 225 large format leaves of sagas and shorter narratives pertaining for the most part to Norway's kings, or the extant *Möðruvallabók* (ca. 1350), an assortment of family sagas filling 200 leaves. The modern names of these manuscripts derive from the localities where the books were found in the sixteenth and seventeenth centuries. Flatey is a flat island in Breiðafjörður in western Iceland and Möðruvellir is a farm in Eyjafjörður in the north. Compilers might also assemble writings with little or no common thread as, for example, in the partly extant *Hauksbók,* put together in the first decades of the fourteenth century by the lawman Haukr Erlends-son. *Hauksbók* contains among other texts one of the major versions of *Land-námabók.*

In fact, they were viewed as so unimportant that the stiff pages of one of them were cut up into patterns for making clothes.[3] Many medieval manuscripts were similarly damaged, or disappeared altogether, after manufactured paper became available in the sixteenth century. From the seventeenth until the early twentieth century the transcribing of sagas and laws from older documents, including earlier paper manuscripts, became a popular pastime in Iceland. To this custom we owe the survival of many medieval Icelandic texts.

Like the family sagas, the Sturlunga sagas often concentrate on conflict and feud. Yet the two groups differ from each other in social emphasis. Whereas the more numerous family sagas narrate disputes and concerns of all kinds, including petty issues involving obscure local persons, the Sturlunga sagas focus on quarrels among the most powerful chieftains. This feature is especially evident in *The Saga of Thórðr Kakali* (*Þórðar saga kakala*), *The Saga of Thorgils Skarði* (*Þorgils saga skarða*), and *The Saga of the Icelanders* (*Íslendinga saga*). Detailing events of the last decades of the Free State, these narratives frequently touch on issues that affect the political future of the country.

The literary quality of the sagas in the Sturlunga collection varies widely. Some of them, including parts of the longer ones, are gripping tales of people and events. On the other hand, many are collections of loosely connected material. Frequently the accounts are filled, even cluttered, with names and places, as though the authors were determined to record every scrap of information they had accumulated on a subject. If the Sturlunga sagas are burgeoning with factual information, the reader must nevertheless be wary. The authors are certainly not disinterested parties. On occasion they are partial to particular personages and families; at

---

3. A description of this manuscript, *Reykjafjarðarbók* (A.M. 122b, fol.) and a picture of one of the leaves cut to serve as a pattern for a waistcoat is found in Jón Helgason, *Handritaspjall* (Reykjavik: Mál og menning, 1958), pp. 44-45.

times, it seems that the purpose behind a story is to redeem the author's reputation or that of a friend, a kinsman, or an ancestor. Still, the author did not have free rein with his subject, and one is often struck by the seeming objectivity of the sagaman. The Sturlunga sagas were written for a contemporary audience with a knowledge of families, farms, events, and characters. The absence or distortion of essential details in a particular account would have been noticeable.

Sturlunga saga, it seems, was compiled in western Iceland at Skarð, a prosperous farm owned by a family famed for its interest in the law. Whoever the compiler was, he was decidedly concerned about the history of his country during the preceding two centuries. With the goal of creating a chronological history, he integrated various accounts from different sagas and thereby mixed the texts. As customary in Icelandic compilations of the period, he tended to respect the original wording of the sagas and left whole pieces of the older narratives intact. In general his emendations were restrained. This medieval historian shortened some of the originals, spliced together overlapping texts, added a number of transitions, and wrote a few of the shorter narratives. Modern scholars have spent years unraveling his chronological arrangement in order to reestablish the integrity of the separate sagas.[4] Because the sagas in the compilation were contemporaneous, *Sturlunga saga* is usually considered to contain reliable, if at times subjectively reported, information, and it remains a primary source for numerous innovative historical studies on the twelfth and thirteenth centuries.[5] Literary scholars, on the other hand, have often

---

4. *Sturl.* 2, pp. v-li.
5. See, for example, Gunnar Karlsson, "Goðar og bændur," *Saga* 10(1972):5-57, and his "Völd og auður á 13. öld," *Saga* 18(1980):5-30; Helgi Thorláksson, "Stórbændur gegn goðum: Hugleiðingar um goðavald, konungsvald og sjálfræðishug bænda um miðbik 13. aldar," in *Söguslóðir: Afmælisrit helgað Ólafi Hanssyni sjötugum 18. september 1979,* ed. Bergsteinn Jónsson, Einar Laxness, and Heimir Thorleifsson (Reykjavik: Sögufélag, 1979), pp. 227-250, and his "Snorri Sturluson og Oddaverjar," in *Snorri: Átta alda minning,* ed. Gunnar Karlsson and Helgi Thorláksson (Reykjavik: Sögufélag, 1979), pp. 53-88.

judged the texts in this compilation to be less sophisticated than the family sagas.

THE FAMILY SAGAS

The family sagas are called in modern Icelandic *Íslendinga-sögur*, "the sagas of the Icelanders." They have no close parallels in other medieval European narratives, which are mostly in verse and are often of a more epic character than the sagas. Some family sagas tell us about the settlement of Iceland, but most of them concentrate on the period from the mid-tenth to the early eleventh century. In a crisp and usually straightforward manner they describe the dealings between farmers and chieftains from all parts of the country and among families from diverse elements of the society. They explore the potential for an individual's success or failure in the insular world of the Old Icelandic Free State.

Whereas the Sturlunga sagas are mostly about individuals engaging in the power struggles of an emerging overclass and give almost no information about the personal lives of ordinary farmers and local leaders, the family sagas tend to concentrate on precisely these concerns. With regularity the stories focus on private matters and offer insights into personal problems of families and the health, good or ill, of marriages. The family sagas often exaggerate situations of crisis. They deal less with extended kin groups, as the name "family sagas" might imply, than with intraregional disputes in Iceland. Similar actions involving different characters are repeated in different locales. With constantly changing detail the literature presents potential issues and responses that individuals in the society needed to make if they were to succeed. Among the matters stressed were methods of reacting to overly ambitious or otherwise dangerous characters, precedents for various legal positions and modes of action, successful interventions by advocates, different means of settlement, and the principles underlying the establishment and maintenance of ties of reciprocity.

In the oral saga, as elsewhere in oral tales, one may assume that adherence to strict fact was never an issue. Nor was the saga teller required to memorize a fixed text; a general outline of a story that was perhaps of historical origin was sufficient. The medieval audience expected the narrator of a family saga to observe certain strictures. Most important, the saga had to be credible; that is, the story had to be portrayed as possible, plausible, and therefore useful within the context of Iceland's particular rules of social order and feud. The sagas served as a literature of social instruction.

In an earlier book I suggest that feud served as a cohesive and stabilizing force in Old Icelandic society.[6] Because the rules of feuding, as they developed in Iceland, regulated conflict and limited breakdowns of order, violence was kept within acceptable bounds throughout most of the history of the Free State. The ways in which feud operated provided a structure for the sagas. In examining the question of the oral saga I found probable the existence of a preliterate stage of well-developed saga telling employing a compositional technique similar to that found in the extant written sagas.

This simple, easily adaptable technique was based on the use of active narrative particles that occur in no particular order and fall into three categories: conflict, advocacy (frequently brokerage), and resolution. Guided by the parameters of socially recognized conduct, the storyteller or storywriter arranged these action particles in various orders and with different details.[7] By using the particles he translated

6. Jesse L. Byock, *Feud in the Icelandic Saga* (Berkeley, Los Angeles, London: University of California Press, 1982), and my "Saga Form, Oral Prehistory, and the Icelandic Social Context," *New Literary History* 16(1984-1985):153-173. See also Vésteinn Ólason, "Íslensk sagnalist: Erlendur lærdómur," *Tímarit Máls og menningar* 45(1984):174-189; Peter Hallberg, "Forskningsöversikt: Från den nörrona forskningsfronten," *Samlaren* 106(1985):71-72.

7. In *Feud* I term these action particles of a saga story "feudemes." By analogy with linguistic terminology, the role of these indivisible units of action in saga feud is similar to the role of morphemes in language. See also my "Narrative Strategy of Small Feud Stories," in *Les Sagas de Chevaliers (Riddarasögur)*, ed. Régis Boyer, Civilisations 10 (Paris: Presses de l'Université de Paris-Sorbonne, 1985), pp. 405-415.

social forms into written narrative forms. In anthropological terms the particles reflect the phases of Icelandic feud. These discrete units of action, the hallmark of saga style, were a convenient means for an oral or a literate teller to advance the narration of a complex tale. Working within a tradition of known characters, events, and geography, the sagaman chose his own emphasis. He (or she) was free to decide what details and known events to include and what new actions to introduce. These choices not only made for variety in the small clusters of actions that linked together to form chains of saga events, but they also served to distinguish one saga from another. Although the medieval audience probably knew in advance the outcome of a particular dispute, the essence of a tale could be put forward differently each time. This economical and effective technique of forming narrative prose applied to both oral and written saga composition. Freedom from reliance on a fixed memorized text allowed individual authors to incorporate new elements, such as Christian themes and changing ethical judgments.

Thirty or more major family sagas are extant.[8] These texts vary markedly in length; some, like *Hrafnkels saga*, are approximately twenty pages in modern volumes; a few, such as *Njáls saga* and *Laxdæla saga*, fill 300 or more pages. The family sagas are preserved in a wide variety of manuscripts, none of which is an original text definitely attributed to a specific author, despite the educated guesses of scholars.

8. The major family sagas included in the Íslenzk fornrit series are *Egils saga Skalla-Grímssonar*, *Hænsa-Þóris saga*, *Gunnlaugs saga ormstungu*, *Bjarnar saga Hítdælakappa*, *Heiðarvíga saga*, *Eyrbyggja saga*, *Eiríks saga rauða*, *Grænlendinga saga*, *Laxdæla saga*, *Gísla saga Súrssonar*, *Fóstbræðra saga*, *Hávarðar saga Ísfirðings*, *Grettis saga Ásmundarsonar*, *Bandamanna saga*, *Vatnsdæla saga*, *Hallfreðar saga*, *Kormáks saga*, *Víga-Glúms saga*, *Svarfdæla saga*, *Valla-Ljóts saga*, *Ljósvetninga saga*, *Reykdæla saga ok Víga-Skútu*, *Þorsteins saga hvíta*, *Vápnfirðinga saga*, *Hrafnkels saga Freysgoða*, *Droplaugarsona saga*, *Fljótsdæla saga*, *Þorsteins saga Síðu-Hallssonar*, *Brennu-Njáls saga*, *Kjalnesinga saga*, *Þórðar saga hreðu*, *Finnboga saga*, *Harðar saga Grímkelssonar*, and *Flóamanna saga*. Also included are a number of smaller sagas, fragments, and short stories called *þættir* (sing. *þáttr*). Additional *þættir*, which often correspond to narrative "chains," are imbedded in many sagas.

The oldest surviving examples of saga writing are fragments; the earliest are usually dated to the mid-thirteenth century, although it is possible that some fragments predate 1200. Among the presumed oldest fragments are sections from *Eyrbyggja saga, Heiðarvíga saga, Laxdæla saga,* and *Egils saga.* These, like later copies of entire sagas, give no information as to when the earliest versions of the texts were composed; thus dating the sagas has always been a difficult task, and scholarly conclusions are open to question. Decisions on the age of the family sagas have been influenced by different theories of saga origins, a point underscored by Hallvard Magerøy: "A chief argument for placing the production of the family sagas in the thirteenth century is that only by this means can saga literature be seen as a natural branch of European literature in the High Middle Ages."[9]

Copies of complete family sagas are preserved in vellum books dating from the fourteenth and fifteenth centuries.[10] Many other sagas are preserved in paper manuscripts from the sixteenth century and later. In the medieval period there were many more family sagas than have survived. *Landnámabók,* for example, names several that are now lost. Except for *Droplaugarsona saga,* which notes at the end that a certain Thorvaldr, descended from one of the main characters, "told this saga," all the family sagas are anonymous.

The family sagas are a register of the basic values of medieval Iceland's conservative rural society, yet since the mid-twentieth century historians and social scientists have shied away from using them as sources. This curious development is largely attributable to a series of theoretical obstacles against historical analysis raised by a group of Icelandic scholars who have come to be known as the "Icelandic school." The ideas that animated the Icelandic school may be traced, first, to the nineteenth-century German scholar

9. Hallvard Mageröy, "Kvar står sagaforskningen i dag?" *Nordisk tidskrift för vetenskap, konst och industri* 54/3(1978):167.

10. Among these, the fourteenth-century compilation *Möðruvallabók* remains the chief source for many of the eleven sagas it contains.

Konrad Maurer and then, in the early decades of the twentieth century, to Björn M. Ólsen, the University of Iceland's first professor of Icelandic language and literature. Under the commanding leadership of Ólsen's successor, Sigurður Nordal, and strongly reinforced by the writings of other Icelandic scholars such as Einar Ól. Sveinsson and Jón Jóhannesson, the movement itself reached its full international momentum after the 1960s.[11]

The Icelandic school championed "bookprose," a term derived from German *Buchprosa* and first employed by the Swiss scholar Andreas Heusler to denote belief in the written rather than the oral origin of the sagas. The theoretical positions of the bookprosists form the foundation of saga studies in the second half of the twentieth century.[12] In particular, the forceful position of Sigurður Nordal has dominated the issue of the sagas' historical value. While serving from 1951 to 1957 as ambassador from his newly independent country to Denmark, he prepared a detailed position paper, aptly

11. Different aspects of the Icelandic school's bookprose concept, as well as views on the long debate in the first half of the twentieth century between bookprosists and freeprosists, believers in the oral origins of the sagas, have been reviewed by Theodore M. Andersson, *The Problem of Icelandic Saga Origins: A Historical Survey*, Yale Germanic Studies 1 (New Haven: Yale University Press, 1964), and Marco Scovazzi, *La saga di Hrafnkell e il problema delle saghe islandesi* (Arona: Paideia, 1960). See also Peter Hallberg, *The Icelandic Saga*, trans. Paul Schach (Lincoln: University of Nebraska Press, 1962), pp. 49-69; Anne Holtsmark, "Det nye syn på sagaene," *Nordisk tidskrift för vetenskap, konst och industri* 35(1959):511-523; Byock, *Feud*, pp. 7-10. Two collections of older articles pertinent to the debate are Walter Baetke, ed., *Die Isländersaga*, Wege der Forschung 151 (Darmstadt: Wissenschaftliche Buchgesellschaft, 1974); Else Mundal, ed., *Sagadebatt* (Oslo, Bergen, Tromsø: Universitetsforlaget, 1977). See also Else Mundal, "Til debatten om islendingasogene," *Maal og Minne* 1975, pp. 105-126.

12. For an example of bookprose see Carol J. Clover, *The Medieval Saga* (Ithaca: Cornell University Press, 1982). Clover argues that the sagas were not "peculiarly local products" but owe their origin to Latin history and chronicle writing. Even though we have only a minimal knowledge of early and mid-twelfth century vernacular narrative, Clover concludes that "the preclassical [twelfth-century] texts themselves dispel any notion that the form of composition in the classical [thirteenth-century] sagas can be a venerable feature of popular tradition." See also Vésteinn Ólason, "Íslensk sagnalist," p. 179, who notes that Clover's book is "an attempt to strengthen the foundations of the bookprose theory."

entitled "The Historical Element in the Icelandic Family Saga."[13] Nordal's view leaves the historian or any other social scientist with little option but to ignore the sagas; it has successfully discouraged analysis of the social substance in the sagas and of indigenously derived creative elements in Icelandic society. In the past, scholars have disputed specifics in Nordal's arguments,[14] but the basic bookprosist position against historical use of the sagas remains intact, inhibiting the innovative kinds of socioliterary analysis which could deepen the study of saga and society. It is worth reviewing some of Nordal's statements in order to understand the division among saga critics concerning the historical value of the sagas. According to Nordal, a historian's interest should be confined to the limited facts of a chronicle; as literature the sagas lie beyond the scope and competence of the historian:

> A modern historian will for several reasons tend to brush these Sagas aside as historical records. He is generally suspicious of a long oral tradition, and the narrative will rather give him the impression of the art of a novelist than of the scrupulous dullness of a chronicler. Into the bargain, these Sagas deal principally with private lives and affairs which do not belong to history in its proper sense, not even the history of Iceland. The historian cuts the knot, and the last point alone would be sufficient to exempt him from further trouble. It is none of his business to study these sagas as literature, their origin, material, and making.[15]

The modern reader may find this attitude to history limited, and perhaps even naive, but it was not so regarded when Nordal was formulating his position in the first half of the twentieth century. Nordal wrote at the end of a period during which scholars were attempting to separate truth

13. Sigurður Nordal, *The Historical Element in the Icelandic Family Sagas*, W. P. Ker Memorial Lecture 15 (Glasgow: Jackson, Son, and Co., 1957).
14. For example, Óskar Halldórsson, *Uppruni og þema Hrafnkels sögu*, Rannsóknastofnun í bókmenntafræði við Háskóla Íslands, Fræðirit 3 (Reykjavik: Hið íslenska bókmenntafélag, 1976), disputes on folkloristic and archaeological grounds many of Nordal's statements about *Hrafnkels saga*.
15. Nordal, *Historical Element*, p. 14.

from fantasy in early Norse sources. Time and energy were spent determining the veracity and the chronology of reported events in Scandinavia's earliest historical period.[16] Debates raged over small issues: Did the Icelander Kjartan Óláfsson (*Laxdæla saga*) have an affair with Princess Ingibjörg of Norway, sister of King Óláfr Tryggvason, while she was being courted by a foreign prince? Was the description of the fight at Vínheiðr (*Egils saga*) an accurate portrayal of the tenth-century battle at Brunanburh in northern England?[17] Few of these issues, however, remain sources of vigorous dispute, and researchers can profit greatly from what the sagas tell of private lives and affairs of medieval people.

The determination of the saga's origin was more than just an obscure academic question, yet hardly any attention has been directed to the relationship between bookprose and Icelandic nationalism. An attempt to analyze the viewpoint of the Icelandic bookprosists is well served by taking into consideration the political climate at the time their theory was being formulated and propounded. The late nineteenth and the first half of the twentieth century in Iceland were marked by intense agitation for independence from Denmark. The island had not been independent since the end of the Free State in 1262-1264; afterward it was ruled first by the Norwegians and then, after 1380, by the Danes. At first foreign

16. In order to determine the chronology of events in medieval Scandinavia, historians of the early twentieth century began implementing a stricter source criticism than had been practiced in earlier studies. The Swedish historian Lauritz Weibull spearheaded this movement with a series of critical studies questioning a number of sources previously presumed reliable, among them the family sagas: Lauritz Weibull, *Kritiska undersökningar i Nordens historia omkring år 1000* (Copenhagen: J. L. Lybeckers Forlag, 1911), and his *Historisk-kritisk metod och nordisk medeltidsforskning* (Lund: C. W. K. Gleerup, 1913). For further discussion see Rolf Arvidsson, "Source-Criticism and Literary History: Lauritz Weibull, Henrik Schück and Joseph Bédier: A Discussion," *Mediaeval Scandinavia* 5(1972):96-138; Ove Moberg, "Bröderna Weibull och den isländska traditionen," *Scripta Islandica* 25(1974):8-22.
17. For a discussion of the academic side of these debates see Andersson, *Icelandic Saga Origins*, pp. 41-50.

control was not particularly onerous.[18] Especially during the period of Norwegian suzerainty, Iceland functioned under its own code of laws and the Althing maintained a good measure of legislative power. Later the country went through some dark periods, especially after the Protestant Reformation when the power of the Danish monarchy increased. By the end of the sixteenth century royal authority had taken on many characteristics of absolute rule, which in effect deprived the Althing of much of its legislative power. With the formal introduction of absolutism in 1662, all legislative power was officially vested in the Danish king, and the yearly Althing became a court of appeals until it was replaced in 1800 by a court in Reykjavik.

The eighteenth century was a low point in Icelandic history. The country was ravaged by an epidemic of smallpox and by famine brought on by volcanic eruptions. In 1801 the second largest island in Europe had only 47,000 inhabitants.[19] At the same time foreign dominance blocked Iceland's economic growth. The Danish trade monopoly, established in 1602,[20] became so unresponsive to Iceland's needs by the middle of the eighteenth century that during the famine year of 1784 the island was required to export food.[21] Trade policies instituted in Copenhagen continued to stunt economic development until well into the nineteenth century. Only in 1854 did the Icelanders begin to enjoy the same foreign trade rights as the Danes.

Despite such problems, the Icelanders managed over the centuries to hold onto their language, culture, and literacy,

18. There were some relatively prosperous periods in Iceland in the late Middle Ages when Scandinavian control over the island weakened and German and English merchants came for fish and sulfur. See Björn Thorsteinsson, *Enska öldin í sögu Íslendinga* (Reykjavik: Mál og menning, 1970).

19. *Mannfjöldi, mannafli og tekjur* (Reykjavik: Framkvæmdastofnun ríkisins, 1984), p. 9.

20. Gísli Gunnarsson, *Monopoly Trade and Economic Stagnation: Studies in the Foreign Trade of Iceland, 1602-1787*, Skrifter utgivna av ekonomisk-historiska föreningen i Lund 38 (Lund: Studentlitteratur, 1983).

21. In the period 1783-1785 famine claimed the lives of approximately one fifth of the population.

and in the mid-nineteenth century the situation began to change. In 1845 the Althing was reestablished in Reykjavik as an advisory body. Although the king renounced absolutism in Denmark in 1848, for a time there was no diminution of royal authority in Iceland. The ensuing struggle, led for decades by Jón Sigurðsson (d. 1879), is narrated with emotion by Thorkell Jóhannesson, professor of history at the University of Iceland in the first half of the twentieth century:

> The Danes refused to recognise the justice of Iceland's claim for self-government while united with Denmark under the person of the king, a claim based on the ancient rights of the country first stipulated in the *Gamli sáttmáli* [the covenant of union with the king of Norway] of 1262. Drafts for an Icelandic constitution were frequently submitted by the Danish authorities, but the Althing, led by Jón Sigurðsson, remained firm in its demands. In 1871 the king at last issued an act defining the status of Iceland within the Danish realm, but the Icelanders refused to recognise its validity because they had not been consulted. In 1874 . . . Iceland was granted a new and better constitution, although the Icelanders were by no means wholly satisfied. The Althing was given legislative power conjointly with the Crown, domestic autonomy and control of the national finances. The executive authority in Iceland, however, was vested in the governor (*landshöfðingi*), but he was responsible to the Minister for Icelandic Affairs, who lived in Copenhagen and was answerable not to the Althing but to the Danish Rigsdag. Despite Icelandic dissatisfaction, the existence of a conservative government in Denmark until the end of the century prevented any further changes. In 1901 a liberal ministry took office in Denmark, with the result that in 1903 a Minister for Icelandic Affairs was appointed to reside in Reykjavík and to answer to the Althing. This was a great step forward, but the independence movement was now stronger than ever and dissension still continued.[22]

Toward the end of the nineteenth century towns began to grow in Iceland. In 1880 the country had only three town-

22. *Iceland 1946* (handbook published by the Central Bank of Iceland), ed. Thorsteinn Thorsteinsson (Reykjavik: Ríkisprentsmiðjan Gutenberg, 1946), p. 43.

ships whose inhabitants together numbered 3,630 and accounted for only 5 percent of the entire population.[23] With all its attendant problems and benefits, urbanization had progressed rapidly by 1920, when seven townships with 29,000 inhabitants accounted for 31 percent of the total population.[24] Yet, despite the growth of towns, the island was largely a rural land of fishermen and farmers. Reykjavik, the capital, with a population soon growing past 30,000, was the country's administrative and commercial center, proud of its new university founded in 1911.

By 1918 Iceland had gained complete internal autonomy. The island's foreign affairs, however, continued to be conducted by Copenhagen, and the Danish king remained head of state. The country did not become completely independent until 1944, when it declared a final separation from Denmark, just before the end of World War II. The movement for independence engendered a nationalistic phase which influenced many aspects of Icelandic cultural life in the twentieth century, including the socialist movement. Characteristic of many social and intellectual currents in Iceland between the wars, the novelist, Halldór Kiljan Laxness, published in two volumes in 1934-1935 one of his most renowned books, *Sjálfstætt fólk* (*Independent People*).[25] This work both extolled the virtues of the nation and treated Icelandic nationalism with irony.[26] Nationalism spilled over into analyses of the national treasure, the family sagas. A problem that stirred Icelandic intellectuals was how to remove the

23. *Iceland 1966* (handbook published by the Central Bank of Iceland), ed. Jóhannes Nordal and Valdimar Kristinsson (Reykjavik: Ísafoldarprentsmiðja, 1967), p. 27.
24. Ibid.
25. Halldór Kiljan Laxness, *Sjálfstætt fólk*, 2 vols. (Reykjavik: E. P. Briem, 1934-1935; 2d ed., Helgafell, 1952), and his *Independent People: An Epic*, trans. J. A. Thompson (New York: Alfred A. Knopf, 1946); See Vésteinn Ólason's essay, *Sjálfstætt fólk*, Bókmenntakver Máls og Menningar (Reykjavik: Mál og menning, 1983).
26. The title *Independent People* is probably ironic. A more determinedly nationalistic work by Halldór Laxness is *Íslandsklukkan*, 2d ed. (Reykjavik: Helgafell, 1957).

sagas from the realm of traditions of unlettered storytellers
and place them in the front rank of world literature while
still contending that they were Icelandic in origin.
To provide the sagas with so rich a luster was an uphill
battle. Since the late Renaissance, educated Icelanders had
been of two minds about the sagas. Some, probably the ma
jority, venerated the stories.[27] Others tended to look down
on the native sagas as crude quasi-historical tales, hardly on
a par with the great literary traditions of Europe. One scholarly eighteenth-century Icelander characterized the sagas as
stories about "farmers at fisticuffs (*bændur flugust á*)."[28] Almost
everyone considered them the product of an old oral tradition. By the twentieth century, however, perception of the
sagas began to change among educated Icelanders. In particular, the bookprosists' view that the sagas are a written
creation gained ascendancy.
At this time many Icelandic intellectuals lived in Reykjavik or Copenhagen. They frequently moved back and forth
between the two cities, and many of them were strong na-
tionalists. From this cultured urban milieu the bookprosists
drew their leaders, who at times found themselves at odds
with older scholars such as Finnur Jónsson[29] and with the
more conservative Icelandic farmers. These modern-day
farmers, many of whom lived on the farmsteads mentioned
by name in the sagas, believed in the accuracy of the sagas,

27. Among them were Icelandic scholars in Copenhagen such as Arn-
grímur Jónsson lærði (the Learned) and Árni Magnússon.
28. Jón Helgason, *Jón Ólafsson frá Grunnavík*, Safn Fræðafjelagsins um
Ísland og Íslendinga 5 (Copenhagen: S. L. Möller, 1926), pp. 181, 195. The
original is contained in Jón Ólafsson frá Grunnavík, *Historiam Litterariam
Islandicam* (1740), unpublished notes in manuscript AM Add. 3, fol. See
Katalog over de oldnorsk-islandske håndskrifter, ed. Kommissionen for det Arnamagnæanske Legat (Copenhagen: Gyldendalske Boghandel, 1900), vol. 1,
pp. 425-426.
29. One is reminded of Finnur Jónsson's statement, "I will uphold and
defend the historical reliability of the sagas, however 'grand' this may
sound, until I am forced to lay down my pen," in his *Norsk-Islandske kultur-
og sprogforhold i 9. og 10. årh.*, Det Kgl. Danske Videnskabernes Selskab,
Historisk-filologiske Meddelelser 3, pt. 2 (Copenhagen: A.F. Høst, 1921),
p. 141.

which they were in the habit of reading. Laxness, who won the Nobel Prize in Literature in 1955, playfully touches on this element of division among Icelanders in *Atómstöðin* (*The Atom Station*), a novel, published in 1948, treating the tensions in Icelandic society at that time. His main character, a young woman who was brought to Reykjavik from the countryside to be a maid in a wealthy household, says, "I was taught never to believe a single word in the newspapers and nothing but what is found in the sagas."[30]

The stakes were high. A defined literary origin did more than furnish the credibility for what Nordal describes as "one of the most powerful literary movements in recorded history."[31] The literary basis of the sagas equipped Iceland with a cultural heritage worthy of its status as an independent nation. Here the Icelandic intellectuals were following a well-established pattern: a similar development had occurred in several European countries in the nineteenth century. In Germany and Norway, for example, folktales and fairy tales were embraced as a national heritage that could be appreciated by a literate culture. A difference was that the Icelanders were moving toward full independence in the twentieth century. Particularly after World War I the nineteenth-century national romantic adoration of oral heritage was no longer flourishing. The bookprosists were influenced by the intellectual currents of their own day. They wrested the sagas from their base within oral culture and reinterpreted the origin and nature of the national texts in a manner compatible with contemporary literary criticism.

Nordal was, of course, aware that the sagas are not an ordinary medieval literature, yet he circumvents the issue of their historical content by concentrating on the far more limited issue of authorship. He justifies the social content of the stories as satisfying the medieval audience's demand for the

30. Halldór Kiljan Laxness, *Atómstöðin* (Reykjavik: Helgafell, 1948; 2d ed., 1961), pp. 58-59. The English version is *The Atom Station*, trans. Magnus Magnusson (Sag Harbor, N.Y.: Second Chance Press, 1982).
31. Sigurður Nordal, *Hrafnkels saga Freysgoða: A Study*, trans. R. George Thomas (Cardiff: University of Wales Press, 1958), p. 57.

appearance of "historical reality." Within this limited context he believes that the artistic success of the writers lay in their ability to meet the audience's desire for realism. That the thirteenth-century author was equipped for this undertaking was never doubted by Nordal, though he did not pursue the obvious implications of his statements:

> Not only through their access to older written sources, but in certain other ways too, the writers of the Family Sagas were better off than might be expected when describing times so long past. The changes in the social and material conditions, in housing, clothes, weapons, seamanship, and so on, were not very remarkable from the tenth to the thirteenth century, and obvious anachronisms in such descriptions are rare. The writers were quite conscious of the distance in time, and they had a considerable historical sense.[32]

Nordal is quite right: medieval Icelandic society was marked by a strong element of cultural continuity. As it evolved from older *goðorð* to more stratified arrangements, Iceland—escaping as it did foreign invasion, religious wars, and rapid social or economic upheaval—was at most points in its history part of an unusually stable cultural continuum.[33] From the eleventh century the island gradually entered into less marginal membership in the distant and richer European medieval culture, losing its self-confident and secure position in the more parochial Norse world. Change came most quickly in the thirteenth century with periods of political disequilibrium, particularly from the 1230s to the 1260s.[34] Despite the turmoil caused by these changes, Iceland remained completely rural, with the majority of the

---

32. Nordal, *Historical Element*, p. 29.

33. Continuity is discussed by Gunnar Karlsson, "Goðar og Bændur," pp. 5-57, especially p. 35; Jesse L. Byock, "Cultural Continuity, the Church, and the Concept of Independent Ages in Medieval Iceland," *Skandinavistik* 15/1(1985):1-14.

34. Einar Ól. Sveinsson, *The Age of the Sturlungs: Icelandic Civilization in the Thirteenth Century*, trans. Jóhann S. Hannesson, Islandica 36 (Ithaca: Cornell University Press, 1953); Jesse L. Byock, "The Age of the Sturlungs," in *Continuity and Change: Political Institutions and Literary Monuments in the Middle Ages*, ed. Elisabeth Vestergaard (Odense: Odense University Press, 1986), pp. 27-42.

population scattered in accordance with the centuries-old settlement pattern, based on family landholding. The country retained much of its traditional law, culture, and social structure throughout the transition leading to Norwegian control and even beyond the end of the Free State.

CONCLUSIONS

Past theories have not treated the sagas as representations of the social processes of medieval Iceland. The early Icelanders, during the two centuries of a completely oral culture, were intelligent and capable enough to establish an efficient system of courts, laws, and institutions that differed from those they had known in their homelands. If we acknowledge these achievements, then we must also admit the likelihood that they could develop a form of narrative suitable for telling stories about themselves and about important events in their daily lives and in the life of their society. The sagas are not like histories or chronicles written in Latin; they are stories that tell of blood feud and conflicts over shared hayfields, horse fights, love, dowries, taunts, and the like. They are an indigenous development, the product of a long tradition of storytelling which responded in both preliterate and literate times to the particular needs of Iceland's insular population.

The various small stories that together form a saga are linked by the logic of dispute, the pulls of obligation, and the brokering of aid. They reveal the different ways in which disputes were started and resolved in medieval Iceland. Within this context saga tellers were able to develop character and to explore new ideas brought in from Europe. They were free to consider all aspects of social intercourse in their culture, including the ramifications of love, the souring of friendship, and the development of new concepts. The context was sufficiently broad to include Christian concepts and beliefs. Beginning in the late twelfth century and ending in the early fourteenth, saga writing became a national passion in Iceland. As new and often foreign elements became important to the society they too were incorporated into this creative form of narration, thus enriching the oral saga as it was transformed into a written genre.

The arguments that the sagas could not be both oral and sophisticated are based on a form of long discredited anthropological reductionism which maintains that without writing people lack the ability to produce complex oral narratives. Whereas in the past it was assumed that the introduction of reading and writing was in itself an overwhelming cultural change,[35] evidence from the postcolonial world has given us a wider perspective from which to assess the transition of cultural elements from an oral to a written state.[36] One does not have to look outside medieval Iceland for proof that adaptation to writing was rapid. Sometime between 1140 and 1180 an unknown Icelandic grammarian wrote an essay that has come to be called "The First Grammatical Treatise."[37] This vernacular book, which provides a modified Latin alphabet for Icelandic as well as an accurate phonologically based system of orthography, was written "in order to make easier writing and reading which have now become common in this land."[38]

In chapters 8 through 11 of this book I examine certain sagas for information about social behavior and social patterning. These same texts have long been analyzed for their literary nature and structure. Instead of demanding that one field of inquiry overshadow the other, it is far more productive to acknowledge the complementary possibilities of different approaches. The sagas are indisputably a major literature. They are at the same time the indigenous social

35. See, for example, Axel Olrik, "Epische Gesetze der Volksdichtung," *Zeitschrift für deutsches Altertum und deutsche Literatur* 51(1909):1-12, whose laws distinguishing between oral and written narrative periodically haunt saga studies.

36. Walter J. Ong, *Orality and Literacy: The Technologizing of the Word* (New York: Methuen, 1982).

37. *The First Grammatical Treatise*, ed. Hreinn Benediktsson, University of Iceland Publications in Linguistics 1 (Reykjavik: Institute for Nordic Linguistics, 1972).

38. Ibid., p. 209.

documentation of a medieval people and, as such, they contribute a wealth of information about the functioning of a tradition-bound island culture.

4

Evolution of a New Society

Among them [the Icelanders] there is no king, but only
law.

—Adam of Bremen (11th century)

Then that decree was sent to Iceland on the advice of the
Cardinal [William of Sabina], since he called it beyond belief that that land was not subject to some king, as were
all the others in the world.

—*The Saga of Hákon Hákonarson* (13th century)

In contrast with most northern European medieval societies,
a distinctive governmental order developed in tenth-century
Iceland. Its consensual system of decision making, marked
as it was by a minimal government hierarchy, differed considerably from systems that evolved to govern large areas
elsewhere in northern Europe. To form a conceptual model
of the way early Iceland functioned, this chapter reviews
information about the settlement of Iceland and considers
the nature of the assemblies and courts; its final section covers the eventual breakdown of Iceland's independent system
of government.

My goal in setting up this model is to explain the associations that underlay the governmental processes of medieval Iceland. The formulation, by illuminating the distinctive
features of authority in the island country,[1] allows us in

---

1. For a model of a different Norse immigrant society see Eleanor Searle,
Predatory Kinship and the Creation of Norman Power 840–1066 (Berkeley, Los
Angeles, and London: University of California Press, 1988).

chapter 5 to turn to the question of how chieftains acquired wealth, particularly in the form of land. The model, which is expanded in chapter 6 by an examination of the legal and extralegal relationships between chieftains and farmers, serves in the remainder of the book as a background for understanding the position of the church and for analyzing saga examples of the exchange of wealth and the operation of power.

THE EFFECT OF EMIGRATING FROM EUROPE

Icelanders emerged as a separate people because they chose to migrate overseas. Their lives and ambitions were shaped less by dynamics analogous to those found in their homelands than by the forces created by their new setting. The country's innovative social model may be traced to the conditions of the settlement. As noted earlier, the absence of an indigenous population freed the settlers from the need to cluster, giving them the flexibility to settle wherever they wished without an initial competition for resources. A fundamental ingredient in the development of Icelandic governmental order and decision making is that Iceland was an immigrant society of freemen formed at a time when Scandinavian kings were enlarging their authority at the expense of the traditional rights of freemen.

This society, Richard Tomasson argues, shares some of the characteristics of other "new societies" formed in later periods by overseas migrations of Europeans. In these offshoot societies, which sociologists call "fragments" of larger and older groupings, the influence of kin and traditional community lessened, and law took precedence over kinship as the source of authority.[2] By detaching itself from a "whole" or parent society, a fragment may lack the stimulus to take part in the developing social issues of the mother

2. Richard F. Tomasson, *Iceland: The First New Society* (Minneapolis: University of Minnesota Press, 1980), p. 4.

culture. European fragment societies experienced an internal transformation; philosophical concepts current in the mother country at the time of separation were played out in a manner not possible in the homeland within the confines of the European continuum.[3] Inward-looking and freed from those confines, the fragment society often developed in a form "unrecognizable in European terms."[4]

Iceland in the late ninth century looked especially attractive to Norse colonists, in part because of the growing resistance to viking expansion in some parts of Europe. In England, as well as in Ireland, native populations under leaders such as Alfred the Great were counterattacking and defeating the invaders. In Scandinavia, the expansion of royal authority continued throughout the viking period. In particular, Norway, the homeland of most of the Icelandic settlers, was in the late ninth century experiencing major political and social adjustments. The long-standing tradition of local independence was challenged by Haraldr hárfagri (Fairhair), a petty king from southeastern Norway who became the first ruler to seek control over the entire country. Allied with the earls of Lade (Hlaðajarlar) from the northern Trondelag region, Haraldr subjugated regional petty kings, local leaders, and free farmers. Although he then claimed to be Norway's overlord, in actuality he seems to have controlled mainly the southwestern coastal region. In other parts of the country his sovereignty appears to have been nominal, with real power being held by jarls, petty kings, and local military leaders called *hersar* (sing. *hersir*).

According to Snorri Sturluson, the thirteenth-century Icelandic author of *Heimskringla* (*A History of the Kings of Norway*), King Haraldr levied taxes on men who traditionally had owned their lands as inalienable family possessions, thus disturbing age-old customs of allodial, or family, landholding (*óðal*). The character of Haraldr's overlordship, especially

---

3. Louis Hartz, *The Founding of New Societies* (New York: Harcourt, Brace, and World, 1964), p. 6.
4. Ibid., p. 4.

his policy concerning *óðal* rights, is one of the issues most disputed by students of Norway in the Middle Ages.[5] Historians today generally believe that Snorri and other saga authors overstated Haraldr's tyranny. Nevertheless, it is instructive to consider the financial policies and hierarchical governmental arrangements which thirteenth-century Icelanders believed Haraldr introduced into the mother country at the time of Iceland's settlement and the establishment of its Althing system of government (*ÍF* 26, ch. 6):

> King Haraldr claimed possession of all *óðal* land wherever he gained power and had each farmer, powerful or not, pay him a tax for the land. He appointed a jarl in each *fylki* [province] who would give judgments at law and collect the fines and the land tax; the jarl would keep a third of the tax for his food and living expenses. Each jarl would have four or more *hersar* under him, and each of the latter would have a revenue of twenty marks. Each jarl would provide the king's army with sixty soldiers and each *hersir* would provide twenty men.

Haraldr's long reign (ca. 885-930) roughly coincided with the period of Iceland's settlement. According to Icelandic narratives, many landowners reluctant to accept Haraldr's demands left Norway. Some went to Iceland and some to Norse settlements in the Shetlands, the Orkneys, the Hebrides, England, Scotland, and Ireland. From the viking settlements in the British Isles a few of the displaced Norwegians returned to raid the coast of Norway, a challenge that Haraldr answered by mounting an expedition (ca. 890) against the Shetlands, the Orkneys, and the Hebrides. This countermove, if it indeed occurred, seems to have stimulated a new wave of emigration from these islands to more distant Iceland. Later medieval Icelandic writers who stress Haraldr's greed for power may have exaggerated his influence on the Icelandic *landnámsmenn*. Yet clearly it was the growth of royal authority in Norway to which Icelandic writers attributed the decisions of many of their forefathers to leave

5. See Per Sveaas Andersen, *Samlingen av Norge og kristningen av landet 800-1130*, Handbok i Norges historie 2 (Bergen: Universitetsforlaget, 1977), pp. 84-91.

that country. And Haraldr's autocratic actions may indeed have impelled some men to seek a fresh start in a newly discovered land.

THE SETTLEMENT OF THE LAND AND
THE ESTABLISHMENT OF ORDER

When first discovered in the mid-ninth century, Iceland was attractive to land-hungry people accustomed to the rugged North Atlantic climate. There had been no prior exploitation of resources and, in the beginning, valuable land was free for the taking. A small number of Irish anchorites (*papar*, sing. *papi*) were in Iceland when the first Norse settlers arrived, but these solitary monks soon left of their own accord or were driven out.[6] The fjords and coastal waters teemed with the food resources of the North Atlantic seaboard, and in the early period the island was fertile. After a few generations of rapid deforestation and extensive livestock raising, however, the productivity of the land began to decline.

The earliest *landnámsmenn*, often shipowners who arrived as the heads of families with dependents and slaves, took huge portions of land, sometimes even entire fjords; Helgi the Lean, for example, claimed all of Eyjafjörðr in the north. Within a few years, however, disputes arose between the initial settlers and those who arrived a little later. According to the *Hauksbók* version of *Landnámabók*, the latecomers accused the early arrivals of taking too much land and asked King Haraldr to mediate. Whether or not the king did intervene is not known for certain, but *Landnámabók* reports that an agreement was reached: "King Haraldr Fairhair got them to agree that no man should take possession of an area larger than he and his crew could carry fire over in a single day. They should make a fire while the sun was in the east. Then they should make other smoky fires so that one fire could be seen from the next, but those made when the sun

6. See *Íslendingabók* (ÍF 1), ch. 1.

was in the east would have to burn until nightfall. Then they should walk until the sun was in the west and make other fires there" (H294). The procedure was different for women wishing to claim land. *Hauksbók* tells us that a woman could take only as much land as she could walk around, while leading a two-year-old well-fed heifer, from dawn to sunset on a spring day (H276).

The pattern of rural life which developed early in Iceland's history remained unchanged for centuries. Both *Laxdæla saga* and *Landnámabók*, with their intense interest in the genealogies of people and land, give an idea, even if fictionally presented, of the leveling process that occurred in Icelandic society in the first formative generations. Unnr in djúpúðga (the Deep-Minded), also called Auðr, daughter of a powerful Norwegian military leader and wife of a viking king said to have been slain in Ireland, claimed for herself a huge and valuable area in the Breiðafjörðr region in western Iceland. To maintain control over her followers, including freedmen, she shared her land with them. But after Unnr's death, around 900, the situation changed drastically. Although her family retained a certain prominence, the new generations descended from her followers no longer honored its claims to regional hegemony. Clearly there was no reason to do so, for the way land was apportioned in early Iceland did not encourage a system of vassalage.

In the succeeding generations, as the original land claims throughout the island were divided up into many farms, there became little to distinguish landholders from one another or to support claims to authority made by leading families among the settlers. After this leveling, land became, through a patrimonial type of ownership (see chapter 5), the sole possession of the family that held it. Ties of interdependence, which formed when the first settlers transferred parcels of property to latecomers, soon disappeared in the absence of any external threat sufficiently alarming to bind the local farmers into European-style defensive units commanded by local aristocrats. The leading families of the original settlers soon realized that their claims to authority and regional control had little viability in a dispersed rural society of landholders enjoying the rights of freemen. According to *Íslendingabók*, within approximately sixty years all the usable land was taken. With the closing of the frontier, the second- and third-generation Icelanders recognized the need for some form of governmental structure. Turning to the king of Norway to settle disputes was a dubious practice if Iceland was to be independent. Further, the settlers who came from various Scandinavian and Norse-Celtic areas brought with them the legal customs under which they had lived. With the steady increase in population the colonists more frequently came into contact with one another, and the lack of a common law must have created serious problems.

In particular, legal differences disrupted the solidarity of the extended families that had migrated to Iceland but whose members had settled in different parts of the country.[7] The problems could probably have been tolerated had not the idea of some form of unified state appealed to the self-interest of the colonists. The initiative for establishing the Althing, the national assembly, seems to have come from a large and powerful kin group which traced its ancestry to an early ninth-century Norwegian *hersir* named Björn buna. The idea, developed years ago by Sigurður Nordal, that kinship with Björn was the basis for selecting those who were first chosen to be chieftains is still intriguing.[8] The children of all Björn's sons, among them the matriarch Unnr the Deep-Minded, came to Iceland; Ari the Learned may have been one of Björn's many descendants.

The actual events that lay behind the founding of the Ice-

7. Family grouping was traditionally an important concept in Norse society and, in *Grágás*, kinship is reckoned out to the fifth degree, to the *thriðjabræðri*, or fourth cousin. GG Ia, pp. 173-174 (ch. 97), p. 194 (ch. 113); Ib, pp. 25-26 (ch. 143); II, p. 75 (ch. 61), p. 113 (ch. 87), p. 341 (ch. 300); III, p. 450 (A.M. 315 A, ch. 3).
8. Sigurður Nordal, *Íslenzk menning* (Reykjavik: Mál og menning, 1942), pp. 111-119; see also Preben Meulengracht Sørensen, *Saga og samfund: En indføring i oldislandsk litteratur* (Copenhagen: Berlingske forlag, 1977), pp. 19-20.

landic government are not recorded and can only be surmised. According to Ari in *Íslendingabók*, a man named Úlfljótr was sent to Norway, probably in the 920s, to adapt the West Norwegian law of the Gula Assembly (Gulathing) to Icelandic exigencies. Some modern scholars, doubting the authenticity of Ari's story, question the existence of Thorleifr inn spaki, an important figure in Ari's account, and the age of the Gulathing.[9] They suggest that the Gulathing and its law, rather than being ancient tradition, came into existence after the establishment of the Althing in Iceland. Even Ari's intent in telling the story raises questions. Because of his own political and family ties, Ari may well have exaggerated in his writings the importance of Norwegian influence. If Úlfljótr did undertake such a trip, his task was probably to seek clarification on certain matters about which the Icelanders, in fashioning their own laws, were unsure, rather than to bring back an entire legal code. Most important, the laws of the Gulathing and the Free State's *Grágás* show few consistent similarities. Jakob Benediktsson sums up the dissimilarity between them: "Norwegian legal traditions applied only to a limited extent to the society that was being created in Iceland. In many areas establishing new constitutional arrangements and new legal procedures was unavoidable. The innovations were then little by little hallowed by custom."[10]

Whatever the truth in Ari's story, a decentralized government specifically designed to satisfy Iceland's needs was created about 930. Approximately thirty-six men became *goðar*,[11] apparently on the basis of kinship alliances (some among the descendants of Björn buna) and local prominence. These

9. Sigurður Líndal, "Sendiför Úlfljóts: Ásamt nokkrum athugasemdum um landnám Ingólfs Arnarsonar," *Skírnir* 143(1969):5-26.

10. Jakob Benediktsson, "Landnám og upphaf allsherjarríkis," in *Saga Íslands* 1:171. See also *Laws of Early Iceland: Grágás I*, trans. Andrew Dennis, Peter Foote, and Richard Perkins, University of Manitoba Icelandic Studies 3 (Winnipeg: University of Manitoba Press, 1980), pp. 8-10.

11. The exact number of the first chieftaincies is uncertain, although later Icelandic writings treated the number as having been fixed at thirty-six.

chieftains served in some capacity as religious as well as secular leaders. Scholars sometimes translate the term *goði* as priest-chieftain; it is derived from the Old Norse word *goð*, which means "god." Probably it stems from the responsibilities of early chieftains as priests and keepers of the local temples. It must be stressed that the written sources from the later Christian period do not give reliable information about pagan religious practices.[12]

Although scholars generally agree that no other governmental or societal structure could have served as a direct model for the Icelandic chieftaincy, the word *goði* was not new. It may have been written in runes in Norway around the year 400, and it is found on several Danish rune stones from the island of Fyn dated to the ninth and perhaps to the early tenth century.[13] *Landnámabók* also refers to one Thórhaddr from Mæri(n) as a temple priest (*hofgoði*) in Norway (S297, H258). In Iceland, Thórhaddr settled in the East Fjords. In the absence of a recognized priesthood, the chieftains seem to have been responsible for hallowing the local assemblies and performing official sacrifices. For a religious life centered on ceremonial cult acts, these duties may have been substantial, at least in the earlier period. The religious functions of the *goði* lent an aura of importance to the individual, distinguishing him from neighboring rich and powerful farmers.

The *goðar* were made officially responsible for holding the local things, or assemblies. All Icelandic things were *skapthing*,[14] meaning that they were governed by established procedure and met at regular legally designated intervals at predetermined meeting places. Except for the *leið* (discussed

12. Olaf Olsen, *Hørg, hov og kirke: Historiske og arkæologiske vikingetidsstudier* (Copenhagen: Gad, 1966).

13. Jakob Benediktsson, "Landnám," p. 172; Ludvig Wimmer, *De danske runemindesmærker*, vol. 2 (Copenhagen: Gyldendalske boghandels forlag, 1899-1901), pp. 346-351, 352-361, 368-383; Hallvard Mageröy, *Norsk-islandske problem*, Omstridde spørsmål i Nordens historie 3, Foreningene Nordens historiske publikasjoner 4 (Oslo: Universitetsforlaget, 1965), pp. 31-33.

14. *GG* Ia, p. 140 (ch. 82); II, p. 277 (ch. 245).

below), no special announcement was required for meetings
of the different things. We do not know the composition of
the assemblies and their courts before the constitutional reforms of the 960s; thereafter their design becomes much
clearer, as both assemblies and courts are discussed in *Grágás*. From the beginning, however, the most important local
assembly was the springtime thing (*várthing*) which met each
year in May and might last a week. Three local chieftains
were responsible for each *várthing*, and all the thingmen of
the three were required to attend. By the mid-tenth century
there were perhaps twelve *várthing*, distributed rather evenly
throughout the country. Only two of them, the Kjalarnes
Thing and the Thórsnes Thing, are known to have preceded
the establishment of the Althing. After the island was divided into quarters (ca. 965), a thirteenth *várthing*, along with
three additional *goðorð*, was added in the Northern Quarter.

The *várthing* were mostly concerned with legal affairs. At
these assemblies cases between local farmers, between local
chieftains, and between chieftains and farmers were tried, if
they could not be settled out of court. Each *goði* named
twelve *bændr* who served as a panel of judges, much like a
jury. As chieftains took no official part in the judicial process
beyond naming the twelve judges, they were free to participate in litigation and out-of-court maneuverings. In addition to its judicial duties, the *várthing* was empowered to set
the local value of the standardized ounce (*thinglagseyrir*). It
also could legislate certain local provisions, but to what extent and in what way are unknown.[15]

The three chieftains responsible for the *várthing* were
equally responsible for the *leið*, the fall assembly usually
held in August. The *leið* had no judicial function and could
be held by each chieftain individually, in which instance the
meeting was attended largely by a chieftain's thingmen. Its
purpose was mainly to report to those who had stayed home
what had taken place at the summer Althing and to announce any new laws.

15. Ólafur Lárusson, *Lög og saga* (Reykjavik: Hlaðbúð, 1958), p. 76.

The Althing was the annual meeting of all *goðar*, each accompanied by some of his thingmen. This crucial gathering, which met at Thingvöllr (the Thing Plain) in the southwestern part of the island, lasted for two weeks in June, during the period of uninterrupted daylight and usually mild weather. Its business was more than governance of the country. At the time when travel was easiest hundreds of people from all over Iceland, including peddlers, brewers of ale, tradesmen, and young adults advertising for spouses, converged on the banks of the Axe River, the Öxará, which runs through the site of the Althing. Thingvöllr, with its large lake and the mountains in the distance, is a site of great natural beauty. For two weeks the ravines and lava plains became a national capital. Friendships and political alliances were initiated, continued, or broken; information was passed; promises were given; stories were told; and business was transacted.

A major feature of the Althing was the meeting of the legislative or law council, the *lögrétta*.[16] Here the chieftains reviewed old laws and made new ones. Only chieftains had the right to vote in the *lögrétta*, but each brought two advisers with him to council meetings. When two or more men shared a *goðorð* only one at a time attended the *lögrétta* and performed the chieftain's other official duties at the Althing. The *lögrétta* was also empowered to grant exemptions from the law. It acted for the country in foreign affairs by making treaties, such as the one with the Norwegian king Óláfr (1015-1030, the saint) delineating the status of Icelanders in Norway and of Norwegians in Iceland.

Formal government at the Althing was public. The *lögrétta* and the courts were held in the open air. At the *lögrétta* the participants sat on benches arranged in three concentric circles. The *goðar* occupied the benches of the middle circle while their advisers sat on the inner and outer benches. In

16. In *Íslendingabók*, ch. 5, Ari reports that Hænsa-Thórir was outlawed at the Althing (ca. 965), indicating that a judicial court sat there. Nothing is known about this court, which would have existed before the reforms.

Map 2. Quarter boundaries and assembly sites during the Free State period (ca. 930-1264).

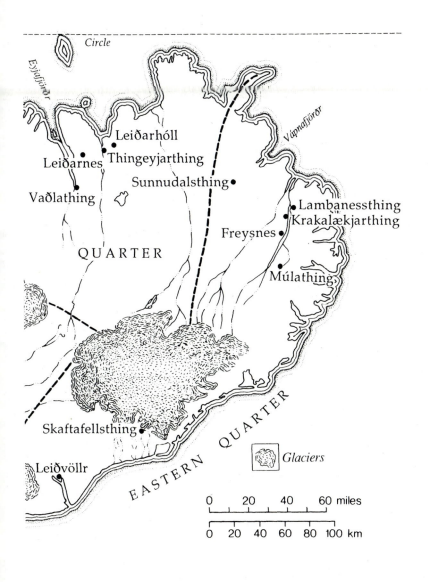

Circle

Eyjafjörðr

Vápnafjörðr

Leiðarhóll

Leiðarnes   Thingeyjarthing

Vaðlathing   Sunnudalsthing

Lambanessthing
Krakalækjarthing

Freysnes

QUARTER

Múlathing

Skaftafellsthing

Leiðvöllr

Glaciers

E A S T E R N   Q U A R T E R

```
0        20        40        60 miles
```

```
0    20   40   60   80   100 km
```

this way each chieftain sat with one adviser in front of him and another behind him. The only fixed buildings at Thingvöllr were a small church, which had been built after the conversion, and a farm. A second small church was added, probably in 1118. Most people pitched tents, but *goðar* and other important personages maintained turf booths from year to year; these they roofed with homespun for the duration of the meeting.

From the beginning of the Free State until its end the only significant national official was the lawspeaker (*lögsögumaðr*), who was elected chairman of the *lögrétta* for a three-year term. Annually at the Law Rock (*lögberg*) the lawspeaker recited a third of the laws from memory. Attendance was required of each *goði* or two stand-ins, selected from among the advisers at the *lögrétta*.[17] They and other interested people sat on the surrounding grassy slope, probably offering emendations or corrections and taking part in discussions of legal issues. Among other duties, the lawspeaker had to announce publicly any laws passed by the *lögrétta*. When needed, the *lögrétta* could also call on the *lögsögumaðr* to furnish any part of the law its members needed in considering legislation. If faced with a difficult point of law or a lapse of memory the *lögsögumaðr* was required to consult five or more legal experts (*lögmenn*).[18] Although the position of lawspeaker was prestigious, it brought little or no official power to its holder, who was allowed to take sides and to participate in litigation and in feuds as a private citizen. We do not know to what extent the lawspeaker decided what to recite, and the choice may have provided him with some leverage. The names and duties of the lawspeakers are preserved in the sources. Ari the Learned dates events by naming the current lawspeaker.

The position of "supreme chieftain" (*allsherjargoði*) was largely ceremonial. It carried with it the duties of hallowing the Althing and setting boundaries for the different sections

17. GG Ia, p. 216 (ch. 117).
18. GG Ia, p. 209 (ch. 116).

of the assembly area. The hallowing marked the official opening of the assembly. The position of *allsherjargoði* was held by the individual who owned the hereditary *goðorð* of Thorsteinn Ingólfsson, the son of Iceland's first settler Ingólfr Arnarson. It is possible that the honor was given to Thorsteinn and his descendants in recognition of services rendered at the time the Althing was established.

The constitutional reforms of the mid-960s were carried out in the wake of a serious clash between two powerful chiefs, Thórðr gellir and Tungu-Oddr.[19] As a consequence of the court system's inability to contain the violence of this conflict, the Icelanders reorganized the judicial system so that the courts could more successfully regulate feud. The original law had specified that a case of manslaughter[20] be tried at the local assembly nearest the scene of the killing, but a defendant from outside the district could hardly expect to have his rights upheld in the home territory of his accuser. To remedy this potential for disorder, the law was altered. Such cases were now permitted to be brought to the Althing where four new courts, one for each quarter, were established. These quarter courts (*fjórðungsdómar*; sing. *fjórðungsdómr*) met yearly at the Althing. They were courts of first instance, that is, individuals from any quarter could begin an action at the Althing rather than at a local *várthing* as long as the matter was of more than minimal consequence. The quarter courts also served as appellate courts: a case that was deadlocked at a *várthing* could be referred to one of them at the Althing.

The founding of the quarter courts was only one of the reforms. The island itself was divided into quarters, a

---

19. The confrontation between the two men is reported with somewhat differing details in *Íslendingabók* and in *Hænsa-Þóris saga* (*ÍF* 3), pp. 1-47.

20. Manslaughter (*víg*) differed from murder (*morð*). If a killing was publicly acknowledged by the perpetrator shortly after the act, it was *víg* and could be atoned for through compensation. *Morð* was a concealed and unacknowledged slaying (*GG* Ia, pp. 154-157 [ch. 88]; II, pp. 348-349 [ch. 315]). *Morð* was a shameful act. See also Klaus von See, *Altnordische Rechtswörter: Philologische Studien zur Rechtsauffassung und Rechtsgesinnung der Germanen. Hermaea*, (2d ser.), 16 (Tübingen: Max Niemeyer Verlag, 1964), pp. 21-22.

change that required fixing the number of full chieftaincies at thirty-nine. The Western, Southern, and Eastern quarters each held three springtime assemblies, each under joint control of three chieftains, making a total of nine chieftains in each quarter. At the same time a fourth *várthing* was added to the Northern Quarter, where geographical conditions required four assemblies, one more than in each of the other quarters. The Northern Quarter thus had twelve *goðar*, although its three new chieftains were not empowered to appoint judges to the quarter courts. To maintain a balance of power among the quarters at the Althing, the title of *goði* was conferred upon three new chieftains each from the Eastern, Western, and Southern quarters, bringing the total number of *goðar* officially participating at the Althing to forty-eight. These nine new *goðar* sat in the national legislative assembly but were not allowed to nominate judges to the quarter courts or to take part in the local assemblies as chieftains.[21]

Through these measures the Icelanders, after a trial period of three decades, remedied the most serious inadequacies of the original system of government. The reforms of the mid-960s reaffirmed the essentially decentralized nature of the earlier structure, based as it was on the relationship of mutual dependency between chieftain and farmer. The more centralized judicial system resulting from these reforms is the one we know from the laws and the sagas. It made Iceland into one jural community, that is, a maximal group which had the obligation to end fighting by peaceful settlement and the machinery to arrange such resolutions. Within Iceland's nontribal jural community, the *goðar* and their cluster of followers were the major cohesive subgroupings.

The quarter assembly (*fjórðungathing*), devoted entirely to the legal affairs of each quarter, was a further innovation instituted sometime after the reforms of the mid-960s. The four *fjórðungathing*, about which there is little information,

---

21. For a discussion of the different types of *goðorð* see Björn Sigfússon, "Full goðorð og forn og heimildir frá 12. öld," *Saga* 3(1960):48-53.

were overshadowed by the courts at the Althing. Although it is generally held that they were soon discontinued, Ólafur Lárusson has argued that they functioned for a longer period than has been assumed.[22] The quarter assemblies are not counted among *skapthing*, and *Grágás* names them only once and does not mention them as having been regularly constituted.[23]

People quickly came to regard the quarter courts at the Althing as better suited than the local assemblies to solve serious problems. A case was normally heard in the court of the quarter in which the defendant was domiciled. Built into this system of annual Althing courts was the concept of impartiality, embracing an intense desire to avoid partisanship. The sources are unclear as to whether thirty-six judges sat in each of the four courts at the Althing or whether a total of thirty-six judges were chosen for all the *fjórðungsdómar*.[24] Since the courts at the *várthing* had thirty-six judges, most experts now believe that the quarter courts at the Althing had the same number.

The panel of judges functioned as a kind of jury, with the power to examine facts, weigh evidence, and deliver a verdict. The national character of the Althing courts is apparent in the composition of the panel of judges. The holders of the "old and full chieftaincies," as the thirty-six prereform *goðorð* came to be known, each nominated judges from their own assembly districts. These judges, required to be free males at least twelve years of age, to have a fixed domicile, and to be responsible for their commitments and oaths, were then apparently assigned by lot to each of the quarter courts.[25] An individual who initiated an action at the

22. Ólafur Lárusson, "Nokkrar athugasemdir um fjórðungaþingin," in *Lög og saga*, pp. 100-118, esp. pp. 117-118.

23. *GG* II, p. 356 (ch. 328).

24. Jakob Benediktsson, "Landnám," p. 180; Jón Jóhannesson, *A History of the Old Icelandic Commonwealth: Íslendinga saga*, trans. Haraldur Bessason, University of Manitoba Icelandic Studies 2 (Winnipeg: University of Manitoba Press, 1974), p. 66.

25. *GG* Ia, p. 38 (ch. 20).

Althing or a person who was summoned there thus entered one of four courts, whose panels of judges were drawn from all four geographical divisions of the country.

The Althing convened on a Thursday evening, and on the following day all judges were appointed. On Saturday the nominees could be challenged and disqualified for various reasons, such as kinship. The process, governed throughout by strict rules of procedure, was open to public scrutiny. The system of seating judges further discouraged regionalism: farmers became acquainted with issues and disputes in other quarters, and decisions were standardized throughout the country. In this way a large segment of the politically important population took part in the decision-making process. Verdicts had to be almost unanimous to avoid legal deadlocks; that is, if six or more judges were in disagreement the case was legally deadlocked. In that event the panel entered two opposing judgments, each favoring one party to the dispute. A final verdict was not possible until a court of appeals was later established. Although every freeman had access to the courts, success in judicial cases often depended on a litigant's ability to muster political support. Settlements usually required negotiations among influential individuals, especially *goðar*.

Because a consensus at court was not always possible, after another thirty-five years (ca. 1005) the court system of the Althing was again altered by the establishment of a court of appeals, called the Fifth Court (*fimtardómr*). As in the other courts, the jury was composed of farmers.[26] The new addition proved to be effective as a court of last instance, in which verdicts were determined by a simple majority. Establishment of the Fifth Court was the penultimate reform of the governmental structure in the Old Icelandic Free State; the final alteration was to expand membership in the *lögrétta* to include the two Icelandic bishops, who, unlike the *goðar*, were not permitted to bring advisers with them.

The regularity and the dependability of the Icelandic

26. GG Ia, p. 77 (ch. 43).

courts reveal the society's desire that parties quickly find acceptable and publicly approved solutions to disputes. Both local and Althing courts offered Icelandic leaders an outlet for their ambitions, and to a large extent the events at these courts reflected the political situation of the country. Farmers and chieftains met there to settle differences, to broker their power, and to advocate the positions of those individuals whose cases they were supporting. Legal assemblies became political arenas where leaders contested with one another for status.

The presence of such elaborate court and assembly structures gave the individual Icelander many alternatives in responding to a grievance. Ideally, two individuals could resolve personal differences by compromise. One party to a dispute might offer *sjálfdæmi*, self-judgment, allowing the other party to fix the terms of the settlement. *Sjálfdæmi* was granted when the party offering it assumed that the opponent would act with moderation, or when the opponent was so strong that he could demand the right to set the terms. Less frequently, *hólmganga*, a formal duel, and *einvígi*, unregulated single combat, were used as direct methods of resolving disputes.[27] The duel was outlawed in Iceland at the beginning of the eleventh century, probably because it embodied outdated values incompatible with the system of negotiation and compromise which by then had become firmly entrenched.

An injured party frequently had other options. For instance, the aggrieved could engage in a blood feud. More so than in other types of action, resort to blood vengeance depended on the support of kinsmen. Hoping, perhaps, to avoid the consequences of blood feud or to end a feud, an individual could turn to the formal legal system with its prescribed rules for summoning, pleading, announcing, and so on. Then there was the less formal option of arbitration,

27. Olav Bø, "Hólmganga and Einvígi: Scandinavian Forms of the Duel," *Mediaeval Scandinavia* 2(1969):132-148; Marlene Ciklamini, "The Old Icelandic Duel," *Scandinavian Studies* 35(1963):175-194.

which tended to introduce into a quarrel the influence of new, often more neutral parties. Each of these techniques of settling disputes could be interconnected. For example, arbitrated settlements were most effective when announced (published) at an assembly, and many court cases were, as Andreas Heusler has noted, a stylized form of feud.[28] At different times contending parties might be involved in all aspects of settlement including violence, legal redress, and arbitration.

The close connection between political and legal success in Iceland was owing in part to the institutionalized concept that the government bore no responsibility for punishing an individual for breaking the law. Criminal acts were regarded as private concerns to be settled between the injured and the offending parties or their advocates. In keeping with this procedure, penalties were paid in the form of damages to the successful party. The duty to exact vengeance in cases of manslaughter fell on the kin of the slain, who, if he or she wished to act, had to choose among the different available methods of processing a claim.

The court and assembly structures in Iceland were unusually extensive, but freemen in Norway as well as in the rest of Scandinavia and in Anglo-Saxon England possessed many rights analogous to those enjoyed by Icelandic farmers. These rights, however, were valid in a more limited sphere than in Iceland. The relationship between farmers and their leaders in Norway was part of a local and national system of decision making which took into consideration the prerogatives and designs of kings and other military, political, and, later, clerical leaders. Focusing on the traditional Norse-Germanic rights of freemen, the Icelanders in the tenth century developed those rights in isolation from the privileges of kings and from the other higher strata of viking society. They expanded the ancient concept of the local freemen's assembly and, in the process, created a body of law

28. Andreas Heusler, *Das Strafrecht der Isländersagas* (Leipzig: Duncker and Humblot, 1911), p. 103.

that in its entirety was distinct from anything that had previously existed in Scandinavia. This governmental system maintained social order for several hundred years. Only in the thirteenth century did it break down, creating a situation in which the Norwegian Crown could successfully claim hegemony over Iceland.[19]

CHANGE AND CONTINUITY

In the late twelfth and thirteenth centuries, Icelandic society experienced changes in the balance of power. As part of the evolution to a more stratified order, the number of chieftains diminished and the power of the remaining leaders grew. By the thirteenth century six large families came to monopolize the chieftaincies. The destabilizing effect of the increase in the power of individual leaders from these lineages was especially evident in the period 1220-1260, which is often referred to in modern studies as the Age of the Sturlungs.[30]

From our vantage point it is clear that these "large" or "big" leaders (called *stórgoðar* or *stórhöfðingjar* in modern studies) were in the process of forming a new social class, though they often continued to use the term *goðar* in reference to themselves. The thirteenth century was a time of transition, but the extent of the change brought on by the advancement of the *stórgoðar* to a new level in the social or-

29. According to Snorri Sturluson's account in *Heimskringla* (chs. 124-125), the Norwegian king Óláfr Haraldsson (later the saint) in the early eleventh century showed some interest in controlling Iceland, but the matter came to nothing. According to *Íslendinga saga* (*Sturl.* 1, ch. 38), the threat of Norwegian military aggression became a serious possibility in the thirteenth century (especially ca. 1220), though an attack was never undertaken. See Magnús Már Lárusson, "Þrístirnið á norðurlöndum," *Skírnir* 141(1967):28-33.

30. Einar Ól. Sveinsson, *The Age of the Sturlungs: Icelandic Civilization in the Thirteenth Century*, trans. Jóhann S. Hannesson (Ithaca: Cornell University Press, 1953); see also Jesse L. Byock, "The Age of the Sturlungs," in *Continuity and Change: Political Institutions and Literary Monuments in the Middle Ages*, ed. Elisabeth Vestergaard (Odense: Odense University Press, 1986), pp. 27-42, for an expansion of this section.

der is difficult to judge. The difficulty exists because the movement was much less of an upheaval than it might have been; the rise in social complexity was evolutionary rather than revolutionary. The *stórgoðar* did not overthrow an existing governing elite; instead, as Gunnar Karlsson notes in his pioneering study on the subject, they simply moved up the ladder.[31]

Abandoning many of the traditional concerns of the *goðar* in local administration, the *stórgoðar* began to aspire to regional control in the late twelfth and early thirteenth centuries. Later on, during the most troubled years of the Sturlung period (ca. 1230-1262), *stórgoðar* attempted to extend their spheres of influence over ever larger geographical areas. With dreams of ruling princely domains, they tried to establish new positions of executive authority, positions that for centuries had been only a remote possibility in Iceland's kingless society. Among the most ambitious of these leaders, a major struggle for national power ensued.

Yet the most serious strife of the troubled Sturlung years lasted little more than a generation, and the extent of disruption is probably exaggerated in the contemporary sources. *Sturlunga saga*, the major source for this period, is not the story of a contented people. It dwells on the violence and the greed for political power which characterized the lives of the thirteenth-century leaders. The picture is made particularly clear in *Íslendinga saga*, the central and longest saga in the Sturlunga compilation. *Íslendinga saga* recounts events from 1183 to 1264, and its author, Sturla Thórðarson, was himself a member of the Sturlung family. As an important leader he played an active role in the events of the last decades of the Free State. A man whose fortunes as a leader alternately rose and fell, Sturla had had firsthand experience of the dangers and treacheries about which he wrote.

Sturla Thórðarson probably wrote *Íslendinga saga* near the end of his life, in the years 1271-1284, that is, in the period after the Icelanders had submitted to Norwegian overlord-

---

31. Gunnar Karlsson, "Goðar og bændur," *Saga* 10(1972):42-43.

ship. Sturla's work is not a general history of the thirteenth century but a retrospective description of the struggles for power among leaders in the preceding half century. Although he mentions many *bændr* and their leaders the *stórbændr* (large or big farmers), his interests are elsewhere. As a historian Sturla is concerned principally with the activities and the fate of the new *stórgoðar* group of leaders to which he himself belonged. In particular he recounts the fortunes of members of his large and quarrelsome family. Neither Sturla nor the authors of many other sagas in the Sturlunga compilation try to hide or to soften the cruel realities of political intrigue. The result is a political history of a few powerful families, whose fortunes *Sturlunga saga* follows closely over generations.

Despite its narrow focus *Sturlunga saga* gives us much information from which we can judge the extent of change. We see that the troubles of the period did not alter the traditional pattern of scattered settlement or remove the farmers' grip on landownership. These are aspects of continuity essential to the cultural focus and economic makeup of the society. Numerous features of the traditional system of reciprocity between farmers and their local leaders (see chapter 6) remained in operation until the end of the Free State, and probably for an even longer time. This continuity in the arrangement of the local power structure was possible because the more enterprising of the *stórbændr* performed in the thirteenth century many of the leadership functions that had formerly been prerogatives of the more numerous local *goðar*. The *stórbændr* were cut from the same cloth as the ambitious *bændr*, typified by Thorgils Oddason from Staðarhóll (d. 1151) and Thórðr Gilsson from Staðarfell,[32] who in earlier centuries had gained control of chieftaincies. The opportunity for such individuals to assume roles of the earlier *goðar*,

---

32. Thórðr Gilsson was active in the first half of the twelfth century. He was the father of the *goði* Hvamm-Sturla, who became influential later in the century. Sturla in turn was the father of the three Sturlusons, Thórðr, Sighvatr, and Snorri.

including solving disputes between neighboring farmers, increased during the Sturlung period. At that time, as Gunnar Karlsson notes, a region "could be without a *stórgoði* for years, either because he was staying in Norway or because he had been killed and no one had the authority to succeed him."[33]

Although occasionally assuming pretensions of rulers, the *stórgoðar* were unable to establish effective regional states. Especially in the last decades of the Free State, their careers tended to be short and their hold on power became insecure as their feuds increased. Rather than setting up effective administrations dependent on sheriffs, bailiffs, and other functionaries of a central political hierarchy, individual leaders usually did not have the time or the authority to replace older forms of government.

Those *stórgoðar* who succeeded in exercising regional control usually did so through the expedient, but inefficient, means of directing several existing chieftaincies. In such situations *stórbændr* often acted as representatives of the farmers. This development offered the new leaders only limited military and financial backing, and *stórgoðar* were frequently forced to rely for support on their families. But here also the *stórgoðar* experienced problems. The custom of prominent men openly keeping concubines diversified the kin group, making the degree of relatedness of kin at the same generational level much less close than it otherwise might have been. For example, Snorri Sturluson (d. 1241) had two legitimate children, Jón Murti (d. 1231) and a daughter Hallbera. His best known son Órækja (d. 1245) was illegitimate.[34] Snorri's brother Thórðr Sturluson (d. 1237) was separated from his first wife and had a son and a daughter by his second wife. In between the two marriages, he had several concubines. With one of these, named Thóra, he had three

33. Gunnar Karlsson, "Goðar and Höfðingjar in Medieval Iceland," *Saga-Book of the Viking Society for Northern Research* 19(1977):368.
34. *Íslendinga saga* (*Sturl.* I, ch. 16).

daughters and three sons, one of whom was Sturla Thórð-arson, the *stórgoði* and author of *Íslendinga saga*.

Stórgoðar families usually had no preestablished system of hierarchy and no well-defined system of inheritance, and, like the Sturlungs, they were not cohesive political groups. If one family, or one group within a family, did gain control of several chieftaincies, these *goðorð* were often distributed among relatives including half siblings, both legitimate and illegitimate. Such kinsmen might be uncooperative and might even be inimical, as often happened with the Sturlungs. The resulting confusion made Iceland in the mid-thirteenth century fertile ground for the expansionist policies of the Norwegian Crown. Aided by Norway's archbishop, the king offered Iceland's *bændr* a stable, if unpalatable, alternative to the turmoil caused by the quarrels of the *stórgoðar*, and the Icelanders at a series of local assemblies in 1262-1264 accepted the offer. In turning to a king who resided an ocean away, the farmers were able to preserve many of the rights that were being threatened by the ambitions of the *stórgoðar*. During the first decades of Norwegian control, Iceland fared reasonably well, largely because the acceptance of Norwegian suzerainty caused little social dislocation. If not fully independent, Iceland, nevertheless, functioned as a semiautonomous region in respect to law. The agreement, by which representatives from the northern and southern regions swore allegiance to the king, was called the Old Covenant (*Gamli Sáttmáli*).[35] It guaranteed that the king would show deference to the Icelanders: "In return the king shall let us enjoy peace and the Icelandic laws."[36] The last phrase seems not to have precluded the right of Norwegians to alter the

35. In 1262-1264 the rest of the Icelanders swore allegiance to the king, using this or a similar covenant. For different manuscript versions of the covenant see *DI*, vol. 1, pt. 3 (Copenhagen: S. L. Möller, 1862), pp. 619-625; vol. 9 (Reykjavik: Hið íslenzka bókmentafélag, 1909-1913), pp. 1-4; vol. 10 (1911-1921), pp. 5-8. I cite the A version of the covenant (vol. 1, pp. 620-621).

36. "Hier j mot skal konungr lata oss naa fridi og jslendskum laugum," *DI*, vol. 1, p. 620.

existing Free State laws; it suggests that the Icelanders would have the right to accept or reject new legislation. Thus much of the traditional legislative power remained with the Icelanders, even though the king was free to modify older laws or to propose new ones. After the strong-willed empire builder King Hákon Hákonarson died in 1263, his son King Magnús lagabætir (the Law Mender, d. 1280) became king. Magnús showed himself to be a wise and conciliatory ruler who usually avoided offending the Icelanders. He allowed them a measure of autonomy and was willing to replace *Járnsíða*, the unpopular Norwegian inspired lawbook introduced in 1271. In 1280 a second Norwegian law code called *Jónsbók* was submitted to the Icelanders, who initially opposed it, even though it retained many traditional features of *Grágás*. After much debate among Icelanders and royal pressure, *Jónsbók* was accepted in 1281 at the Althing by a majority vote of the *lögrétta*. In the decades immediately following the introduction of *Jónsbók*, the king normally refrained from repressive use of his new powers, and Iceland enjoyed a period of peace and relative prosperity.

5

Sources of the Chieftains' Wealth

> There was neither public revenue nor public expenditure, neither exchequer nor budget. No taxes were levied by the Republic, as indeed no expenses were incurred on its behalf.
>
> —James Bryce

In early Iceland the methods by which land was acquired had a decidedly predatory stamp. Perhaps more than in other societies with better resources and additional opportunities, an increase in the size of an individual's landholdings often depended on taking a neighbor's property. As a result, the success of one Icelander routinely signaled the impoverishment of another. With this idea in mind, the question of how best to define Iceland's system of wealth exchange, in particular the means by which land was acquired, is paramount throughout the following discussion. So also is a basic fact: the income a chieftain received from performing legally designated governmental duties was too little and too irregular to explain how successful chieftains amassed the wealth necessary to purchase support, pay compensation awards, exchange gifts, make loans, and provide feasts and hospitality.

This chapter surveys the different sources of income which contributed to the wealth of chieftains. It begins with a short discussion of several pertinent factors and proceeds to an assessment of the relative value of the income that a chieftain derived from his position as a governmental leader. This privileged income included revenues generated by the few taxes, profits from carrying out official services, and advantages reaped from the exclusive right to set prices on imported goods. The second part of the chapter considers sources of wealth which were not controlled solely by the *goðar* but were available to all prosperous farmers in the community. These nonprivileged sources include trade and the control of valuable property such as *staðir* (sing. *staðr*), the most important of the church farmsteads.

BACKGROUND INFORMATION

Several factors are fundamental to an understanding of Iceland's political economics. One is that a tax designed specifically for maintenance of governmental leaders was not imposed until near the end of the Free State.[1] This levy, called *sauðakvöð* or *sauðatollr* (sheep tax), is mentioned several times in *Sturlunga saga*.[2] *Sauðakvöð* seems to have been a forced impost rather than a regularly collected tax.[3] It was employed most often as an expedient by *stórgoðar* in dire need of funds.[4]

Another factor is that the introduction in the thirteenth

1. Björn Thorsteinsson, *Íslenzka þjóðveldið* (Reykjavik: Heimskringla, 1953), p. 101. Several minor taxes first appear in the later Free State period. Among the more important was a form of thing tax, *thingtollr*; this tax is mentioned, for example, in *DI*, vol. 1, pt. 1, p. 276. For a listing of the different *tollr* see Björn Thorsteinsson, "Tollr," *KLNM* 18, cols. 452-454.

2. All the references to the *sauðakvöð* or *sauðatollr* appear toward the middle of the thirteenth century: *Sturl.* 1, *Íslendinga saga*, ch. 79, in 1230; *Sturl.* 2, *Þórðar saga kakala*, ch. 37, in 1245; *Sturl.* 2, *Þorgils saga skarða*, chs. 14, 55, and 58, in 1252 and 1255.

3. The editors of *Sturlunga saga*, Jón Jóhannesson, Magnús Finnbogason, and Kristján Eldjárn, infer from ch. 37 of *Þórðar saga kakala* that *sauðatollr* might have been collected yearly (*Sturl.* 2, p. 299, n. 1). This conclusion is only a guess; the source on which it is based is unclear and does not specify a regular collection.

4. An extreme example of the rapaciousness of the later chieftains is the conduct of Snorri Sturluson's ambitious son Órækja in his attempt to establish himself in the West Fjords. Órækja's collection of taxes takes on the aspect of a military requisition (*Sturl.* 1, *Íslendinga saga*, ch. 93).

century of a tax on farmers such as *sauðakvöð*, as well as the aggressive stance that some *goðar* took at this time against foreign merchants, may have had as much to do with general economic conditions in Europe as with contemporaneous Icelandic political arrangements. Around 1200, when Icelandic leaders were becoming more ruthless, Europe was experiencing inflation. This situation led those in power in many places in the medieval West to squeeze people within their reach.

An additional factor is that the Icelanders never had a sufficiently large or stable source of silver to replenish the precious metals brought by the first settlers. Over the years, traveling Icelanders and successful traders brought to the island new supplies of silver, but by the eleventh century the reserve seems to have been sharply reduced. From the earliest period Icelanders substituted commodities for silver, and several mediums of exchange—ranging from silver to livestock, woolen cloth, and dairy products—coexisted in medieval Iceland. In particular, homespun cloth (*vaðmál*) replaced silver as a more common unit of exchange, with each grade equivalent to a weight of silver, though the ratios fluctuated over the years.

The principal monetary unit was the *lögeyrir* (law ounce), which equaled six ells of homespun cloth two ells wide (an ell seems to have been a little more than 49 cm or approximately 19.5 inches). The ratio of the law ounce to an ounce of silver varied from 8:1 in the eleventh century to 6:1 in the latter half of the thirteenth century, with a ratio of 7.5:1 recorded in the twelfth century. Prices of goods were calculated in *thinglagsaurar* (standardized ounces), whose values were set at the local springtime assemblies and thus varied from district to district. Usually the standardized ounce was equal to three or four ells of homespun cloth.[5] Livestock

5. For standards of values and equivalents and pricing policies, see Jón Jóhannesson, *A History of the Old Icelandic Commonwealth: Íslendinga Saga*, trans. Haraldur Bessason, University of Manitoba Icelandic Studies 2 (Winnipeg: University of Manitoba Press, 1974), pp. 328-335; Bruce E. Gelsinger, *Icelandic Enterprise: Commerce and Economy in the Middle Ages* (Columbia: Uni-

were also frequently used as currency. The value of a cow was set at each district assembly, a practice that again made prices widely different. Taxes and tithes were paid mostly in butter, cheese, livestock, and other farm products. Icelandic economic arrangements were to a large degree dictated by the climate and the nature of the land. Because Iceland is situated between two different air masses, the cold dry polar front and the warm, damp southern front, and between two different oceanic currents, the North Atlantic drift and the East Greenland polar current, its temperature and weather are exceedingly unstable. This variability and the short growing season at Iceland's northern latitude limited vegetation to grasses, mosses, lichens, and sedges. Wood became a scarce commodity; birch, the only tree that grew naturally in medieval Iceland, was stunted and twisted because of the constantly changing temperature. The first settlers found an advantage in the absence of dense forests. The land was easy to clear and the scrub birch offered a ready supply of fuel. The grasses and shrubs were immediately suitable for pastoral farming. Problems, however, were not long in coming. The population seems soon to have reached the limits of what the land could support; the overgrazing that followed caused serious erosion. Although reliable data for Icelandic climate in the Middle Ages are scarce, the evidence suggests that during the period 870-1170 the climate was unusually mild and thereafter grew colder. A cooling of the climate would have further limited the productivity of the land, especially at higher elevations.[6]

The Icelanders early had to adapt to the confines of a

---

versity of South Carolina Press, 1981), pp. 33-44; Magnús Már Lárusson, "Íslenzkar mælieiningar," *Skírnir* 132(1958):208-245; Finnur Jónsson, "Islands mønt, mål og vægt," in *Mål och vikt*, ed. Svend Aakjær, Nordisk kultur 30 (Stockholm: Albert Bonniers förlag, 1936), pp. 155-161. See also Asgaut Steinnes, "Mål, vekt og verderekning i Noreg i mellomalderen og ei tid etter," in ibid., pp. 123-127.

6. A. E. J. Ogilvie, "The Past Climate and Sea-ice Record from Iceland, Part I. Data to A.D. 1780," *Climatic Change* 6(1984):149.

limited amount of productive land. The interior of the island has extensive lava plains and in the winter is too cold for habitation, and more than 11 percent of the island is covered by glaciers. The settlers did not develop any significant new farming technology to increase the productivity of the finite habitable areas along the coast and in the sheltered valleys. Although some farmers, especially in the south, cultivated cereal crops such as barley on a small scale, the summer growing season was too short, too cold, and too wet for extensive plantings. Instead, the *bændr* became settled pastoralists, raising livestock and producing dairy products. The harvesting of hay was vital in order to feed as many cattle and sheep as possible during the long winter; numerous saga feuds begin with quarrels over especially fertile meadows and their harvests. As erosion and overuse diminished the quantity of productive land, its value increased. Land became a scarce commodity which was all the more valuable because of the limited supply of alternative sources of wealth. The general scarcity of land in Iceland was different from circumstances found in many contemporaneous European lands, where large tracts of forest and uninhabited wilderness provided the medieval population with room to expand.

SOURCES OF INCOME AVAILABLE ONLY TO CHIEFTAINS

The sources of a *goði*'s wealth in the early period have never been explored, principally because the major historical writings, *Landnámabók* and *Íslendingabók*, give little specific economic information. *Grágás* is only slightly more informative. Legally prescribed taxes and other sources of income allotted to a chieftain in *Grágás* are noticably small. They could not have enabled a *goði* either to amass or to maintain large holdings of property, numbers of livestock, or supplies of readily transferable wealth.

Taxes

Relying principally on information from historical and legal sources, students of medieval Iceland have usually assumed that chieftains in the early centuries found little financial advantage in their official position. In keeping with this view, a disproportionate share of the comparatively small space given to discussion of wealth exchange in current historical writings is devoted to *thingfararkaup* (the thing tax) and *hoftollr* (the temple tax). *Thingfararkaup*, which literally means the fee or bargained price (*kaup*) for traveling to the Althing, was the most lucrative assessment a chieftain could legally impose. Upon demand, each *thingfararkaupsbóndi* (thing-tax-paying-farmer) who possessed for each person in his household a minimum amount of property—a cow, a boat, a net, for example—had to pay the thing tax to his *goði*.[7]

According to Ari in *Íslendingabók* (ch. 10), Gizurr Ísleifsson, Iceland's second bishop, carried out a census, probably at the end of the eleventh century, and determined that there were 38 "hundred" *thingfararkaupsbændr*. If the term "hundred" stood for 120, as was customary, then the number of substantial farmers at this time was approximately 4,560. So large a number of property-owning free farmers is an indication of the social leveling that had transpired in Iceland in the centuries following the settlement. The figure also suggests the political importance of the *thingfararkaupsbændr*, individuals who, from all accounts, looked after their own rights and interests. They controlled most of the island's productive land, and almost all the population, estimated at approximately 60,000, lived on their farms. The wealth and authority of the *goðar* were surely dependent on

---

7. GG Ia, p. 159 (ch. 89); II, p. 320 (ch. 287); III, p. 173 (A.M. 135 4to, *Arnarbælisbók*, ch. 10), pp. 431-432 (A.M. 125 A 4to, ch. 25). The specifics of *thingfararkaup* are not completely clear in *Grágás*. See Sveinbjörn Rafnsson, *Studier i Landnámabók: Kritiska bidrag till den isländska fristatstidens historia*, Bibliotheca Historica Lundensis 31 (Lund: C. W. K. Gleerup, 1974), pp. 135-136, esp. n. 9.

their relationship to these farmers, but the legally defined elements of this relationship only hint at how the *goðar* operated.

At the local springtime assembly a chieftain was permitted to require each ninth *thingfararkaup* farmer among his thingmen to accompany him to the Althing. The *goði* then collected the tax from the thingmen who stayed at home and used the funds to compensate those who accompanied him to the Althing. This payment to the farmers was also called *thingfararkaup*. The size of *thingfararkaup* varied, probably in accordance with the distance from home to the Althing. Although we lack specific information, it seems doubtful that a chieftain could set the tax above the amount assessed by competing local leaders and still retain the support of his thingmen. Because a *goði* incurred heavy expenses on a trip to the Althing, any revenue from *thingfararkaup* might be, and probably was, canceled out by the costs incurred.

The only other major tax available to the early *goðar* was *hoftollr* (the temple tax). Most of the little that is known about *hoftollr* comes from *Eyrbyggja saga*, which, like all the family sagas, was written in later Christian times and therefore is not a trustworthy source for information about specific preconversion religious practices. *Eyrbyggja saga* (ch. 4) describes the temple tax: "All persons were required to pay a tax to the temple priest on all his trips, in the same manner that thingmen now must accompany their leaders. But at his own expense the *goði* was required to oversee the upkeep of the temple so that it did not deteriorate and to hold in it sacrificial feasts."[8] This passage suggests that the profit from *hoftollr* was limited. In return for dues, the chieftain bore the expense of maintaining the temple.

Again as with *thingfararkaup*, if one *goði* raised his demands, the interests of other *goðar* would have been served

---

8. Another reference to *hoftollr* is found in *Vápnfirðinga saga* (ÍF 11), where the person immediately in charge of the temple is a priestess. According to the saga, "all the farmers were required to pay to the temple a temple tax" (ch. 5).

by their asking less from their thingmen. Because *thingfar-arkaup* and *hoftollr* brought chieftains little surplus wealth, scholars have long postulated that a *goði* realized little or no income from possession of a *goðorð*. The concept that a chieftaincy did not offer financial advantage, but instead may have been a drain on a chieftain's resources, originated in Konrad Maurer's extensive study of the origin of the Icelandic state (1852).[9] The idea promulgated by Maurer and taken up by later scholars has survived well over a century without being seriously challenged. The concept was firmly established by 1883, when it was defined by the Arnamagnæan Commission which compiled the index for *Grágás* III: "In accepting the tax [*thingfararkaup*] it does not appear that the chieftain had an income."[10]

Since Maurer, numerous scholars have commented on the chieftains' limited financial prospects. In *Íslenzk menning*, a study of Old Icelandic civilization, Sigurður Nordal, in discussing the apparent paucity of income from either *thingfararkaup* or *hoftollr*, judges the economic viability of the *goðorð*: "But even if the chieftain had employed the magnificence and authority [of the *goðorð*] to its full extent, then his position would in general have been an expense for him rather than a profit."[11] Jón Jóhannesson in *A History of the Old Icelandic Commonwealth* writes that chieftains enjoyed a small income from maintaining the temple and from levying certain dues (*lausatekjur*), but he found the information about the *thingfararkaup* unclear. Like Nordal, Jón Jóhannesson concludes: "The office of a chieftain does not appear to have been a lucrative position, considering the many expenses involved."[12] Ólafur Lárusson in *Lög og saga* suggests that some *bændr* avoided *thingfararkaup* by following their chieftain to

9. Konrad Maurer, *Die Entstehung des isländischen Staats und seiner Verfassung* (Munich: Christian Kaiser, 1852), finds that a *goðorð* "even demanded monetary sacrifices" (p. 102).

10. *GG* III, p. 702.

11. Sigurður Nordal, *Íslenzk menning*, vol. 1 (Reykjavik: Mál og menning, 1942), p. 124.

12. Jón Jóhannesson, *History*, p. 62.

the Althing. He agrees that the office of the chieftaincy was "not especially remunerative."[13] Jakob Benediktsson, in his essay in *Saga Íslands*, points out the dual nature of the thing tax: "The *goðar* seem both to have received payment of *thingfararkaup* from those who stayed home and at the same time compensated those who went to the thing, and it cannot be seen whether they had any profit from these transactions."[14] In *Íslenzka þjóðveldið*, Björn Thorsteinsson agrees that chieftains had relatively little revenue from temple dues and from *thingfararkaup*: "These payments were rather low and covered little more than the cost of sacrifices and of travel to the thing."[15] The same writer later maintains a similar view of *thingfararkaup* in *Ný Íslandssaga*.[16] In *Íslenzk miðaldasaga*, a survey of Iceland's medieval period, he restricts his major treatment of chieftains' wealth to the twelfth and thirteenth centuries, when chieftains along with *stórbændr* exercised control over church property. In the discussion of the early period, Björn Thorsteinsson notes briefly the connection between a chieftain's wealth and his role in the operation of society: "The chieftains had their main source of income in the control of the law."[17] Unfortunately he does not elaborate on the observation. Kirsten Hastrup also stresses the importance of law within the society but gives no indication of how the *goðar* used the law to their financial benefit.[18] She writes: "Just as it is difficult to extract from the sources information about the economy and about the nature of the relations of production, so is it also difficult to get a

13. Ólafur Lárusson, *Lög og saga* (Reykjavik: Hlaðbúð, 1958), p. 71.
14. Jakob Benediktsson, "Landnám og upphaf allsherjarríkis," in *Saga Íslands* 1:174. This otherwise comprehensive essay tracing Icelandic history through the 900s devotes little attention to the issue of wealth beyond looking briefly at *thingfararkaup* and commenting on rental income.
15. Björn Thorsteinsson, *Íslenzka þjóðveldið*, p. 101.
16. Björn Thorsteinsson, *Ný Íslandssaga: Þjóðveldisöld* (Reykjavik: Heimskringla, 1966), p. 85.
17. Björn Thorsteinsson, *Íslenzk miðaldasaga* (Reykjavik: Sögufélag, 1978), p. 52.
18. Kirsten Hastrup, *Culture and History in Medieval Iceland: An Anthropological Analysis of Structure and Change* (Oxford: Clarendon Press, 1985), pp. 118-121, see also p. 13.

clear picture of actual political power and political actions. This is why the analysis of the politico-administrative system will be made on structural principles, that is, in terms of legal values and civil rights."[19]

In *Studier i Landnámabók*, Sveinbjörn Rafnsson discusses the financial aspect of the *goði-bóndi* relationship. Although agreeing with other scholars that "*thingfararkaup* goes continually through a chieftain's hands," he attempts to establish an additional connection between the earlier *thingfararkaup* and the taxes introduced at the end of the Free State.[20] He suggests that *thingfararkaup*, though in itself not profitable, may have set a precedent for the later thirteenth-century *sauðakvöð*. This line of reasoning, however logical, fails to answer the basic question: How did the *goðar* survive from the 900s until the 1200s, when a profitable tax first came into use? Although the precedent of farmers paying *goðar* was established by the earlier tax, the two levies are quite dissimilar: *thingfararkaup* was payment by specific individuals for a specific purpose; *sauðakvöð* was a general levy providing leaders with income. It may be true that *thingfararkaup* smoothed the way for the implementation of later taxes, but in the tenth and eleventh centuries Icelandic farmers were not so primitive that they did not know how taxes worked.

Furthermore, the fact that farmers at the end of the Free State understood how taxes functioned does not mean that they accepted the right of the *stórgoðar* to impose them. To the contrary, *bændr* in the thirteenth century clung to their centuries-old privileges. Later sagas in the Sturlunga compilation tell us that in the 1240s and 1250s the farmers were often reluctant to accept the new claims of the *stórgoðar*. At times, as in the *Saga of Thorgils Skarði*, the *bændr* openly refused to furnish these leaders with supplies. For example, Thorgils skarði and Thórðr kakali, two *stórgoðar* who claimed control over large regions, faced strong opposition from the *bændr* when they tried to levy taxes; in the end both suc-

19. Ibid. p. 106.
20. Sveinbjörn Rafnsson, *Studier*, p. 134.

ceeded only to a limited extent. Even when his power was finally assured, Thórðr's right to tax the farmers in his territory was not well established. When Thórðr and his rich enemy Kolbeinn ungi agreed to travel to Norway and lay their case before the king, part of the arrangement was that Thórðr's travel expenses should be paid by Kolbeinn, since Thórðr's thingmen apparently refused to pay taxes to defray the costs.[21]

Price Setting

Besides taxes the chieftains had certain other privileged sources of wealth, such as the right to set prices on wares that foreign merchants brought into Iceland. Ostensibly the purpose of this practice was to control the greed of foreign merchants, as suggested in *Grágás*, though neither the date nor the enforceability of the following clause is known: "It is said in our laws that men shall not buy expensive Norwegian goods from merchants at their ships until those three men who set the rate within each district boundary have done so."[22]

Although some windfall profits might have accrued from price setting, it was not as lucrative as one might expect because, in most instances, the Norwegian merchant retained the advantage. If dissatisfied with a chieftain in a particular region, the merchant could try to find a more compliant chieftain in that area or he could sail to another place

---

21. *Sturl.* 2, *Þorgils saga skarða*, ch. 14. The question of whether or not Thorgils skarði and other *stórgoðar* were affluent is debated by Helgi Thorláksson, "Stórbændur gegn goðum: Hugleiðingar um goðavald, konungsvald og sjálfræðishug bænda um miðbik 13. aldar," in *Söguslóðir: afmælisrit helgað Ólafi Hanssyni sjötugum 18. september 1979*, ed. Bergsteinn Jónsson, Einar Laxness, and Heimir Thorleifsson (Reykjavik: Sögufélag, 1979), pp. 227-250; and Gunnar Karlsson, "Völd og auður á 13. öld," *Saga* 18(1980):5-30. Helgi Thorláksson in "Stórbændur," p. 229, doubts that Thorgils skarði was in great need. Gunnar Karlsson in "Goðar og bændur," *Saga* 10(1972):43-44, and "Völd og auður," pp. 14-19, takes the opposing view, arguing that Thorgils was for years troubled by a lack of funds.

22. GG Ib, p. 72 (ch. 167).

on the coast. In only a few years a *goði* could acquire a bad reputation if he pressed the merchants too hard for a price advantage or demanded more than a small share in the profits. For a *goði* the value of the privilege probably was that it gave him first choice of imported goods. This advantage was significant in a society in which gift giving, loans of precious items,[23] and displays of hospitality were used to increase political stature. Expensive feasts and expansive hospitality figure prominently in the literature, and we can often judge the quality of a relationship by noting whether the host sent his guest off with "good gifts."[24]

Only a few sagas narrating events before the thirteenth century—for example, *Vápnfirðinga saga*, *Hænsa-Þóris saga*, and *Ljósvetninga saga*—mention price setting. An account in *Vápnfirðinga saga* may offer some insight into the relationship between local *goðar* and Norwegian merchants. The story goes that one summer a ship captained by a Norwegian named Hrafn and his partner, an Icelandic *bóndi*, puts into Vápnafjörðr in the Eastern Quarter. The Icelander goes home to his farm, leaving the Norwegians to find lodgings for themselves. Two young chieftains from the local region, Brodd-Helgi, a highly ambitious man, and his more moderate friend Geitir, learn of the merchants' arrival (ch. 4):

> Brodd-Helgi rode to the ship and invited the captain to lodge with him.
> The Norwegian answered that he would not lodge with Helgi, as "it has been said to me that you are arrogant and greedy for money. But I am humble and a man of few needs, and the two do not go together."
> Brodd-Helgi tried to buy some valuable objects from the

23. *The Saga of Gísli Súrsson* (ch. 15) mentions a valuable imported tapestry which was lent for a feast.
24. Aaron J. Gurevich, "Wealth and Gift-Bestowal among the Ancient Scandinavians," *Scandinavica* 7(1968):126-138; William Ian Miller, "Gift, Sale, Payment, Raid: Case Studies in the Negotiation and Classification of Exchange in Medieval Iceland," *Speculum* 61(1986):18-50; and Helgi Thorláksson, "Snorri Sturluson og Oddaverjar," in *Snorri: Átta alda minning*, ed. Gunnar Karlsson and Helgi Thorláksson (Reykjavik: Sögufélag, 1979), pp. 53-55.

merchant because he was a man given to lavish display. But Hrafn replied that he had no wish to sell goods on credit.

Brodd-Helgi said, "You have made my journey here a wasted endeavor, refusing my lodgings and refusing my trade."

Geitir came next to the ship and found the captain, telling him that it was unwise to have fallen out with the most notable man in the district.

The Norwegian answered, "It had been my intention to lodge with some *bóndi*, but will you now see to my needs, Geitir?"

Geitir did not quickly agree, but in the end he took the Norwegian in.

The crew also found lodgings for themselves. Rollers were put under the keel and the ship was dragged ashore and set up for the winter. The Norwegian was given a storage shed for his wares; he sold his goods slowly.

The Norwegian merchant is later murdered, and Geitir and Brodd-Helgi plan to divide the goods (see chapter 10).

In 1215 Sæmundr Jónsson of Oddi and Thorvaldr Gizurarson of Hruni, two powerful leaders, dangerously overstepped the bounds of tradition by imposing terms that the Norwegian merchants found unfair. The foreigners' indignation suggests the unusualness of the proceeding.[25] A planned retaliatory invasion sponsored by Norwegian authorities was only narrowly averted through the diplomacy of Snorri Sturluson.[26] That disputes over pricing should arise around 1200 may be attributed to factors outside Iceland. Beginning in the late twelfth century the cost of goods imported to Iceland began to rise, a result of widespread inflation in Europe.

For the Icelanders the increase in the cost of imports was especially distressing because the prices they received for their exported goods did not rise similarly. Nor were the

25. Earlier, in 1203, Snorri Sturluson tried to set the price on flour imported by an Orkney merchant. This attempt also resulted in dissension (*Sturl.* 1, *Íslendinga saga*, ch. 15). A still earlier dispute with Norwegians, lasting from 1170 through 1180, seems also to have touched on issues of trade. See Jón Jóhannesson, *History*, pp. 181-182.

26. Jón Jóhannesson, *History*, p. 242.

Icelanders in an advantageous position to negotiate better trade terms. After the mid-twelfth century almost all their overseas trade was handled by Norwegians who seem to have at times colluded on fixing the prices of goods. The Icelanders themselves had little direct contact with the foreign markets where their import goods were purchased and their export goods sold. Whatever their temporary resistance to paying the prices demanded by foreigners, they really had no other options. In the long run, they had to come to terms with the Norwegian merchants or receive no imported goods.

Additional Privileged Sources of Wealth

Another irregular source of wealth available to a *goði* was the assets to be gleaned from managing a court of confiscation or execution (*féránsdómr*) for the benefit of claimants.[27] The *féránsdómr* was usually held two weeks after the closing of the thing at which a judgment had been obtained. The property to be confiscated was called *sektarfé*. Men who could prove their claims had first right to the property, and then the chieftain could take his fee. For the service of officiating at the confiscation of property against a lesser or a full outlaw, the chieftain was legally entitled to a remuneration of one cow or one ox four winters old. The remaining property was divided among the men of the district or of the quarter.

In itself the chieftain's fee was small, especially in view of the dangers inherent in leading a prosecution for someone else and then confiscating the defendant's property. Should a *goði* be in the position of confiscating the property of an outlaw with himself as the injured party, however, he would receive not only his fee but also a claim to a substantial part of the remaining property. Furthermore, he would be in a favorable position to determine the specific allotments. The

27. *Grágás* has many references to *féránsdómr*. See for instance: GG Ia, pp. 83-88 (chs. 48-51), p. 108 (ch. 59), pp. 112-116 (ch. 62), pp. 118-119 (chs. 66-67), p. 120 (ch. 69), p. 125 (ch. 77).

possibility of combining roles made the practice of buying the claims of others a potentially profitable source of wealth for chieftains. Several other irregular sources of income were available. For instance, when a foreigner died without an heir or a partner, certain rights of inheritance accrued to chieftains.[28] Another source of income was in assuming the role of trustee (*fjárvarðveizlumaðr*). Chieftains settled issues of inheritance and managed the property rights of widows, minors, and unmarried women. Although the *goðar* were advantageously placed to undertake such tasks, they did not monopolize the administration of guardianships or inheritance cases. The right of each family to manage its own affairs was a basic tenet of Icelandic law.

SOURCES OF INCOME AVAILABLE TO ALL FREEMEN

The *goðar* shared access to certain sources of wealth with all prosperous landholders. Two of these, trade and rental of land to tenant farmers, were available from the first years of the settlement. Another source of income, the revenue generated by *staðir*, became available only after the introduction of the tithe in 1097. In the twelfth and thirteenth centuries, control of these church farmsteads became increasingly concentrated in the hands of prominent leaders, especially the *stórgoðar* but also the *stórbændr*.

The Tithe and Staðir

A marked change in the chieftain's flow of revenue resulted from introduction of the tithe. Iceland's was the first national tithe in all Scandinavia; it also was the first tax in Iceland's history which assessed an individual's economic

---

28. GG Ib, pp. 197-198 (ch. 249); Alan Berger, "Lawyers in the Old Icelandic Family Sagas: Heroes, Villains, and Authors," *Saga-Book of the Viking Society for Northern Research* 20(1978-79):72-75.

circumstances, thus providing a basis for graduated taxation. An important feature of the tithe law was that a *goðorð*—an otherwise marketable commodity that could be bought or sold—was declared to be "power, not wealth," and thus tax-exempt: "Velldi er þat en æigi fe."[29] Possessions of the church, including farms on which church buildings stood, were exempt from the tithe. As noted earlier, this advantageous tax-exempt status had important consequences. Families in the twelfth century often donated large parts of their landholdings to the church under agreements allowing them to retain administrative rights over the property for themselves and their heirs.

The tithe, which did not discriminate between men and women, was required of all heads of households who qualified as *thingfararkaupsbændr*. Persons holding less property than the *thingfararkaupsbændr* were required to tithe only when they had no dependents. As Jón Jóhannesson points out, "This regulation is noteworthy because of its implicit leniency towards people in the lower income categories; to some extent it must have provided a counterbalance to the higher tithe-rate for smaller amounts of property."[30]

The tithe was divided into four parts: one for the bishop (*biskupstíund*), the second for the priest's services (*preststíund*), the third for the upkeep of the church building (*kirkjutíund*), and the fourth for the poor (*fátækratíund* or *thurfamannatíund*). A person in control of the farm on which the church stood received the part set aside for maintenance of the church. A person who controlled or owned a farmstead with a church on it, whether or not the farm was a *staðr*, was often in a position to collect two quarters of the tithe. For example, the proprietor of the farm naturally kept the *kirkjutíund*, and he could also get the *preststíund* if he had himself, a family member, or a servant ordained as a priest. The advantages that

29. *GG* III, p. 44 (*Skálholtsbók*, ch. 28). See also *GG* Ib, p. 206 (ch. 255), II, p. 47 (ch. 37). The more traditional view, noted earlier, is that the *goðorð* was not taxed because it was unprofitable.
30. Jón Jóhannesson, *History*, p. 173.

the tithe offered chieftains suggest that from the first many
goðar perceived this tax as a means of increasing their
wealth. Through the lögrétta at the Althing the chieftains
gave their consent to the tithe and then manipulated its
operation in their favor. If the chieftains were indeed instrumental in introducing
the tithe, they did not create the situation that made the new
law agreeable to them as well as to many farmers. The custom of lay administration or hereditary wardship of
churches—a custom that granted a level of control almost
equivalent to ownership—began shortly after the conversion, when landowners, both bœndr and goðar, built churches
on their property. Churches, after being consecrated in the
name of the deity or of his saints, were returned to the
guardianship of secular individuals and their heirs by a form
of enfeoffment resembling a feudal contract. Theoretically
the ownership of the property passed to the church. In practice the control of the land, along with the added benefits
that came from the presence of a church building, was regarded by secular landholders as a hereditary administrative
right. Yet there were some limitations on the owner of a
staðr: the church building had to be properly maintained,
the land could not be sold, and the owner was required to
keep a list (máldagi) of all church property.

Besides tithe payments, some church owners could also
collect dues, called tollar and skyldir, from churchgoers.
These small payments may have become standard in the
thirteenth century, and some of them, such as the church
candle tax (ljóstollr or lýsitollr) may well have been fairly lucrative.[31] Unfortunately, little is known about these minor
taxes.[32] Added together, the different church-related pay-

---

31. GG III, p. 144 (Belgsdalsbók, ch. 32), p. 191 (Arnarbælisbók, ch. 17).
See Magnús Már Lárusson, "Fabrica: Island," KLNM 4, col. 121; Jón Jóhannesson, History, p. 176. For examples of lýsitollr, see DI, vol. 1, pt. 1,
p. 276; pt. 3, p. 597.
32. Magnús Stefánsson, "Kirkjuvald eflist," trans. Björn Teitsson, in
Saga Íslands 2:77.

ments formed an important source of wealth for owners of churches and *staðir*.

Many studies have stressed the control of *staðir* as the principal source of wealth for the *stórgoðar* in twelfth- and thirteenth-century Iceland.[33] This conclusion is sound in certain respects, but when accepted as a general rule it becomes misleading. The tithe did not establish the *goðar* as leaders. Traditions of leadership were firmly in place when in the late eleventh century the chieftains used their lawgiving power to reap benefit from a new form of revenue, one that also offered a nontaxable shelter for existing wealth. On the other hand, some families, particularly the Oddaverjar and the Haukdælir in the south, profited to an inordinate degree from management of *staðir*. The increased wealth such families derived from control of church property hastened the evolution toward increased social complexity.

The same was not true throughout the country; especially in the West Fjords and in Eyjafjörðr in the north, gaining control of *staðir* was not an absolute prerequisite for power. Attempts by individuals or families to achieve hegemony over local areas had been a feature of the Icelandic body politic long before the effect of tithing and *staðir* was felt. In the tenth century, for instance, Guðmundr the Powerful from Eyjafjörðr in the north probably controlled two *goðorð*. Likewise, the chieftain Hafliði Másson in the northwest had become very powerful by the early twelfth century, before the tithe became a factor. The historian Björn Sigfússon has pointed out, with good reason, that the success of neither of these men depended on church-related wealth.[34]

33. Björn Thorsteinsson has been instrumental in drawing attention to the importance of *staðir* for those chieftains of the postconversion centuries who in modern studies are often called church *goðar* (*kirkjugoðar*). His emphasis on class structure, however, may be misleading. See, for example, his *Ný Íslandssaga*, pp. 207-208. Gunnar Karlsson, "Völd og auður," pp. 5-30, notes that both *stórbændr* and *stórhöfðingjar* owned *staðir* and that possession of *staðir* alone did not assure the authority of a *stórgoði*; see esp. pp. 9-11.

34. Björn Sigfússon, "Full goðorð og forn og heimildir frá 12. öld," *Saga* 3(1960):57. In stating his premise—that church influence, whether direct or

In summary it may be said that *staðir* were only one kind
of productive property. Still lacking is an understanding of
the processes by which ambitious individuals acquired valuable property, including *staðir*.

Trade

During the period of independence Iceland imported sta-
ples such as barley, wheat, timber, and linen, as well as all
manner of luxury goods. A number of Icelanders, among
them Gizurr Ísleifsson (later bishop), Hallr Thórarinsson
from Haukadalr, and Thórhallr Ásgrímsson, are known to
have participated at times in trading voyages, but few Icelanders devoted themselves entirely to overseas trade. Although trading voyages may have benefited individuals,
they never gave rise to a merchant class or supported a governing group.[35]

As the Icelanders, from early on, specialized in the exploitation of sheep by-products, exports were chiefly raw
wool, different grades of homespun cloth, and a type of
rough woolen cloak (*vararfeldr*). Through this specialization

---

indirect, has been considerably exaggerated in modern scholarship—Björn
Sigfússon specifically (pp. 56-57) takes issue with past scholars such as Árni
Pálsson and Jón Jóhannesson, who stressed the importance of the church's
role in altering the conditions in the twelfth and thirteenth centuries.

35. For a discussion of export and import trade, see Jón Jóhannesson,
History, pp. 305-317; Björn Thorsteinsson, "Handel: Island," *KLNM* 6, cols.
118-119; Gelsinger, *Icelandic Enterprise*, pp. 12-16. Gelsinger characterizes Icelandic trade in the different periods as follows: "Trade of the settlement
period must have been barely sufficient for the needs of the colonists, but
it pointed the way to prosperity in the following century" (p. 151). In the
following century, however, in the formative years 930-1022, "Icelandic merchants did not depend primarily upon that occupation for their livelihood.
Trade was carried out more from motives of necessity than of profit" (ibid.,
p. 152). In the next centuries foreign trade in the hands of Icelanders dwin-
dled. One reason was that "around the beginning of the eleventh century,
land probably became a better investment because the shortage of free labor
would have grown less extreme as the population expanded" (ibid., p. 160).
Gelsinger concludes: "What is remarkable about the Icelandic Commonwealth's foreign trade is not that it ended in failure but that it persisted,
despite limitations, for almost four centuries" (ibid., p. 180).

they obtained, at least in one area of production, a comparative advantage that lowered their costs, making it feasible for them to participate in international trade. The goods were produced by a widespread cottage industry, and woolen products became a useful vehicle of exchange within the country. Along with merchandise derived from sheep raising, some trade was conducted in other farm products, for example, horses, hides, and sometimes cheese. Also there was a limited trade in sulfur and exotics such as white falcons.

The lack of wood of sufficient quality to build large ships was from the start an almost insurmountable obstacle to the development and maintenance of a competitive merchant fleet. The *landnámsmenn* brought with them many ships, but later generations were unable to replace them; as the centuries passed the number of seagoing vessels steadily decreased. By the thirteenth century it was rare for Icelanders to own large ships.[36] Most of the Icelanders who became full-time international merchants moved abroad, operating principally out of Norway. Often working in conjunction with Norwegian partners, they seem not to have confined themselves to trade with Iceland but to have operated in many northern European seaports. Some of these traders returned to Iceland. Although merchants from throughout the Norse lands, including the Orkneys, traded in Iceland, most of them came from Norway. The apparatus supporting the Iceland and the Greenland trade, including credit arrangements, merchant guilds or brotherhoods, and trade towns with warehouses and workshops, was centered in that country.

Even for well-equipped foreign merchants, the Iceland trade was a difficult and time-consuming venture. The strength and coldness of the winter winds and the danger to shipping from drift ice restricted sailing and enforced a seasonal rhythm in trading activities. Foreign traders arrived

36. In one example of rare ownership, the Norwegian Jarl Skúli gave a ship to Snorri Sturluson in 1220 (*Sturl.* 1, *Íslendinga saga*, ch. 38).

in Iceland during the summer and had to find lodgings on farms for the long northern winter before spring made it easier to return to the continent. Once in Iceland a foreign merchant needed a base from which to trade, and a chieftain's or a *stórbóndi's* farm was the logical choice. In return the Icelander probably received some payment. Such arrangements, which provided entertainment, news of the outside world, access to prestige goods, and foreign contacts, added to the stature of individuals within the local community.

Nevertheless, the chieftains' income from trade should not be overemphasized. Although better able to compete than their fellow Icelanders for the modest gains of trade, the chieftains played only a passive part in controlling the flow of goods or in regulating prices when compared with the role played by foreign merchants. The schedule of trading and the choice of goods, as well as the quantity and quality of articles traded, were in the main determined by the merchants. Only in the mid-fourteenth century, when the trade in stockfish (*skreið*, dried cod) was first developed,[37] did Europe discover in Iceland a product of great commercial value. Because of stockfish, Europeans with sufficient means—Norwegians until 1410-1430(?), then English and German merchants—made the capital investment necessary to establish a lively trade.[38] The specifics of the financing are not known, but the German Hansa merchants in particular, with their connections throughout northern Europe, were in an advantageous position to finance export of Iceland's fish, the demand for which seems to have increased as stockfish became a staple food, especially during the long Lenten fast.

Once started, Iceland's stockfish trade grew rapidly. By the second half of the fourteenth century the export of *skreið* and the industry that grew up around it had become firmly entrenched. Dried cod remained the principal export, al-

---

37. Björn Thorsteinsson, "Fiskhandel: Island," *KLNM* 4, cols. 370-372.
38. For a discussion of Icelandic *skreið* export and the role played by German merchants see Gelsinger, esp. pp. 181-194.

though the trade diversified in the fifteenth century when English merchants showed interest in acquiring fish oil, *vaðmál*, falcons, and sulfur as well as perhaps wool and hides.[39] About this time the English, themselves, began to fish the Icelandic waters. Because the Icelanders lacked the large quantities of salt necessary for curing and for making brines, they were unable to expand their trade by exporting in quantity salmon, herring, or trout.

The development of the stockfish trade introduced into Iceland a new source of income and new forms of employment which may have led in the fourteenth century to some social and economic changes. The Black Death epidemic certainly brought change. The plague arrived in Iceland in 1402, causing an upheaval of property ownership and sharp changes in people's circumstances. The epidemic lasted two years, possibly killing two-thirds of Iceland's population. The stockfish trade and the plague, however, are well beyond our period of inquiry. More pertinent is the determination that the wealth of the early *goðar* was not founded on trade.

Rental Land

Beginning in the colonization period, large landowners faced the problem of how best to work their new holdings. The early settlers brought slaves with them, and in the first century after the *landnám*, slavery may have provided a partial solution. As a source of labor in Iceland, however, slavery had serious limitations, and its practice diminished rapidly. Historically, slavery tends to be an efficient institution chiefly in countries where field agriculture allows for economies of scale and where work can easily be supervised.[40] In Iceland, where farmers engaged predominantly in cattle

---

39. Björn Thorsteinsson, *Enskar heimildir um sögu Íslendinga á 15. og 16. öld* (Reykjavik: Hið íslenzka bókmenntafélag, 1969), pp. 32-35.
40. Trout Rader, *The Economics of Feudalism* (New York: Gordon and Breach, 1971), pp. 40-42.

and sheep raising, efficient use of slave labor was not possible. Pasturage and other chores connected with animal husbandry called for a wide dispersal of the work force and required a high degree of personal initiative. In the eleventh century slavery all but ceased. A major reason for a quick end to slavery was that tenant farming was a more feasible alternative.[41] It is apparent that renting of land was a widely established practice by the late eleventh century, when the sources become more reliable. As Björn Thorsteinsson notes, the status of the *goðar* must have been connected with land-ownership and rents: "It was not large households and important groups that secured power and reputation for the chieftains over the centuries, but the ownership of land and the income from rental property."[42] *Grágás* supports this observation. It contains a detailed entry on renting (*fjárleigur*) which treats matters such as contracts of sale, hire, or loan, settlement of debts, found property, livestock, and so on.[43] A longer entry in *Grágás* concerns matters of landownership (*landbrigða-þáttr*), stipulating rights connected with different types of land, buying and selling property, joint interests, hunting and fishing, and others.[44]

Extensive tenant farming was possible because many sizable family holdings included rentable property, especially outlying lands (*útjörð*, pl. *útjarðir*). In particular, a main or head farm, termed *aðalból* in *Grágás* and *höfuðból* in the later, part Norwegian *Jónsbók*, played a pivotal role in the Icelandic system of land distribution. These farms existed because the original landholdings from the settlement days were not continually being divided as the years passed. In many instances they were solidified into *aðalból*, which had a pre-

41. Jakob Benediktsson and Björn Thorsteinsson have argued that tenant farming existed, and was important, from the very start of the settlement. Although a reasonable guess, this view is unfortunately not supported by firm proof. See Jakob Benediktsson, "Landnám og upphaf allsherjarríkis," p. 164, and Björn Thorsteinsson, *Ný Íslandssaga*, p. 124.
42. Björn Thorsteinsson did not pursue the issue (*Ný Íslandssaga*, p. 123).
43. *GG* Ib, pp. 140-161 (chs. 221-226); *GG* II, pp. 210-290 (chs. 171-262).
44. *GG* Ib, pp. 76-139 (chs. 172-220); *GG* II, pp. 408-538 (chs. 389-460).

scribed minimum size. Information about the exact size of these patrimonial holdings is known only from documents dating from the fifteenth century. At about that time, though probably much earlier, the minimum was set at sixty hundreds (a hundred was equivalent to the value of one cow). *Jónsbók*, with its mixture of Norwegian and Icelandic law, stresses the retention of the land by the original kin group, though we cannot be sure that the relevant entries were operative during the earlier Free State.

Many scholars have connected *aðalból* with allodial land-holding,[45] a tradition of ownership common in Norway whereby certain land was the possession of a patrilineal descent group defined in relationship to a specific ancestor who was a landholder. Björn Thorsteinsson and Sigurður Líndal, for example, stress the importance of family landholding.[46] They point out that from the *landbrigða-þáttr* section of *Grágás*, one may unequivocally determine that the *landnámsmenn*

45. Magnús Már Lárusson, "Odelsrett: Island," *KLNM* 12, cols. 499-502, and "Á höfuðbólum landsins," *Saga* 9(1971):40-90. Sveinbjörn Rafnsson (*Studier i Landnámabók*, pp. 142-151) discusses the issue of landownership, emphasizing the importance of *aðalból* and *höfuðból*. In part three of his book he argues that the purpose of *Landnámabók* was to verify the actual twelfth- and thirteenth-century possession of land. He points out that verification was necessary because of legal restrictions whereby land remained inalienably connected with the family that had originally owned it. See also Jakob Benediktsson, "Markmið Landnámabókar: Nýjar rannsóknir," *Skírnir* 148(1974):207-215; Hallvard Magerøy, *Norsk-islandske problem*, Omstridde spørsmål i Nordens historie 3, Foreningene Nordens historiske publikasjoner 4 (Oslo: Universitetsforlaget, 1965), pp. 24-28. Björn Thorsteinsson, *Íslensk miðaldasaga*, pp. 34-36, describes the different types of landholdings. See also Gurevich, "Wealth and Gift-Bestowal," pp. 126-127; his "Representations of Property during the High Middle Ages," *Economy and Society* 6(1977):1-30, and his "Edda and Law: Commentary upon *Hyndlolióð*," *Arkiv för nordisk filologi* 88(1973):77-83. See also chap. 8, "The Importance of Land in Saga Feud," in Jesse L. Byock, *Feud in the Icelandic Saga* (Berkeley, Los Angeles, London: University of California Press, 1982), pp. 143-160. Kirsten Hastrup, *Culture* (pp. 72-75), emphasizes the importance of the *ætt* (kin group). She connects *ætt* land with *óðal* land (pp. 190-192, 201-204), suggesting that the right of potential heirs to influence "major economic transactions in which the present owner might engage himself was to be seen as a modification of the idea of private ownership according to a latent principle of *ætt*-ownership" (p. 190).
46. "Lögfesting konungsvalds," in *Saga Íslands* 3:77-79.

understood the fundamental concept of Norwegian allodial landholding. Without doubting that a form of family landholding is being dealt with, one should, nevertheless, point out that in *Grágás*, at least as it is preserved in the thirteenth-century texts, the term *óðal* itself is never used. On the other hand, the term *aðalból*, which means head farm, is spoken of in connection with matters of inheritance in a way that demonstrates acceptance of the proprietory claims of kin groups.[47] Unlike allodial land, however, an *aðalból* was not the exclusive possession of a patrilineal descent group. Allodial land passed to often remote agnates, but Icelandic heirs seem to have been mostly drawn from immediate cognate kinsmen. Potential heirs at each generation were defined by their relationship to the present holder or to the immediately preceding holder. Normally the property was inherited by an eligible male; other family members, including women, divided the chattels, the outer farms, and the lands exceeding the accepted minimum size of an *aðalból*.

An *aðalból* tended to remain under the management of a family member, or at least it could be neither sold nor rented without specific agreement by the legally responsible male heirs. Thus land could technically be alienated from a family only if the heirs agreed to a transfer. Such an agreement, unless well compensated, would be disadvantageous to the heirs, and their consent was undoubtedly difficult to obtain. The practice of maintaining *aðalból* and *höfuðból* ensured the presence of many substantial farmers whose outlying rental farms (*leiguból*) provided their owners with an important source of income.

SUMMARY

The focus on landownership as the principal source of a chieftain's income requires an important qualification: the *goðar* by no means monopolized the ownership of land. Pos-

47. GG Ib, p. 78 (ch. 172), p. 150 (ch. 223); II, p. 226 (ch. 185), p. 415 (ch. 389).

session of substantial parcels of land was the major source of wealth for the many well-off *bændr*, who far outnumbered the *goðar* in their midst. Further, the chieftains never enjoyed special privileges or exclusive rights either to use or to benefit from public or private land.

Each source of income considered in this chapter contributed to the wealth of the *goðar*. None of them, however, explains the full extent of the chieftains' wealth or power. What has remained unexplored in Icelandic studies is the underlying system of wealth acquisition by which aspiring *goðar* amassed property, including *staðir*. This system was dependent on the dynamics of the *goði*-thingman relationship and processes such as advocacy.

6

Consensual Governance

All societies have authority structures and values concerning the allocation of authority. In stateless societies, the proper unit for the analysis of such phenomena is not the total society, where we are likely to mistake lack of a central political hierarchy for egalitarianism, but the maximal decision-making unit (or some cohesive subgrouping within it).

—Robert A. LeVine

In Iceland, where no such need of defence existed, where there was no foreign enemy, and men lived scattered in tiny groups round the edges of a vast interior desert, no executive powers were given to anybody, and elaborate precautions were taken to secure the rights of the smaller communities which composed the Republic and of the priest-chieftains who represented them.

—James Bryce

The medieval Icelanders possessed a well-developed vocabulary for describing social and political stratification. They employed the words and the attendant concepts when writing the kings' sagas about the rulers of Norway and Denmark or when composing saga histories about other Norse lands, such as *Orkneyinga saga*, an account of the Norse earls of Orkney. But when Icelanders wrote about their own society, whether in sagas, laws, or stories, the roles and the vocabulary of statehood seldom appear. This striking contrast is the result of a central development in early Iceland: leadership evolved in such a way that a chieftain's power and the resources available to him were not derived from an

103

exploitable realm. Territorial lordship, an element of authority which permeated the Western concept of landownership and legal and economic jurisdiction, was largely absent in early Iceland; the lord-peasant relationship, so prevalent elsewhere in the medieval West, barely existed.

In more stratified European societies, religious and military hierarchies provided models for structuring social, legal, and political relationships. Iceland developed differently. In place of overlordship, the early Icelanders, with their focus on law, developed their own set of mechanisms for maintaining order. As they modified traditions and customs they had known in their homelands, a new system of law and political behavior emerged. It compensated for the absence of executive institutions that accompanied territorial leadership in other Norse lands. This chapter concentrates on basic relationships that underlay the operation of Iceland's system of consensual governance. One, the *goði*-thingman bond, was defined by law. Another, which can best be described by the term "advocacy," was not legally defined. It found its authority in private contractual agreements whereby one person, not necessarily a chieftain, gave support to another by speaking or acting for him, and so became involved as a third party to a dispute. The usefulness of advocacy was reinforced by the presence of additional extralegal arrangements, such as political friendships and frequent recourse to arbitration.

In principle, the legal *goði*-thingman bond was created by a voluntary public contract which did not depend upon a geographical base. A key factor that has received scant attention in previous studies is that this relationship provided little sense of either permanency or protection to either leader or follower. For an ambitious individual, at least in the early centuries, becoming a *goði* was not entry into a formally defined class. To become a *goði*, a *bóndi* did not undergo formal investiture; there was no oath of office, no swearing before a deity. The *goði* was answerable only to minimal guidelines set by law and to the pressure of public opinion.

Possession of a *goðorð* granted a leader little formal authority over his followers. Although it would be naive to assume that all social systems function according to their laws, in the instance of early Iceland, it appears that a chieftain, in accordance with *Grágás*, had little power to command a thingman to act against his will. Instead, a chieftain's power rested, to a large degree, on the consent of his followers. Thingmen, for their part, could formally demand very little of their *goði* beyond requiring that he carry out the few duties prescribed in the laws. These responsibilities included holding thing meetings and setting prices on imported goods. Such duties assured the availability of arenas for settlement of disputes and helped to prevent friction among the farmers. In fulfilling these obligations the *goðar* had little latitude, for in most instances they were accountable to their followers and to other chieftains.

Advocacy arrangements existed alongside, and sometimes in place of, *goði*-thingman and kinship ties. These agreements established between any two individuals a set of third-party contractual obligations, which could be freely entered into by advocates and clients living in any part of the quarter or, for that matter, in any part of the country. Unlike the *goði*-thingman bond which was defined in the laws, advocacy was an informal, extralegal association that came into being in response to specific needs. Functioning as a form of third-party intervention, it assumed unusual prominence in early Iceland because both farmers and chieftains frequently required more assistance than public institutions offered.

The fact that government was often permitted to operate by means of private intervention, particularly at the assemblies, provided many opportunities for advocates. Some of these, especially chieftains, increased their influence to the point where they became power brokers. Such individuals, who were often also called on to act as arbitrators, did not constitute a separate class or a semiofficial body, for theirs was a temporary role. They were farmers and chieftains who enjoyed credibility and inspired the trust of others. Examples mentioned in the sagas of especially powerful advocates, who frequently acted as power brokers, are the chieftains Snorri goði, Jón Loftsson, Guðmundr dýri, and Guðmundr the Powerful, and the prominent *bóndi* Njáll Thorgeirsson.

Sometimes advocates, even as brokers, acted out of highmindedness (*drengskapr*), charging no fee for their efforts to solve the problems of others. The motivation for such acts might be desire to end conflict, to enhance one's prestige or to reaffirm kinship, political alliances, or *goði*-thingman ties. But at other times an advocate might set a fee which was often substantial, perhaps even requiring the transfer of property or inheritance rights in return for his services. The fee, which made it worth the while of a third party to intervene in the affairs of others, is frequently referred to in the sagas by the term *sæmð*, meaning honorable recompense. *Hallfreðr's Saga* (*Hallfreðar saga*) offers an example of how an advocate, in this instance a kinsman and a *goði*, was engaged. Hallfreðr, a cantankerous poet, has slept with another man's wife. In a confrontation the next day he kills one of the husband's kinsmen, named Einarr. The husband initiates a lawsuit against Hallfreðr; when Hallfreðr is summoned to the local Húnavatn thing, his brother Galti asks him (ch. 8):

> "What do you intend to do about this case?"
> Hallfreðr replied, "I intend to seek the aid of my kinsman Thorkell [Thorgrímsson, a *goði*]."
> In the spring thirty of them rode north to Hof [Thorkell's farm in Vatnsdalr] and spent the night. Hallfreðr asked Thorkell what support he could expect from him. Thorkell responded that he would take on the case if he were offered some *sæmð*. [The kind of payment is not disclosed.]

Seeking an advocate was a basic step in building the partisan support required for success at the assemblies. People often turned first to kinsmen, as Hallfreðr did, since kinship was a basic field of relationships that provided a claim to potential supporters. Shared blood, however, beyond providing an entry to ask for assistance was no guarantee that support would be forthcoming. If only partly reliable during feud, kinship relationships did have more dependable features throughout the Free State: cognatic kinship ties remained important in determining inheritance rights and deciding who should take the responsibility for seeking vengeance. Like the *goði*-thingman relationship, kinship ties were often augmented by extralegal arrangements, for once a right or a duty had been ascertained, a farmer or a chieftain might need help in validating his claim or carrying out his responsibility. In the absence of court-appointed officials to warrant that justice be done, who was to supply the assistance? Private advocates filled the void by undertaking specific aggressive or defensive action. These voluntary relationships, whether entered into with an individual's regular chieftain or with another leader, supplied the support required to achieve a sense of security. A large part of saga narrative is devoted to descriptions of people seeking advocates, and individuals are routinely shown protecting their rights through specific advocacy agreements, rather than simply relying on the *goði*-thingman bond or on kinship.

Third-party advocacy relationships complemented rather than supplanted *goði*-thingman alliances and kinship ties. Informal, voluntary, and sometimes covert, the different advocacy roles provided a framework within which individuals could manipulate political forces at different stages of a dispute. Icelandic feuds tended to be long-lived, surviving many attempts at resolution; at times they continued for generations. Settlements, both those that were final and those that were temporary, were frequently arrived at through arbitration.[1]

---

1. On arbitration see Andreas Heusler, *Das Strafrecht der Isländersagas* (Leipzig: Duncker and Humblot, 1911), esp. pp. 40-41, 73-95, and his *Zum isländischen Fehdewesen in der Sturlungenzeit*, Abhandlungen der königlich preussischen Akademie der Wissenschaften, Phil.-hist. Klasse 4 (Berlin, 1912), pp. 43-58; Lúðvík Ingvarsson, *Refsingar á Íslandi á þjóðveldistímanum* (Reykjavik: Bókaútgáfa Menningarsjóðs, 1970), pp. 319-380; William Ian Miller, "Avoiding Legal Judgment: The Submission of Disputes to Arbitration in Medieval Iceland," *American Journal of Legal History* 28(1984):95-134; Jesse L. Byock, "Dispute Resolution in the Sagas," *Gripla* 6(1984):86-100,

The Old Icelandic legal and narrative texts about the Free State contain many terms for arbitrators and arbitration. Sometimes arbitration is referred to as *jafnaðardómr*, a case judged by one or more umpires. More often the term *görð*, meaning simply arbitration, is used. A settlement or reconciliation brought about through arbitration was called *sætt* or *sátt* (the forms are used interchangeably; the pl. for both terms is *sættir*), and arbitrators or peacemakers were frequently called *sáttarmenn* or *görðarmenn*. Arbitrators were often influential advocates who possessed the wide-ranging family and political alliances required to arrange compromises. So it is in the example above from *Hallfreðr's Saga*; Thorkell, after having taken on Hallfreðr's case, chooses to seek an arbitrated settlement rather than to defend his client in court: "Now men came to the thing. When Hallfreðr and Galti arrived they went to Thorkell's booth and inquired what was to happen. Thorkell replied, 'I will offer to set up an arbitration [*görð*], if both sides will accept this. Then I will try to arrange a settlement [*sætt*].' "

In many instances when arbitration had a chance of success, supporters of both sides united to aid the arbitrator. A famous example is from *Eyrbyggja saga* (ch. 10) where Thórðr Gellir arbitrated between two local groups, the Thórsnesingar and the Kjalleklingar. Usually the farmers and chieftains who backed the arbitrator were concerned with achieving a compromise that adjusted for the new status quo but did not seriously disturb the existing balance of power. Here again consensus came into play, since compromise resolutions often involved many people. These and other *sættir* had a chance of success because they were based on a common standard of compensation or blood money recognized throughout the island as suitable recompense for torts and physical injury. Like arbitration, which in many instances served to promote the common good, advocacy was intended to accomplish specific goals.

---

and *Feud in the Icelandic Saga* (Berkeley, Los Angeles, London: University of California Press, 1982), pp. 102-106, 260-265.

Advocacy and arbitration tended to cool hotheadedness by taking the conduct of a quarrel out of the hands of the original, perhaps more emotionally engaged, rivals and entrusting decisions to third parties. That is what eventually happens in Hallfreðr's case. Hallfreðr's brother is attacked at the thing and killed by the brother of the woman he seduced. When the killer is allowed to get away, Hallfreðr doubts the commitment of his advocate Thorkell and instead challenges the husband to a *hólmganga*. Reason prevails, and in the end Hallfreðr withdraws his challenge to the duel, and the husband agrees to let Thorkell resume arbitration. Thorkell pronounces that the killings of Einarr, the husband's kinsman, and Galti, Hallfreðr's brother, cancel each other out, with the provision that Hallfreðr's visit with the wife made up for any difference that might have existed between the two fallen men. For his scurrilous verses against the husband, Hallfreðr has to pay one article of value. When Hallfreðr shows reluctance to do so, Thorkell chides him; Hallfreðr then gives the husband an arm ring of great value.

Perhaps because of its efficacy, advocacy became the accepted procedure for guiding conflict and violence into legal channels—into the courts or into private arbitration. This development, which influenced the alignments of the political networks between leaders and the social networks between leaders and followers, was determined largely by the status of the free farmers. Icelandic *bændr* could demand that their chieftains show restraint, even during feuds and settlements. Thingmen were not beholden to their leaders as were the warrior-retainers of a *comitatus* in other northern cultures. Thingmen were mostly landowners and householders whose interests were better served by compromise solutions than by pitched battles. Advocacy, brokerage, and arbitration facilitated problem solving by compromise rather than by military victory. Reliance on these processes helped to make it possible for feud to take the place of war in Iceland.[2]

2. Definitions of feud and distinctions between feud and war are dis-

The absence of pitched battles does not mean that the island inhabitants eschewed all forms of militant show, only that they ritualized the actual use of force. Parties to a dispute that was moving toward resolution frequently assembled large numbers of armed *bændr*. Sometimes these groups confronted each other for days at assemblies and at other gatherings, such as a court of confiscation (*féránsdómr*), where the successful party was trying to enforce a judgment at the home of the defendant. Although opposing sides often clashed briefly, and a few men might be killed, protracted battles were consistently avoided. It was not by chance that the parties showed restraint. Leaders really had few options if they hoped to retain the allegiance of a large following, since the *bændr* were not dependable supporters in a long or perilous confrontation. They had no tradition of obeying orders, maintaining discipline, or being absent from their farms for extended periods. The *goðar*, for their part, were seldom able to bear the burdens of campaigning. They lacked the resources necessary to feed, house, equip, and pay followers for more than a brief period.

Rather than signaling the beginning of war, a public display of armed support merely revealed that significant numbers of men had chosen sides and were prepared to participate in working toward an honorable resolution. With chieftains and farmers publicly committed, a compromise resting on a collective agreement could be reached. Conforming to the expected practice, third parties, termed *góð-viljamenn* (men of goodwill) or *góðgjarnir menn* (well-wishing men), intervened between the armed groups, publicly displaying *góðgirnd* or *góðgirni* (the words normally mean goodness, kindness, or benevolence). Consider the description from *The Saga of Thorgils and Hafliði* (*Þorgils saga ok Hafliða*) of the gathering of men for a court of confiscation after Haf-

---

cussed by Jacob Black-Michaud, *Cohesive Force: Feud in the Mediterranean and the Middle East* (Oxford: Basil Blackwell, 1975), esp. pp. 1-32.

liði Másson succeeded in obtaining a judgment of outlawry against Thorgils Oddason in the year 1120 (ch.

> 20): And as the time approached for holding the *féránsdómr* [at Thorgils' home], Thorgils gathered men around him, assembling almost four hundred in all. Hafliði had from the north a picked band of one hundred men, each chosen for his manliness and equipment. And in a third place the men of the district gathered together for the purpose of intervening with *góðgirnd*. The leaders of this group were Thórðr Gilsson and Húnbogi Thorgilsson from Skarð. With them were also other *góðgjarnir menn*, Guðmundr Brandsson and Örnólfr Thorgilsson from Kvennabrekka, with two hundred men for the peacemaking.

Góðgjarnir menn might simply be concerned neighbors. Frequently, as in the above example, they were chieftains and ambitious *bændr* who, by stopping a violent clash, often enhanced their own reputations. One of the *góðgjarnir menn* in the above example, Thórðr Gilsson, was a *bóndi* who became a chieftain. His son was the famous chieftain Hvamm-Sturla (see chapter 8). In some instances, after separating the opposing sides, *góðgjarnir menn* served as arbitrators, thus improving their own status by arranging suitable resolutions. For approximately three centuries, or until the last decades of the Free State, there were in Iceland no pitched battles with casualties comparable to those that routinely took place elsewhere in medieval Europe. Avoiding warfare, the Icelanders esteemed political flexibility and legal acumen.

THE FLEXIBILITY OF THE *GOÐI-* THINGMAN RELATIONSHIP

From the ninth century to the twelfth the concerns of free farmers dominated the spectrum of governmental activity. Legal and administrative decisions were fashioned within the context of a widespread belief in the inviolability of the rights of freemen. These rights were contained in a system of law which served less to protect privileges than to allow the individual to exercise specific rights. The *goðar*, in their capacity as advocates, enjoyed no legal authority to act in defense of their supporters; conversely, they were under no obligation to do so. This situation left a *goði* open to prosecution by other freemen, a factor that apparently discouraged rashness on the part of leaders.

Being a *goði* was a professional vocation with entrepreneurial overtones. In an island society with limited economic opportunity, *goðar* were individuals poised to intervene, upon request and when remuneration was likely, in the disputes of others. They and influential farmers who chose to play the role of advocates were experts in conducting feud, whether arbitrated, adjudicated, or fought. For reasons of self-interest, kinship, political obligations, or payment, a *goði* was willing to help others. Although the law in Iceland held out the promise of equal rights, the political reality was that only consensus among leaders, representing their followers, could make the complex legal system work satisfactorily. As a result of the advocacy process, violence was reduced to an acceptable level; rash acts and overbearing conduct became marginal.

From early on a major threat to Iceland's internal cohesion was the possibility of regional fragmentation. The lay of the land, with its uninhabitable interior, isolated fjords, and remote valleys, made communications difficult and might easily have fostered the growth of regionalism. The Althing system of government, however, successfully countered this danger. When situations started to get out of hand, regional antagonisms or serious feuds triggered the safety mechanisms of the jural community. In particular, brokerage and arbitration came into play. In extreme instances, as in the major feud between Thórðr Gellir and Tungu-Oddr in the mid-960s, legislated constitutional change was deemed necessary: the quarter courts were instituted to lessen the likelihood of future escalations of regional confrontations.

The unusualness of the Icelandic system of consensual governance has, over the years, caused confusion as to how best to describe the authority of the *goðar*. The uncertainty stems to a large degree from the very nature of the *goðorð*. As the basic cohesive subgroupings within the social order delineated by the reach of the Althing, these associations of chieftains and thingmen were not geographically defined. In the past, scholars, attempting to interpret conditions in Iceland in terms appropriate to northern Europe, have tended not to concentrate on this distinguishing characteristic or on processes such as advocacy. Likening the authority of a *goði* to the power of an overlord, they have compared the *goðorð* with the small political entities or petty kingdoms that flourished in early viking Norway or early Ireland. In keeping with this comparison, early Iceland has often been characterized as a union of petty states.[3]

The concept of *goðar* as leaders of small states reflects the outward aspects of the politics of confrontation among chieftains while failing to take into account the complex relationship between chieftains and farmers. Unlike petty kingdoms in Norway or Ireland, which often fought to defend or extend their borders, a *goðorð* had no defined boundaries. Icelandic chieftaincies were units of power not based on the resources of an exploitable realm. Differing from the Norwegian and Irish leaders, who lived surrounded by followers sharing a common loyalty, the chieftains lived interspersed among farmers who might be thingmen of other, sometimes rival, *goðar*. Thingmen of competing *goðar* might also be advocacy clients of chieftains other than their own, as well as clients of prominent *bændr* who themselves might be thingmen of still other *goðar*. In order to understand Iceland we must remember that farmers and chieftains had many choices. One possibility is exemplified in Thórólfr Lamefoot's advocacy arrangement with Snorri goði, described in *Eyrbyggja saga* (see chapter 9). Thórólfr, who is under no du-

3. For example, Ólafur Lárusson, *Lög og saga* (Reykjavik: Hlaðbúð, 1958), p. 61, writes: "The Icelandic republic was at all times a kind of federation. The dominion of the Icelandic chieftaincies, the *goðorð*, corresponds to small Norwegian kingdoms." See Jesse L. Byock, "Governmental Order in Early Medieval Iceland," *Viator* 17(1986):20. Icelandic arrangements are also not easily compared with modern democratic ones. See Gunnar Karlsson, "*Goðar* and *Höfðingjar* in Medieval Iceland," *Saga-Book of the Viking Society for Northern Research* 19(1977):358-370.

ress, enters into an agreement with Snorri whereby Snorri, as Thórólfr's advocate, prosecutes Thórólfr's own son, Arnkell goði, who happens to be Snorri's major rival. *The Saga of Guðmundr Dýri (Sturl.* 1), written shortly after the death of Guðmundr dýri (the Worthy) in 1212, gives a detailed and basically reliable picture of *goði*-thingman alliances in the region of Eyjafjörðr in the Northern Quarter at the end of the twelfth century. The two accompanying maps (3a and 3b) portray the networks of crisscrossing ties, with chieftains relying for support on farmers, some of whom lived far away from their *goðar*. In this Sturlunga saga, at least five chieftains are claiming the allegiance of farmers while at the same time feuding over land and power. The leaders (marked by boxes) did not control territorial entities but, in keeping with centuries-old Icelandic traditions, lived scattered among thingmen loyal to other chieftains. The networks of public *goði*-thingman associations pictured on the maps do not reflect advocacy-client agreements, which were often covert.

At least in the early centuries, a chieftain was both a *bóndi* and a *goði* or, more precisely, he was a *bóndi* who controlled all or part of a *goðorð*. Because the sagas and other sources refer to a chieftain as *goði*, *bóndi*, *goðorðsmaðr* (literally, *goð-orð*-man), or *höfðingi* (leader, pl. *höfðingjar*), it is at times difficult to decide whether a man is or is not a chieftain. For most of the Free State's history the *goðar* lived as prosperous farmers among farmers without the distinction of being a legally defined class.

The closeness between *goðar* and *bændr* was maintained by routine intermarriage. The ties were further strengthened through the common and respected tradition of concubinage with women from *bændr* families. Through such arrangements, illegitimate children were often provided with substantial property. In this environment the *goðar* were not under pressure to establish lineages along the exclusionary lines of many European aristocracies.[4] Since chieftaincies

4. Jenny M. Jochens, "En Islande médiévale: A la recherche de la famille nucléaire," *Annales: économies, sociétés, civilisations* (1985):95-112.

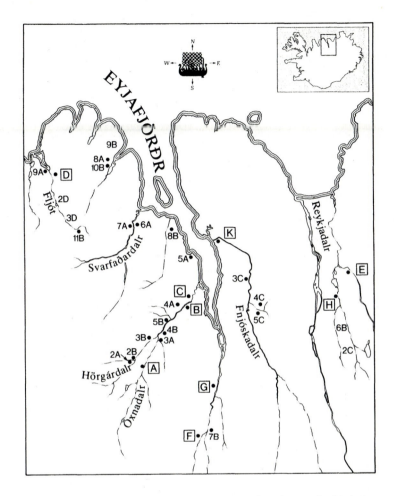

Map 3a. Eyjafjörðr (ca. 1190), showing locations of chieftains (marked by boxes) and their thingmen as mentioned in *The Saga of Guðmundr dýri*. A chieftain and his thingmen are designated by a letter and numbers: **A** stands for a chieftain; 2A, 3A, and so on stand for that chieftain's thingmen.

could be bought, shared, traded, or inherited during much of the Free State's early history,[5] a *goðorð* was obtainable by ambitious and successful *bændr*. It was a marketable com-

---

5. *GG* Ia, pp. 141-142 (ch. 84).

The following list of chieftains and their thingmen mentioned in *Guðmundar saga dýra* includes only chieftains (marked on the map by boxes) and thingmen whose areas of residence and affiliation can be verified from the saga. The numbers and letters refer to designations on map 3a.

A. *Guðmundr dýri at Bakki*
  2A. Söxólfr Fornason at Myrkárdalr
  3A. Thorvaldr at Bægisá
  4A. Kálfr Guttormsson at Auðbrekka
  5A. Hákon Thórðarson at Arnarnes
  6A. Sons of Arnthrúðr at Sakka (later sent to Ögmundr Thorvarðsson)
  7A. Sumarliði Ásmundarson at Tjörn
  8A. Thorsteinn Halldórsson at Brekka
  9A. Nikulás Bjarnarson at Grindill

B. *Önundr Thorkelsson at Laugaland* (he later moves to Langahlíð [5B], and Thorfinnr, his son and follower, moves to Laugaland)
  2B. Erlendr Thorgeirsson at Myrká
  3B. Björn Steinmóðarson at Öxnahóll
  4B. Tjörvi at Rauðalækr
  5B. Langahlíð
  6B. Halldórr or Björn Eyjólfsson (farms in Reykjadalr not specified)
  7B. Einarr Hallsson at Möðruvellir (shares *goðorð* with Önundr)
  8B. Helgi Halldórsson at Árskógr
  9B. Björn Gestsson at Sandr (location approximated)
  10B. Eyvindr and Sighvatr Bjarnarson at Brekka
  11B. Rúnólfr Nikulásson at Mjóvafell (residence of father)

C. *Thorvarðr Thorgeirsson at Möðruvellir*
  2C. Halldórr or Björn Eyjólfsson (farms not specified)
  3C. Brandr Knakansson at Draflastaðir
  4C. Hallr Ásbjarnarson at Fornastaðir
  5C. Ögmundr Thorvarðsson sneis at Háls (later becomes *goði*)

D. *Jón Ketilsson at Holt* (*goðorð* later given to Guðmundr dýri)
  2D. Thorvarðr Sunnólfsson (farm not specified)
  3D. Már Rúnólfsson (farm not specified)

E. *Eyjólfr Hallsson at Grenjaðarstaðir* (a priest, later abbot of Saurbær); acts as though he were a *goði*. Eyjólfr is a son-in-law of Óláfr Thorsteinsson at Saurbær [F].

F. Óláfr Thorsteinsson at Saurbær (probably a chieftain; may have shared a *goðorð* with Kleppjárn Klængsson)

G. Kleppjárn Klængsson at Hrafnagil (may have shared a chieftaincy)

Farmsteads that changed ownership:

H. Helgastaðir
The first owner, Guðmundr Eyjólfsson, gave the property to his son Teitr. Upon Teitr's death, the property was disputed, but in the end it went to Kleppjárn Klængsson and his son Klængr. A marriage was arranged between Klængr and the daughter of Thorvarðr Thorgeirsson. Kleppjárn and Klængr sold the property to Ásbjörn Hallsson, the brother of Eyjólfr Hallsson.

Farmsteads whose owners changed allegiance from one chieftain to another:

K. Laufáss
Thórðr Thórarinsson was a follower of Thorvarðr Thorgeirsson; his sons were followers of Guðmundr dýri.

modity whose availability helped to reinforce the social order by rewarding enterprising individuals within the system. Norwegian law, in contrast with Icelandic law, distinguished among various ranks of farmers, yeomen, aristocrats, and high government functionaries, such as *árborinn maðr, reksþegn, hauldr, lendr maðr, hirðmaðr, stallari,* and *jarl.* Different monetary values, according to rank and class, were assessed to redress personal injury.[6] In *Grágás* the right to lawful redress for injury and the legal amount prescribed, six marks (48 legal ounces), was the same for all freemen, whether

---

6. "Um rettarfar manna" section of *Den ældre Gulathings-Lov* in *Norges gamle love indtil 1387,* vol. 1, ed. R. Keyser and P. A. Munch (Christiania: Chr. Gröndahl, 1846), p. 71. Moreover, there were noteworthy variations among the classifications of rank in the different Norwegian regions with their diverse laws.

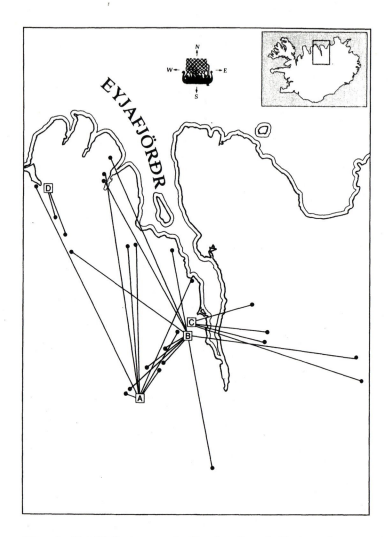

Map 3b. Eyjafjörðr (ca. 1190), showing ties of allegiance between four chieftains and their thingmen as mentioned in *The Saga of Guðmundr Dýri*. The farms of the chieftains are indicated by boxes. The dots indicate only those freemen whose names, farms, and allegiance were given in the saga (see map 3a). Communication between the farms was more difficult than these lines indicate, as the region is highly mountainous.

farmers or chieftains.[7] The sagas, however, show awards being adjusted for the relative respect accorded to different individuals.

The absence of rigid class distinctions between chieftains and farmers in early Iceland is corroborated by the terms of the treaty between the Icelanders and the Norwegian king, Óláfr Haraldsson (1014-1030). The treaty, which was originally oral, was first sworn sometime during Óláfr's reign. Later in the century it was committed to writing when representatives from Iceland came to Norway and swore to it for a third time.[8] A copy of this written version, preserved in Grágás,[9] is the oldest extant Old Norse document about Iceland. Remaining in force until the end of the Free State (1262-1264), the treaty does not differentiate between goðar and bændr but states that "in Norway Icelanders are to have the right [réttr] of a hauldr." Réttr refers to lawful claim for redress possessed by an individual subjected to personal injury. Hauldr (Old Icelandic hǫldr) is a Norwegian legal term for a type of higher yeoman, an owner of allodial land.[10]

Apparently the category of hauldr (pl. hauldar) was acceptable to all leading Icelanders. The older version of the Norwegian Gulathing Law established a time period before an Icelander's social station could be reevaluated: "The Icelanders shall have the rights of hauldar while they are here on trading voyages. If they have stayed here through three winters, then an individual shall be accorded such rights as men bear witness to."[11] The treaty with Óláfr also granted rights to subjects of the Norwegian king when they were in Iceland. Without distinction of Norwegian rank, the Icelan-

7. GG Ia, p. 155 (ch. 88); II, pp. 202 (ch. 169), 313-314 (ch. 282), 390 (ch. 375); III, p. 434 (A.M. 125 A. 4to, ch. 12).

8. Jón Jóhannesson, A History of the Old Icelandic Commonwealth: Íslendinga saga, trans. Haraldur Bessason, University of Manitoba Icelandic Studies 2 (Winnipeg: University of Manitoba Press, 1974), pp. 109-117.

9. GG Ib, pp. 195-197 (ch. 247-248); III, pp. 463-466 (A.M. 136 4to, Skinnastaðabók).

10. Arne Bøe, "Hauld," KLNM 6, cols. 251-254.

11. Den ældre Gulathings-Lov in Norges gamle love, vol. 1, p. 71.

ders gave the Norwegians the same rights enjoyed by Icelandic freemen: "slikan sem landz menn."[12] Adding to the lack of significant distinction between chieftains and farmers in early Iceland was the tradition whereby *goðar* dealt directly with their followers. *Grágás* clearly defines a freeman's right to choose his *goði*,[13] a right characteristic of a nonterritorial concept of authority:[14]

> A man shall declare himself in thing [part of a chieftain's assembly group] with whatever *goði* he wishes. Both he and the chieftain shall name for themselves witnesses in order to attest that he [the farmer] declares himself there, along with his family and household and livestock, in thing [with the chieftain]. And that the other accepts him.[15]

Once a farmer had chosen a *goði* he was not bound to him but had the right to change:

> If a man wants to declare himself out of the thing [relationship with his *goði*], it is the law that he declare himself so at the springtime thing, if he enters into a thing relationship with another *goði* who is a *goði* of the same springtime thing. So also if he enters into a thing relationship with another *goði* who has an assembly group within the same thing district. It is the law that at the Althing he declare himself out of the chieftain's assembly third [a chieftain's following, called a third as there were three chieftains] at the high court at the *lögberg* [the Law Rock], if the *goði* hears [or listens]. If the *goði* does not hear, then he must say it to him directly, and in that instance it is the law that he declare himself out of the thing in the presence of witnesses for himself. And on the same day he must declare himself to be in a thing relationship with another *goði*.[16]

12. GG III, p. 464 (A.M. 136 4to, *Skinnastaðabók*).
13. GG Ia, pp. 140-141 (ch. 83); II, pp. 277-278 (ch. 245).
14. The major territorial restriction was that a farmer could not choose a chieftain outside his quarter of the island. There were, however, a few exceptions: *bændr* who lived on Hrútafjörðr in the northwest were allowed to cross the fjord, and a chieftain could accept a thingman from outside his quarter if permitted to do so at the *lögberg* at the Althing (GG Ia, pp. 140-141 [ch. 83]).
15. GG Ia, p. 137 (ch. 81). See also GG II, p. 273 (ch. 242).
16. GG Ia, p. 140 (ch. 83). See also GG II, pp. 277-278 (ch. 245).

By the same token, a chieftain could break off a relationship with a thingman:

> If a *goði* wishes to declare himself out of thing with a thing-man [thus ending their thing relationship], then he shall notify him [the thingman] a fortnight before the springtime thing or with more notice. And then it is the law that he should tell the man at the springtime thing.[17]

In practice, the free exercise of the right to change leaders—an essential element in chieftain-farmer reciprocity—was tempered by traditions of personal and family loyalties, as well as by practical considerations, such as proximity to a chieftain. Probably freemen did not change chieftains frequently, yet the option was available. *The Saga of Hvamm-Sturla* offers a concise example from the early 1170s of a farmer, Álfr Örnólfsson, switching his allegiance from Einarr Thorgilsson to Hvamm-Sturla, two *goðar* who are involved in a series of contests in the latter half of the twelfth century (see chapter 8). Farmers, particularly rich and prominent ones, could, if dissatisfied, shift their allegiance. In extreme instances, disaffected farmers moved to other areas.[18] Although the laws give the impression that all freemen were required to be in thing with a chieftain, it is probable, especially in the absence of a policing authority, that some freemen chose not to enter into such arrangements.

The status of farmers as free agents seems to have been reinforced by the presence of communal units called *hreppar* (sing. *hreppr*).[19] Composed of a minimum of twenty *thingfararkaupsbændr*, these geographically defined associations of landowners were independent of the *goðar* and later of par-

17. *GG* Ia, p. 141 (ch. 83). See also *GG* II, pp. 278-279 (ch. 247); III, pp. 426-427 (A.M. 125 4to, ch. 65).
18. *Sturl.* 1 offers many examples of farmers moving in the later centuries of the Free State, a time when the territorial authority of the *goðar* was increasing (*Sturlu saga*, chs. 3, 6, 9, 23, 26; *Guðmundar saga dýra*, ch. 4; *Hrafns saga Sveinbjarnarsonar*, ch. 13; *Íslendinga saga*, chs. 6, 13, 18, 32, 33, 52, 53, 56, 59, 81, 83, 146, 166).
19. In 1703, when census figures first become available, there were 162 *hreppar*.

ish arrangements.[20] We do know that the *hreppar* were self-governing, but precisely how they functioned is unclear. Their age and origin are also obscure, although the whole country seems to have been divided into *hreppar* as early as the 900s, that is, before the introduction of Christianity. The *hreppar*, with their overt function of providing fire and livestock insurance for local farmers and of administering poor relief, continued in operation long after the end of the Free State, contributing to social continuity in the rural society.

The uncertain hold of *goðar* on their thingmen and the competition among leaders for the allegiance of *bændr* made it difficult if not impossible for individual chieftains to impose burdensome taxes on their followers. Leaders in other Norse settlements were not so constrained. For example, in Orkney leaders had the right to impose taxes and to demand extensive services from the farmers. Like Iceland, the Orkney Islands were settled by Norwegians during the viking period. The Orkneys, however, were nearer Norway and the British Isles and were threatened by both.

Orkney was ruled by jarls, and *Orkneyinga saga*, written in thirteenth-century Iceland, presents Orkney from early on as a state with a central political hierarchy and a military structure. Along with the accounts of other jarls, the saga tells the story (ch. 13) of Einarr Sigurðarson, who in 1014 seized control over two-thirds of Orkney after his father was killed near Dublin while aiding viking allies against the Irish in the battle of Clontarf:

> Einarr became a strong ruler and assembled a large band of followers. During the summers he was often out raiding and called out large levies of ships and men from throughout the land. The resulting plunder, however, was not consistently rewarding. The farmers became tired of serving, but the jarl held them harshly to their duties and taxes and made sure that no one spoke publicly against him. Einarr was a thoroughly tyrannical man, and all the payments and services

20. Magnús Már Lárusson, "Hreppr," *KLNM* 7, cols. 17-22; Jón Jóhannesson, *History*, pp. 83-89.

that he imposed on the farmers caused a serious famine in his part of the earldom [*jarldómr*].

It does not seem likely that leaders in the Orkneys spent much time advocating the claims of farmers, as happened in Iceland where leaders were solicitous of the demands of *bændr*. The Icelandic respect for freemen's rights was also extended to freedmen and their heirs. The slaves whom the early settlers brought with them were rapidly integrated into Iceland's minimally stratified social order.[21] Most slaves were freed in the tenth century, and by the eleventh slavery had largely died out. Some freedmen became landowners, though the majority probably became tenant farmers. It is difficult to define the latter, called *búðsetumenn* (cottagers who owed work services to their landlords) and *leiglendingar* (land renters not obligated to provide labor), because Icelandic tenant farmers enjoyed most freeman's rights, including the taking of vengeance and the collecting of blood money.[22] According to *Grágás*, only hired hands and impoverished fishermen were denied the right to choose their own *goðar*:

> A man who begins householding in the spring shall declare himself in thing wherever he wishes; it is a household where a man has milking stock. If, however, a man is a landowner he shall declare himself in thing even if he has no milking stock. If he is not a landowner and has no milking stock, he follows the thing choice of the householder in whose care he places himself. If he is living in a fishing hut, then he follows the thing choice of the man who owns the land on which he is living. A man shall declare himself in thing with the *goði* he prefers at the Althing or, if he wishes, at a *várthing*.[23]

21. The number of slaves brought to Iceland is unknown; many of them were probably of Celtic stock (Peter Foote, "Þrælahald á Íslandi," *Saga* 15[1977]:41-74).

22. Tenant farmers and slaves are discussed by Kirsten Hastrup, *Culture and History in Medieval Iceland: An Anthropological Analysis of Structure and Change* (Oxford: Clarendon Press, 1985), pp. 107-118. Hastrup's fine discussion may overemphasize class distinctions.

23. GG Ia, p. 136 (ch. 81). A line from the document "Skipan Sæmundar Ormssonar" (1245) corroborates that the chieftains drew their thing-tax-paying followers from both landowners and tenant farmers: "each *bóndi* who . . ." (*DI*, vol. 1, pt. 2, p. 536). A tenant farmer's exercise of his rights must have varied according to the *hóf* of the landowner.

Since the *goðar* could not claim obedience, they competed among themselves for supporters and advocacy clients. A chieftain's authority depended upon bonds of blood and alliance with members of the society's politically important population, the *thingfararkaupsbændr*. At the same time, the collective wealth of the *bændr* posed a challenge for the chieftains. The private lands and possessions of these farmers were a major source for the wealth required for the *goðar* to function as leaders. How to acquire resources from the independent-minded farmers and still retain their support was a dilemma faced by those seeking power, since checks and balances in the system, discussed in examples in later chapters of this book, worked to protect property owners against overly aggressive chieftains.

ADVOCACY, *VINFENGI*, AND KINSHIP

Chieftains had an advantage over farmers in being closer to the inner workings of the legal system, an advantage that was sustained by the workings of justice in medieval Iceland. The courts were less likely to base judgments on the evidence than to adjust decisions to satisfy the honor and resources of powerful individuals. An ordinary *bóndi* had little chance of success in facing opponents of substance without the help of advocates such as *goðar*. With their stake in maintaining the status quo, the *goðar* dealt in power politics, influencing the course of conflict resolution. Participating as advocates, both aggressively and defensively, permitted them to influence the behavior of others while enjoying the sanction of public opinion.[24] As the *goðar* were not territorial lords, the question remains: What were they? The answer is that they were leaders of interest groups that were continually jockeying with one another for status. The negotiations, political maneuverings, and compromises, strikingly portrayed in the family and Sturlunga sagas, followed a pat-

---

24. For advocacy and its occurrence in saga narrative, see Byock, *Feud*, pp. 37-38, 74-92.

tern of action in which leading individuals, whether prominent *bændr* or *goðar*, gained their own ends by intervening on behalf of others. As advocates they gave counsel, functioned as lawyers, and, in extreme circumstances, were willing to fight.

Chapters 8 through 11 of this book offer a series of case studies exploring different aspects of third-party intervention. From these examples we see that advocacy, in its different forms, had both overt and covert functions. The overt function was to provide clients and their leaders with a mechanism for arriving at the consensus necessary to settle disputes in a way that satisfied law and honor. The covert function was to allow leaders to maintain or increase their own power. *Goðar* were especially well placed to participate in advocacy by playing Iceland's quasi-egalitarian game of upholding rights through open feuding, but anyone who was asked could be an advocate. Advocacy became the keystone of a system of reciprocal arrangements in which people carefully kept track of assistance rendered and maintained a balance of obligations. The social fabric depended upon the maintenance of this balance, a process that forms the basis of much of the action in the sagas.

Some advocates made better use of their advantage than others. Their fame rested on their ability to mediate and to use the law intelligently on behalf of themselves and of others. Through the mechanisms of advocacy, *goðar* and some *bændr* acquired lands and received gifts. Success bred success, and the better an individual's reputation for bringing about advantageous settlements, the more often questions of inheritance, prosecution, and mediation were submitted to him. As Preben Meulengracht Sørensen has noted, "It was in the farmers' own advantage to be thingmen of those *goðar* who could best look after their interests, and the more thingmen that a *goði* could turn up with, the stronger his position at the thing and in armed conflicts."[25]

---

25. Preben Meulengracht Sørensen, *Saga og samfund: En indføring i old-islandsk litteratur* (Copenhagen: Berlingske forlag, 1977), p. 48.

Arriving at an assembly with a large following might even be profitable. Consider the account from *Ljósvetninga saga* (ÍF 10) where two chieftains, Eyjólfr Guðmundarson and Thorvarðr Höskuldsson, are locked in a desperate struggle. One of Thorvarðr's followers has killed Eyjólfr's brother, and Eyjólfr prepares a case. Each of the rival chieftains offers to pay other *goðar* in return for support. Eyjólfr, who is very wealthy, offers his "friend" (see *vinfengi*, below), the chieftain Gellir Thorkelsson, one "eyrir silfrs" (an ounce of silver, one-eighth of a mark) for each man plus half a mörk (mark) for each chieftain whom Gellir can bring with him to the Hegranes Thing (ch. 15 [25]).[26] Further, Eyjólfr offers a gold ring to the chieftain Skegg-Broddi. Thorvarðr, who is less wealthy, also sends a gold ring to Skegg-Broddi.

The advocacy system, together with the temporary interest groups that gathered around Icelandic leaders, diluted the strength of kinship bonds. Kinsmen in the same region might be attached to different and sometimes rival *goðar*. At times they might switch from one advocate to another. Shifting allegiances clouded loyalties during feuds and legal actions; the sagas frequently show kinsmen on opposing sides of feuds. Icelandic kinship arrangements were different from the ancestor-oriented kinship groups that scholars have traditionally postulated for Germanic society. The Icelandic kinship system was unusually egocentric, emphasizing cognatic ties.[27]

Families were basically nuclear with *thingfararkaupsbændr* and their wives living in their own households and forming independent units of production and consumption. Kinship centered on categories of kinsmen rather than on corporate groups. The sagas often distinguish between blood kinsmen (*frændr*) and the nearest affinal male relatives, such as fa-

26. Events described later in the saga show that the two chieftains, although "friends," did not really trust each other (ch. 17 [27]). The chapters refer to the two major manuscripts of the saga.

27. Preben Meulengracht Sørensen, *Saga og samfund*, pp. 30-36; Kirsten Hastrup, "Kinship in Medieval Iceland," *Folk* 23(1981):331-344, and her *Culture and History*, pp. 70-104.

thers-, brothers-, and sons-in-law (*mágar*).[28] Fictive kinship bonds complemented these relationships. They were formed when individuals, after a ritual blending of blood, became, for example, foster brothers (*fóstbróðir*),[29] sworn brothers (*svaribróðir*), or oath brothers (*eiðbróðir*). In the sagas such arrangements, usually including obligations to take vengeance, were frequently more reliable than blood ties.

Iceland was a highly individualistic society in which blood and fictive kinship served principally to form networks of preestablished relationships that could be mobilized according to the talents and resources of the individual. An Icelander could primarily expect support from his nearest relatives—parents, children, siblings, maternal and paternal uncles, and brothers-in-law. Except in matters of domestic conduct, such as incest, kinship in Iceland was rarely prescriptive or proscriptive. For example, there was no proscription against close cooperation among affinal relatives, and in-laws often cooperate against consanguine relatives in legal matters and in feud. This situation would be very unusual in a society that used kinship as a principle for organizing political and legal relations (for example, in so-called patrilineal societies).

Reflecting a distinct patrilineal emphasis, the laws of wergild (*Baugatal*) preserved in *Grágás*[30] seem to be very old. They presuppose a society, such as Norway's, which was organized around agnatic groups, and they are at variance with the information provided in the sagas about how Icelandic society operated. It is not surprising that older concepts of social, political, and kinship organization, such as elements of *Baugatal*, were carried to Iceland. These concepts served as a point of departure for the new society, and, to a certain extent, remnants of all imported concepts remained operative throughout the history of the Free State

28. *Mágar* (sing. *mágr*, fem. *mágkonur*) constituted a category of *sifjar*, a broader term designating general relationship by marriage. *Frændsemi* (blood relationship) is contrasted with *sifjar* (affinity).

29. *Fóstbróðir* also referred to men who were brought up together.

30. GG Ia, pp. 193-207 (chs. 113-115).

and beyond. However, the new associations that emerged in Iceland could not be based on traditional Norse corporate groups because only a few individuals from these groups migrated. Furthermore, the settlers claimed land individually. In order to defend his patrimony from encroachment the landowner in the early period had to look to anyone capable of lending support—cognates, affines, or nonkin landowners who would find an advantage in lending assistance. In this situation support for maintaining landownership claims, the crucial issue in the early period, was provided more by political associations than by kinship groupings. Reciprocity was widespread and advocacy was systematized. Talent in acquiring allies rather than reliance on an external rule of law defined through kinship or through the *goði*-thingman relationship determined how well one would fare in a crisis.

Success in maintaining reciprocal agreements and playing the role of advocate required conformity to a standard of moderation, termed *hóf*. An individual who observed this standard was called a *hófsmaðr*, a person of justice and temperance. The opposite of *hóf* was *óhóf*, a failure to observe restraint denoting excess or intemperance. Adherence to *óhóf* alarmed both friend and foe and called forth the exercise of peer pressure against it. Rarely did one leader succeed in imposing his will on other leaders for very long. The practice of *óhóf* was known as *ójafnaðr*, meaning unevenness, unfairness, or injustice in dealings with others. *Ójafnaðr* disturbed the consensual nature of decision making and set in motion a series of coercive responses; for example, when an individual's greed or ambition threatened the balance of power, other leaders banded together in an effort to counter his immoderate behavior. Action against an unruly man (*ójafnaðarmaðr*), instead of causing an upheaval in governmental authority, led to small adjustments in the balance of local power, as recounted in saga feuds. Without slipping into the realm of *ójafnaðr*, leaders sought to reap profit, status, and perhaps social good from their activities as advocates.

When a leader overstepped the bounds of propriety many people, including members of his own family, could take offense. *Ljósvetninga saga* (chs. 2-3) tells a curious story about the problems that befall two leading *goðar*, Guðmundr the Powerful and Thorgeirr goði, when they grossly manipulate the law to their own advantage. A pair of troublesome brothers are outlawed for three years as punishment for their misdeeds. They go to Norway where they gain the esteem of Jarl Hákon, Norway's ruler. After only two years abroad one of the brothers, Sölmundr, returns to Iceland in violation of his sentence. He brings for the two chieftains, Guðmundr and Thorgeirr goði, gifts that have been provided by the Norwegian jarl to buy protection for the outlaws. Guðmundr is described as a retainer of the jarl, whereas Thorgeirr's interest in the gifts seems only pecuniary.

The situation is difficult because other local men, including Thorgeirr's sons, have strong feelings against Sölmundr. In order to protect him, the chieftains decide to use their legal powers to nullify the earlier court judgment. In preparing the case, the chieftains apparently intend to use to their advantage Thorgeirr's position as lawspeaker, the final arbiter of law in unclear cases. Thorgeirr tells Guðmundr: " 'And I will support you, but you are to defend the case.' Guðmundr replied: 'I cannot speak against this since you have the law in your power.' " Thorgeirr's sons, however, are of a different mind. They kill Sölmundr and, before a settlement is reached, Thorgeirr barely escapes impeachment.

In addition to demonstrating *hóf*, an advocate had to have knowledge of the law in order to be successful, especially when he played the role of power broker. The *goðar* had no monopoly on legal knowledge; in the sagas prominent *bændr* such as Njáll Thorgeirsson and Helgi Droplaugarson show exceptional skill at law. Although they did not possess *goð-orð*, they moved in the circles of the *goðar* and benefited from being advocates and brokers. At times the influence of such *bændr* rivaled the authority wielded by *goðar*, although it is not clear how successful they were in the long run. A *bóndi* was at a disadvantage without the privileges normally enjoyed by a *goði*, especially the ready support afforded by a legally constituted following of thingmen. The story of Helgi Droplaugarson in *Droplaugarsona saga* illustrates this disability. For several years he competes at the law courts as an equal with a local chieftain, whose *goðorð* he apparently covets.[31] Helgi's opponent, however, shows a remarkable ability to absorb damage, a resiliency that Helgi as a *bóndi* finally is unable to equal.

As important advocates, power brokers maintained social stability when feuds escalated and threatened serious disruption. Turning to a broker with wide-ranging alliances was a way for a disputant to involve others, both chieftains and farmers, in his case. A resolution arrived at through such third-party intervention was likely to gain broad social approval. Because the courts required unanimity, or a general consensus, before arriving at a decision, brokerage and arbitration became commonplace. In striving for consensus, advocates and arbitrators frequently relied on ties of contractual political friendship called *vinfengi* and *vinátta*—the two terms are often used in similar ways, although *vinátta* more frequently than *vinfengi* is employed to describe genuine affection.

Vinfengi agreements allowed leaders to achieve the collaboration necessary for social control, and *vinfengi* is mentioned repeatedly in the sagas. Yet, this device for augmenting power has received little attention.[32] *Vinfengi* relationships

31. In Byock, *Feud*, pp. 38-46, a part of this specific *bóndi-goði* confrontation from *Droplaugarsona saga* is examined in light of advocacy and narrative structure.

32. According to the extensive cumulative index of the 22-volume *Kulturhistoriskt lexikon för nordisk medeltid* (Malmö: Allhems förlag, 1956-1978), the word *vinfengi* is never mentioned in any of the many articles devoted to Icelandic society and to the sagas. The entry entitled, "Venskap" (friendship), vol. 19: cols. 647-648, is characteristic of treatment that the concept of friendship has received. The discussion concentrates primarily on the ethical aspects of male bonding, particularly of *vinátta*, while the term *vinfengi* is not mentioned. Under the entry "Lösöre" (chattels), vol. 11: col. 157, which is almost entirely devoted to East Norse law, Bo Ruthström astutely notes that in the Old Swedish legal usage of *vin ok vitne* (friend and

described in *Vápnfirðinga saga* are particularly illuminating. (They are discussed in chapter 10.) The saga portrays a feud between the chieftain Brodd-Helgi, who frequently establishes *vinfengi* based on deceit, and the chieftain Geitir Lýtingsson, who bases his survival on more honorable conduct. A renowned broker, Guðmundr the Powerful, plays a conspicuous role in deciding the outcome of the feud.

Vinfengi and *vinátta* relationships complemented kin or *goði*-thingman obligations and put individuals in a position to demand reciprocity. Here the formal exchange of gifts and the holding of feasts played an important role. The author of *Njáls saga* underscores this importance when in describing the friendship between Höskuldr Hvítanessgoði and Njáll's family he tells us (ch. 17), "their *vinátta* was so great that they invited each other to a feast every fall and gave each other handsome gifts." In a more detailed example from *Vápnfirðinga saga* the chieftain Brodd-Helgi entices a thingman of a rival chieftain with the offer of lodging and a gift of five stud horses (see chapter 10).

In this context, *vinfengi* was yet another way to supplement blood kinship relationships and the nonblood kinship bonds formed by marriage, fosterage, and sworn brotherhood. The number of alternatives available in building temporary relationships made protecting oneself in Icelandic society a complex procedure. In chapter 9, I analyze the choices faced by a freedman, Úlfarr leysingi, who finds himself threatened by a neighboring farmer. Úlfarr turns for support to a local chieftain who, among other signs of friendship, invites him to feasts and gives him handsome gifts. This same episode from *Eyrbyggja saga* also illustrates the

---

witness) *vin* meant modern Swedish *mäklare*, broker or agent. Translations of the sagas tend to gloss over the contractual political nature of *vinfengi*. The specific Icelandic terms are almost always dropped and saga characters become "friendly" with each other or are simply "friends." For examples of *vinfengi* and *vinátta* in the *Íslendingasögur* see "Index" in Byock, *Feud*, p. 290; William Ian Miller, "Justifying Skarpheðinn: Of Pretext and Politics in the Icelandic Bloodfeud," *Scandinavian Studies* 55(1983):339-340.

choices confronting a family of *bændr*, the sons of Thorbrandr, forced into the difficult, but ultimately successful,
position of opposing an ambitious chieftain.

A *vinfengi* arrangement might be concluded between individuals of equal political status, as between chieftains or
between thingmen of different chieftains. *Vinfengi* agreements might also be reached by people of different status.
Such relationships might be kept secret, especially if, as often happened, chieftains and farmers who entered into them
shared nothing but a mutual need for support. Should a
friendship not prove rewarding—by not providing assistance
during a feud, for example—the arrangement could be terminated. *Vápnfirðinga saga* describes how a *bóndi*, Digr–Ketill, terminated a covert agreement of friendship between
himself and a *goði* (see chapter 10). In some ways the extralegal bonds of *vinfengi* corresponded to the lawfully defined "thing relationship" between a *goði* and a *bóndi*, as both
alliances could be ended when one of the parties was dissatisfied.

Chieftains who were careful to cultivate good reputations
as advocates and were successful in their power brokerage
often defined the terms of a friendship before entering into
it. *Njáls saga* (ch. 139) describes in detail how Snorri goði,
one of the cleverest chieftains portrayed in the family sagas,
is supposed to have weighed the options available to him as
a third party well situated to intervene in a coming armed
clash at the Althing. The scene begins when the major prosecutors of the killers of Njáll and his sons come to Snorri's
booth at the assembly to seek assistance in the upcoming
court case. After an initial discussion in which Snorri pre-
dicts that the case will not be settled in court but will turn
into an armed confrontation, one of the prosecutors, Ásgrímr
Elliða-Grímsson, asks Snorri the crucial question:

> "I want to know what help you intend to give us, if it goes
> as you predict."
>   Snorri replied, "I shall make this friendship [*vinátta*] agree-
> ment with you, Ásgrímr, since your honor is at stake. I will
> not go into court with you. If you should come to blows at

the thing, then attack only if you see no danger whatsoever, because there are valiant champions on the other side. But if you give way you should retreat in this direction to join up with us, for I will have drawn up my men in preparation and will be ready to assist you. And if, on the other hand, they are the ones who give way, it is my guess that they will make for the vantage point of Almannagja [a rift in the lava near the Law Rock]. If they make it to that place you will never be able to overcome them. I shall undertake to draw up my men in front and bar them from the vantage point, but we will not go after them if they retreat north or south along the river. And when you have killed as many of their men as it seems to me you can afford to pay compensation for and still keep your chieftaincies and your domiciles, I will come forward with all my men and separate you. If I do that for you, you should follow my instructions."

In this example from *Njáls saga*, Snorri makes clear what he will and will not do in his *vinátta* before entering into the agreement. The account shows how a leader as cunning as Snorri might aid his friend's side to carry out limited vengeance and then, at the right moment, might assume the role of a man of goodwill intent on intervening between the feuding parties in order to terminate the violence. It is obvious here that honor is a related issue.

Christian priests, including many who were not *goðar*, also played the role of advocate.[33] According to *The Saga of Guðmundr Arason the Priest (Prestssaga Guðmundar góða)*, Guðmundr, later (1203) bishop of Hólar, took on a prosecution for a killing in the early 1180s. Like most advocates, Guðmundr depended on the support of others. In this instance he was counting on the assistance of his prominent kinsman, the *goði* Sturla Thórðarson of Hvammr (1116-1183), the father of Snorri Sturluson. Unhappily for Guðmundr, Sturla died soon after Guðmundr won a legal sentence of outlawry against the killer, named Oddr. Guðmundr then faced the dishonor that accrued to one who had obtained a sentence in his favor but had no means of executing the penalty prescribed by law. A solution, in keeping with the nature of

33. As noted in chapter 7, priests were also active participants in feuds.

advocacy, was found when "Almighty God supported him by putting ideas into his mind so that he decided to make a vow that he would give Almighty God all the wealth that came to him because of Oddr's outlawry, as long as the case was brought to an end without peril to Guðmundr's soul" (ch. 8).

Women did not serve as advocates because they were not entitled to lead prosecutions, either for revenge or for material compensation. Their legal impotence is confirmed in *Eyrbyggja saga* (see end of chapter 9), and there is no evidence in *Grágás* that women were permitted to speak publicly at a thing. When present at assemblies, they probably attended as onlookers—the rules concerning judges mention only men[34] —and they were not allowed to serve as members of a *kviðr* (a verdict-giving panel) or to act as legal witnesses.[35] Although a woman could inherit a *goðorð*, she was ineligible to act as a *goði* and had to turn the chieftancy over to a man.[36]

Icelandic women did, however, frequently play an influential role in the workings of advocacy. They contributed to the private consensus underlying decisions that determined relations between families and the outcome of feuds. Perhaps because freeborn Icelandic women maintained a measure of control over their own lives, including their right to own property independently, their opinions frequently carried weight. When acting as heads of households, they were required to tithe "in the same manner as men,"[37] and like men they were subject to outlawry for a wounding or a killing.[38] Some women may have served as temple priestesses in the pre-Christian period.[39] Despite their influence in some areas, Icelandic women played no substantial role in open

---

34. GG Ia, pp. 38-39 (ch. 20).
35. GG Ia, p. 161 (ch. 89); II, p. 322 (ch. 289).
36. GG Ia, p. 142 (ch. 84).
37. GG Ib, p. 206 (ch. 255); II, p. 47 (ch. 37); III, p. 44 (ch. 28).
38. GG II, p. 350 (ch. 318).
39. *Vápnfirðinga saga* (ch. 5) calls a woman named Steinvör a *hofgyðja*, a temple priestess.

political life and did not enjoy legal equality with men. Still, if we are to judge by the sagas, women of property-holding families had sufficient clout to set in motion actions that escalated or prolonged feuds.[40] As the literature suggests, females frequently achieved their objectives by inciting, shaming, or goading their kinsmen into action.

SUMMARY

Advocacy and other private arrangements, in particular *vinfengi*, accommodated petty interests as well as major concerns. As acceptable social mechanisms, they suited the *goðar* in their position as leaders of legally constituted interest groups. At the same time they reinforced the broad range of free farmers' rights, which sometimes competed with the rights of *goðar*. The willingness of advocates to embroil themselves in the problems of others, often simple farmers, gave a wide range of individuals, both advocates and clients, a significant role in the operation of their society. This process, though hardly democratic in the modern sense, gave many freemen a say in determining their own future and served to control violence in a society that permitted almost no governmental control. Third-party interventions, in particular advocacy, became part of a highly stylized form of handling disputes which embraced the principle of compen-

40. The position of women in early Iceland is a subject about which there is a large and growing literature: Rolf Heller, *Die literarische Darstellung der Frau in den Isländersagas*, Saga 2 (Halle [Saale]: Max Niemeyer Verlag, 1958), pp. 98-122; Jenny Jochens, "The Medieval Icelandic Heroine: Fact or Fiction," *Viator* 17(1986):35-50; Roberta Frank, "Marriage in Twelfth- and Thirteenth-Century Iceland," *Viator* 4(1973):473-484; Helga Kress, "Ekki höfu vér kvennaskap: Nokkrar laustengdar athuganir um karlmennsku og kvenhatur í Njálu" in *Sjötíu ritgerðir helgaðar Jakobi Benediktssyni 20. júlí 1977*, ed. Einar G. Pétursson and Jónas Kristjánsson, pt. 1, pp. 293-313 (Reykjavik: Stofnun Árna Magnússonar, 1977); Ólafía Einarsdóttir, "Staða kvenna á þjóðveldisöld. Hugleiðingar í ljósi samfélagsgerðar og efnahagskerfis," *Saga* 22(1984):7-30; Else Mundal, "Kvinnebiletet i nokre mellomaldergenrar. Eit opposisjonelt kvinnesyn?" *Edda* 72(1982):341-371; Gunnar Karlsson, "Kenningin um fornt kvenfrelsi á Íslandi," *Saga* 24(1986):45-77.

sation and employed arbitration so successfully in arriving at compromise solutions that for several hundred years feuds threatening public order were successfully contained.

7

Integration of the Church

The men from Fljót could see that they would not have
their full rights vindicated in a lawsuit against Önundr unless they could depend upon the support of others. So
they went to Bishop Brandr [Sæmundarson, d. 1201] and
sought his advice. The bishop told them that Guðmundr
dýri's assistance had determined the outcome of the most
important lawsuits that had come to the Althing during
the preceding summer. The bishop advised them to seek
a meeting with Guðmundr to see if they could get him to
take on their case.

—*The Saga of Guðmundr Dýri*

Assessing the impact of the medieval church on a society
such as Iceland's is difficult; church practices in Iceland were
often irregular in the light of accepted Roman procedure and
may be interpreted in different ways.[1] In forming a view, one
should consider several key factors. First, the conversion to
Christianity was a peaceful transition. Second, the church
expanded the cultural horizon of the Icelanders by intro-

---

1. Much has been written about the Icelandic church. See for example,
the excellent essays in *Saga Íslands*: Sigurður Líndal, "Upphaf kristni og
kirkju," in *Saga Íslands* 1:227-288, including a bibliography; Magnús Stefánsson, "Kirkjuvald eflist," trans. Björn Teitsson, in *Saga Íslands* 2:57-144,
including a bibliography, and his "Frá goðakirkju til biskupskirkju," trans.
Sigurður Líndal, in *Saga Íslands* 3:111-257, including a bibliography. See also
Jón Jóhannesson's section, "Church and Religion," in his *A History of the
Old Icelandic Commonwealth: Íslendinga saga*, trans. Haraldur Bessason, University of Manitoba Icelandic Studies 2 (Winnipeg: University of Manitoba
Press, 1974), pp. 118-221.

ducing new ideas from the Latin West. Third, Iceland's new church developed for almost two centuries with little external supervision, and during this stage of development it does not make much sense to talk about the Icelandic church as if it had been a full-fledged institution. Economics is a fourth factor. Until well after the end of the Free State the Icelandic church reaped only a small portion of the revenue from the land it ostensibly owned because laymen controlled most of the property. Additionally, one must reckon with the nature of the Icelandic priesthood, for the priests did not form a caste distinct from the society. Their behavior was dominated by secular norms, and they included among their ranks chieftains and influential farmers who had no desire to lose their family lands to church control.

In the following discussion I consider the place of the Icelandic church in the light of Icelandic traditions of social control, established in the early centuries. After covering the conversion of the Icelanders and the development of the church, I go on to the heart of the matter—the role of the clergy and the relation of the church to the secular society.

THE CONVERSION

A few of the *landnámsmenn* had converted to Christianity before coming to Iceland, and others possessed at least a passing knowledge of the new religion. Their acquaintance with Christianity derived from the meeting of cultures which occurred in the viking outposts in northern Europe, especially those in the British Isles. As the majority of the settlers were believers in the old gods, however, organized Christian worship probably died out within a generation or two. It should be stressed that little is known about this period, and it is possible that some individuals and families maintained a belief in the Christian God. A distinction here is that belief may have been relatively easy, but maintaining Christian observance was much more difficult.

In the tenth century, as the island's new social order evolved, the Icelanders worshiped the traditional Norse gods. By far the most important was Thórr, the god of farmers and seafarers. It seems that Freyr, the god of fertility, and to a far lesser extent Óðinn, the god of warriors and aristocrats, were also worshiped. Although personal attachment to the Norse gods varied with the individual, seasonal observances and public rites, such as the hallowing of assemblies, were important formal ceremonies. As noted earlier, the *goðar* seem to have carried out most of the priestly functions in such ceremonies. Iceland's acceptance of Christianity[2] is traditionally ascribed to the year 1000. Information about the transition is contained in a number of overlapping, often late, and sometimes divergent sources.[3] Nevertheless, the basic progression of events as reported in the sources has a certain logic. Beginning approximately in 980, the island was visited by several missionaries. Among the

2. See Dag Strömbäck, *The Conversion of Iceland: A Survey* (London: Viking Society for Northern Research, 1975). See also Jón Jóhannesson, *History*, pp. 118-144. A creative and folkloristic interpretation is offered by Jón Hnefill Aðalsteinsson, *Under the Cloak: The Acceptance of Christianity in Iceland with Particular Reference to the Religious Attitudes Prevailing at the Time*, Acta Universitatis Upsaliensis, Studia Ethnologica Upsaliensia 4 (Stockholm: Almqvist and Wiksell, 1978).

3. The most reliable account of the Christianization of Iceland is from Ari's *Íslendingabók*, ch. 7. Another account is found in the *Historia de antiquitate regum Norwagiensium*, written about 1180 by the Norwegian monk Theodoricus monachus (in Gustav Storm, ed., *Monumenta Historica Norvegiæ* [Christiania: A. W. Brøgger, 1880], pp. 1-68). An Old Icelandic translation of the lost Latin *Saga of King Óláfr Tryggvason* by the monk Oddr Snorrason of Thingeyrar gives an account of the Christianization of Iceland which is largely based on *Íslendingabók*: Oddr Snorrason, *Olav Tryggvasons saga: etter AM 310 gv.*, ed. Anne Holtsmark (Oslo: Selskapet til utgivelse av gamle norske håndskrifter, 1974). Another lost Latin *Saga of King Óláfr Tryggvason* by the monk Gunnlaugr Leifsson of Thingeyrar seems to have been highly credulous and unreliable; it formed the basis for the remaining sources on the Christianization of Iceland. These are *Kristni saga*, ed. Guðni Jónsson, in *Íslendinga sögur*, vol. 1, *Landssaga og landnám* ([Akureyri]: Íslendingasagnaútgáfan, 1953); *Óláfs saga Tryggvasonar en mesta*, 2 vols., ed. Ólafur Halldórsson, Editiones Arnamagnæanæ Ser. A 1-2 (Copenhagen: Munksgaard, 1958-1961); and the account of the conversion in *Njáls saga*, chs. 100-105. A number of other family sagas such as *Laxdæla saga* contribute additional accounts.

first was an Icelander returning from abroad, Thorvaldr
Koðránsson, called the Far Traveler (inn víðförli).[4] Thorvaldr was accompanied by Friðrekr, a German bishop who
had previously baptized him and about whom we know very
little.[5] Thorvaldr met with little success. He became the subject of lampoons and, with Friðrekr, was forced to leave after
being involved in disturbances in which two men were
killed.

During the reign of Óláfr Tryggvason (995-1000), Norway's proselytizing warrior king, the effort to convert Iceland suddenly intensified. Early in his reign King Óláfr sent
an Icelander named Stefnir Thorgilsson home to convert his
countrymen.[6] Stefnir is said to have used so much violence
in destroying the sanctuaries and images of the old gods that
he was outlawed from Iceland. In response to such missionary probes, the so-called kin shame (*frændaskömm*) legislation was passed at the Althing. It called upon families to
prosecute Christians within their ranks if they blasphemed
the old gods or committed other offenses.

After the failure of Stefnir's mission, King Óláfr next sent
to Iceland a German, or perhaps Flemish, priest named
Thangbrandr. He was an experienced missionary already
known for his proselytizing work in Norway and in the Faroes. His mission to Iceland (ca. 997-999) is mentioned in
many sources.[7] Not only was Thangbrandr a preacher but,
according to later stories, he was skilled in the use of spear
and sword. His efforts were only partly successful; he converted several prominent Icelanders but also killed two or
three men who had composed mocking verses about him.
Njáls saga gives a lively, although probably exaggerated, account of Thangbrandr's methods of conversion. According

---

4. Thorvaldr's mission is reported only in *Kristni saga* and in the *Kristni
þáttr* section of *Óláfs saga Tryggvasonar en mesta*, two untrustworthy sources.
    5. *Íslendingabók* (ch. 8) mentions a bishop Friðrekr who came to Iceland
during the heathen period but gives no further information.
    6. Like Thorvaldr's mission, Stefnir's is reported only in *Kristni Þáttr* of
Óláfs saga Tryggvasonar en mesta and in *Kristni saga*.
    7. Sveinbjörn Rafnsson, "Um kristniboðsþættina," *Gripla* 2(1977):19-31.

to the saga, the priest, accompanied by his converts, traversed the countryside, pausing here and there to preach. At one such stop at Fljótshlíð in the south, where Thangbrandr and his group extolled the faith, "Vetrliði the poet and his son Ari spoke most strongly against it, so they killed Vetrliði."[8]

Thangbrandr returned to Norway around 999 without having converted Iceland. In retaliation, King Óláfr became more aggressive toward the Icelanders and took hostage a few of them who were then in Norway. Among the captives were sons or relatives of prominent Icelandic pagans, whom the king threatened to maim or kill unless Iceland accepted Christianity. The king's hostile actions soon had the desired effect in Iceland, for several reasons. A tenet of the Free State's otherwise limited foreign policy was to preserve good relations with Norway. Many Icelanders retained family ties with Norwegians, and Norway was a major trading partner. Emboldened by the king's actions, the Christians in Iceland grew more determined to convert the entire country and to do away with religious traditions offensive to Christians, such as the hallowing of assemblies by heathen rites.

Adherents of the two rival religions formed antagonistic groups, and events moved swiftly. A delegation of important Christians journeyed to Norway and rescued the hostages by promising King Óláfr that they would try to bring about the conversion. At home the Christian chieftains moved toward establishing separate courts and a government distinct from the preexisting system, which was controlled by believers in the old faith. The issues raised by these developments presented a dilemma to thoughtful Icelanders, as division of the country into separate camps raised the danger of war.

Matters came to a head the next summer at the Althing, as those believing in the Norse gods skirmished with the

---

8. ÍF 12, ch. 102. The killing of Vetrliði is mentioned in *Heimskringla*, *Kristni saga*, *Landnámabók*, and *Óláfs saga Tryggvasonar en mesta*. The *Njáls saga* account is probably derived from one of these.

Christians. When a major warlike encounter appeared imminent, a typical Icelandic scenario developed: mediators intervened, and the dispute was submitted to arbitration. The lawspeaker Thorgeirr Thorkelsson, a *goði* from the farm of Ljósavatn in the Northern Quarter, was selected for the delicate job of settling the dispute. Thorgeirr was acceptable to both sides. As lawspeaker he had been constitutionally elected; further, he was a pagan, yet he seemed to have strong ties with members of the Christian camp.

According to Ari's account in *Íslendingabók*, Thorgeirr sequestered himself, lying under a cloak for part of a day and through the following night. Then, before announcing his decision, he received assurances that both sides would abide by his ruling since it "will prove to be true that if we divide the law we will also divide the peace." Ari relates Thorgeirr's decision (ch. 7):

> Then it was made law that all people should become Christian and that those who here in the land were yet unbaptized should be baptized; but as concerns the exposure of infants, the old laws should stand, as should those pertaining to the eating of horseflesh. If they wished, people might sacrifice to the old gods in private, but it would be lesser outlawry [*fjör-baugsgarðr*] if this practice were verified by witnesses. But a few years later this heathen custom was abolished, as were the others.

Within the brief period of the meeting of the national assembly in the summer of the year 1000, the menacing problem of changing religions was resolved, and Iceland averted civil war. Given the decades of strife, both before and after the conversion in neighboring Norway, the peaceful manner in which the Icelanders adopted the new faith has long been considered remarkable. But was it so strange in light of the methods of channeling and resolving disputes which the Icelanders had developed in the preceding seven decades? The process of resolving the antagonisms attendant upon the conversion dispute followed the pattern by which important feuds were settled: third parties intervened and through arbitration a compromise was reached. By the year 1000 the procedure for conflict resolution in Iceland was so well established that an issue as potentially disruptive as a change in religion was resolved with little violence. With so skillful a compromise the Icelanders peacefully accepted the conversion, avoiding a sharp break with the past. Although the pagans were in the majority, they joined the Christians in legislating the adoption of Christianity. We may guess that they feared social upheaval more than they disliked religious change. This supposition is reinforced by the fact that Iceland continued to abide by Thorgeirr's ruling, even though, with King Óláfr's death that same year (1000), Norway partly reverted to paganism. The sense of compromise and political expediency underlying the conversion may be glimpsed in the decision by many of the participants as to when and where they would accept baptism. Some chose not to do so in the cold waters at the Althing; instead, they put off formal acceptance of the faith until they reached hot springs on their way home.

THE DEVELOPING CHURCH

During the next seven or so decades following the conversion, the Icelanders had only a limited knowledge of the new religion. A large part of the training they did receive came from an assortment of foreign priests and itinerant missionary bishops who traveled to the newly converted country. Among them were three foreign teachers, Peter, Abraham, and Stephen, who Ari tells us called themselves Armenian (*ermskir*) bishops.[9] In order to facilitate the observance of Christianity, many chieftains and farmers built churches on their farms at their own expense and considered themselves "owners."[10] In erecting *Eigenkirchen, goðar* ex-

9. *Íslendingabók* (ch. 8). See Magnús Már Lárusson, "On the So-Called 'Armenian' Bishops," *Studia Islandica* 18(1960):23-38.
10. During the period 1030-1153 there were many similarities between the Icelandic and Norwegian churches. In particular, one may mention the private control of churches. Called *hægendis-kirkja* (sing.), "church of convenience" or private chapel, it is what Ulrich Stutz termed *Eigenkirche* (*Ge-*

changed their heathen religious role for that of Christian priest, and they seem to have suffered no diminution in their status and power. Perhaps their authority even grew. Among individuals sharing this dual authority during the following years were Ari the Learned, Sæmundr the Learned from Oddi, Teitr (Bishop Ísleifr's son) from Haukadalr, and Teitr's son Hallr.

When the church owner or warden did not himself become the priest, he could arrange to have a priest serve in his church. By one method the owner entered into a contractual agreement with an impoverished young man willing to be trained for the priesthood. In return for the training and for being supplied with the necessary books and vestments, the youth would remain throughout his life at the owner's church. Such a priest, who was called a *kirkjuprestr*, probably enjoyed little respect. If he ran away, the landowner, whether farmer or chieftain, could demand him back as though he were a runaway slave. Not very much is known about this type of priest, and in any event the practice seems to have diminished sharply in the twelfth century.

The other type of priest, at times called a *thingaprestr*, functioned in the manner of a private chaplain. Such individuals were freemen with clerical training who undertook employment as priests. For a fee including room and board, they would look after one or more churches. These priests normally became members of the household of the church owner, leaving some doubt as to the degree of independence with which they managed their churches. Among them were

---

schichte des kirchlichen Benefizialwesens von seinen Anfängen bis auf die Zeit Alexanders III [1895; repr. Aalen: Scientia, 1961]). In this early period virtually all churches in Norway were some sort of *hægendis-kirkjur* (pl.). Even the main churches and the common churches of more important communities (*höfuðkirkjur*) and the churches of Norwegian leaders and farmers were considered as privately owned, either by a single person (or more properly by a family) or by a group of people. Gradually the *hægendis-kirkjur* were converted into "official" parish churches. My thanks to Per Sveaas Andersen for elucidating this point.

Thorlákr Thórhallsson and Guðmundr Arason, both of whom later became bishops. In the mid-eleventh century a formal church apparatus began to take shape. Gizurr hvíti (the White) was a prominent Christian *goði* who had played an important role in the conversion. Gizurr sent his son Ísleifr (born ca. 1006) to study the new religion at the monastic school in Herford, Westphalia. Ísleifr, one of the first Icelanders to be educated and ordained abroad, returned home to Iceland, married, and became a chieftain like his father. At the Althing some years later, about 1055, Ísleifr was elected Iceland's first bishop. After his election he again went abroad and in 1056 was consecrated by the archbishop of Bremen.

We do not know very much about Ísleifr's episcopate, but it seems that he enjoyed only limited success in making his authority felt. *Hungrvaka*, a major source for information about Ísleifr, says (ch. 2) that Ísleifr the bishop "encountered many serious difficulties during his episcopate stemming from people's disobedience. As an example of the kind of problem caused by lack of faith, disobedience, and immorality among his subjects, the lawspeaker married two women—a mother and her daughter." We are not told whether these unions were concurrent or whether one followed the other. Apparently Ísleifr was not appointed to a specific see, and *Hungrvaka* tells us that he suffered because people showed him little honor or obedience. From his farm at Skálholt in the Southern Quarter he seems to have acted much like the missionary bishops with whom he competed. Possibly referring to the Armenians or to other missionaries from the Eastern church, *Hungrvaka* says (ch. 2) that in "Bishop Ísleifr's day bishops who preached a more lenient doctrine than Bishop Ísleifr came from other countries to Iceland. They therefore became popular with wicked men until Archbishop Aðalbertus [archbishop of Hamburg-Bremen, 1043-1072] sent a letter to Iceland prohibiting people from accepting any of their [these bishops'] services and said that some had been excommunicated and that all of them had gone out to Iceland without his permission."

Ísleifr's eldest son Gizurr Ísleifsson succeeded his father as bishop of Skálholt in what appears to have been a smooth transition. Like his father, Gizurr was elected bishop at the Althing. *Hungrvaka* (ch. 4) reports that Gizurr sought to remedy the problem of disobedience which his father had experienced. Before accepting the office, he received pledges from all the chieftains in the country that they would accept those ordinances that he would enforce. Gizurr went abroad and was consecrated Iceland's second bishop in 1082 in Magdeburg. During his long episcopate (1082-1118) Gizurr was deeply respected and worked to set the church on a more secure footing. He was responsible for the introduction of the tithe in 1097 and provided the Icelandic church with a fixed episcopal seat by willing his farm Skálholt to the church. Transferring land out of family control usually required the approval of potential heirs, a process that might lead to disputes, but we are not told whether Gizurr encountered any such difficulties. At the time of his episcopate people in the Northern Quarter were feeling the need to have their own bishop, and at the beginning of the twelfth century an episcopal seat was established at Hólar in Hjaltadalr. The bishop at Skálholt retained jurisdiction over the inhabitants of the Western, Southern, and Eastern quarters. Jón Ögmundarson was selected first bishop of Hólar by the clergy and laymen of the Northern Quarter. He was consecrated in 1106 by the archbishop of Lund.

For our purposes, the major question is: Did the church significantly alter the basic patterns through which members of the secular society acquired wealth and power? With the establishment of the northern bishopric the Icelandic church assumed the basic form that it was to retain throughout the remaining century and a half of the Free State. The indications are that the church did not supplant Iceland's long-established traditions of secular self governance. Years ago G. Turville-Petre and E. S. Olszewska succinctly described the situation that prevailed after the conversion: "Just as their pagan ancestors had built temples to Thor and Frey, so the Christian *goðar* built churches upon their lands, and maintained these churches as their private property. Until the question of patronage became acute, towards the end of the twelfth century, and until the Icelandic Church, under foreign influence, began to press for separate jurisdiction for the clergy, there were scarcely grounds for a quarrel between Church and State. Ísleifr was not only a bishop, he was also a *goði*, and, it seems, his son Gizurr (died 1118) succeeded him in both these offices."[11] In a similar vein Jón Jóhannesson writes that Bishop Gizurr "saw to it that there were no clashes between the church and the secular leaders, even if it meant that he had to bypass the letter of ecclesiastical law. His church policies remind us of the compromise at the Althing in the year 1000."[12]

Except for the stormy episcopates of Thorlákr Thórhallsson in the Skálholt diocese at the end of the twelfth century and of Guðmundr Arason in the Hólar bishopric at the beginning of the thirteenth century, all Icelandic bishops until 1238 (when Norwegians first filled the two offices) followed Gizurr's example of pursuing a national church policy. From the start the bishops set the example for the integration of the clergy into Icelandic familial life. For example, of the six nuns who can be identified before 1300, one was Gróa (died 1160), the daughter of a bishop, wife of another bishop, and mother of a priest.[13]

THE CHURCH AND SECULAR AUTHORITY

From early on, the Icelandic church was vulnerable to secular interference because of its inability to exercise control

---

11. G. Turville-Petre and E. S. Olszewska, trans., *The Life of Gudmund the Good, Bishop of Holar* (Coventry: Viking Society for Northern Research, 1942), p. xi.

12. Jón Jóhannesson, *History*, p. 148.

13. Gróa, who became a solitary nun in old age, was the daughter of Bishop Gizurr Ísleifsson of Skálholt, the wife of Bishop Ketill Thorsteinsson of Hólar (1122-1145), and mother of the priest Rúnólfr (Roberta Frank, "Marriage in Twelfth- and Thirteenth- Century Iceland," *Viator* 4[1973]:482).

over its property. More than 200 years after Iceland's conversion, the wealth and the authority of the Icelandic church were still largely administered by laymen. As on the continent, the church in Iceland claimed ownership of large tracts of land. The difference was that in Europe the church often enjoyed the social, economic, and political advantages derived from control of valuable property; in Iceland the claim to such control was mostly hollow. Much of the church's property remained under secular control until a compromise was finally arranged in 1297 which returned a portion of the lands to the church.[14]

There is no doubt that the Icelanders looked on their society as a Christian one, and Christian observance is built into the secular law in a fairly thorough fashion. Iceland, nevertheless, lay far from the centers of Roman authority and in few places in medieval Europe, especially in the twelfth and thirteenth centuries, did laymen exercise as much control over the church as they did in Iceland. Beginning with the conversion and continuing into the thirteenth century, chieftains and influential farmers met at the assemblies, where through consensus they regulated almost all points of contention between the church and lay society. Partly because the church was introduced into Iceland by compromise rather than by enforcement through the victory of one side, it early adapted itself to the normative patterns of Icelandic decision making. These patterns had been evolving since the establishment of the Althing in 930, and by the early eleventh century they were firmly in place.

The lack of friction between the early Icelandic church and the secular society was owing in part to the financial benefits that the church brought to many chieftains and prominent farmers. The benefits, which increased after the tithe law was introduced in 1097, fueled the move toward a more stratified society by altering to some degree the dis-

---

14. Magnús Stefánsson, "Frá goðakirkju," pp. 222-226; Jón Jóhannesson, *Íslendinga saga*, vol. 2: *Fyrirlestrar og ritgerðir um tímabilið 1262-1550* (Reykjavik: Almenna bókafélagið, 1958), pp. 89-109.

tribution of wealth. Possession of farmsteads with churches on them became for the chieftains and farmers who owned such lands an important new source of income (see chapter 5). Donations in honor of saints increased the value of many of these churches, and owners could acquire several churches, each with one or more farms attached. Revenue from such property contributed to the success of many of the six extended *stórgoðar* families whose power became so important in the thirteenth century.

Another factor facilitating the smooth integration of the Icelandic church and the Althing system of governance was that, for the formative first century and a half after the conversion, the Icelandic church was left mainly to its own devices. It was not, at this stage, a well-developed institution, and what organization there was enjoyed a large measure of independence from higher church authority. The independent evolution of Iceland's church was fostered by the irregular and difficult communications that distanced Icelandic churchmen from their foreign superiors. The relative unimportance of Iceland in the eyes of continental churchmen may also have been a factor. From the conversion until the beginning of the twelfth century Iceland fell within the archiepiscopal see of Hamburg-Bremen. The archbishop and his chapter were preoccupied with the events taking place in the neighboring kingdoms of Norway, Sweden, and Denmark, as well as in their own north German locality. The situation did not change significantly for Iceland when, in 1104, a new archbishopric for all Scandinavia was established at Lund, in the Danish kingdom. Communications with Lund were irregular. The archbishops in Lund were friendly and helpful to the Icelanders, but Iceland was not a primary or even a particularly important concern of these archbishops, involved as they were in affairs of Denmark and the surrounding countries.

In 1153 a separate archiepiscopal see was established in Norway at Niðaróss (Trondheim). The archbishop of Niðaróss was given jurisdiction over the dioceses of Norway as well as over the Orkneys, the Hebrides, the Faroes, Iceland,

and Greenland. Communications with Norway were usually good, and, although the archbishops in Niðaróss often strongly supported the Icelandic bishops, the influence of these high churchmen on Iceland's lay society was limited. In the late twelfth century the Niðaróss archbishop and Norway's King Sverrir Sigurðarson (1184-1202) were locked in a deadly struggle, during which the king was excommunicated, the country was placed under an interdict, and the bishops were exiled. It was not until well into the thirteenth century that the archbishops and the Norwegian Crown, particularly under Sverrir's grandson, King Hákon Hákonarson (1217-1263), were able to work together effectively in order that both church and Crown might extend their authority to Iceland.

Before the joint intervention of Norway's king and archbishop in Icelandic affairs in the last decades of the Free State, few church demands for more autonomy had been met. A notable exception was that in 1190 the Norwegian Archbishop Eiríkr Ívarsson prohibited the ordination of *goðar* as priests, thus lessening the control of secular leaders over the church.[15] Although this interdiction was never officially made part of Icelandic law, no sure evidence that any new priests were ordained from among the chieftains emerges after 1190. Yet even here change came slowly. Previously ordained chieftain-priests retained their dual function. Temporal leaders continued to assume lower clerical orders, and their sons occasionally assumed higher orders. Further, after 1190 *bændr* who were allied with chieftains continued to serve as ordained priests.

Monastic holdings did not significantly alter the economic or political position of the early Icelandic church, though monasteries did play an active role in Iceland's cultural life. Modern writings about Iceland's monasteries have frequently included assumptions that these religious communities were more important than the verifiable information suggests. In fact, the sources give little information about

15. *DI*, vol. 1, pt. 1, p. 291.

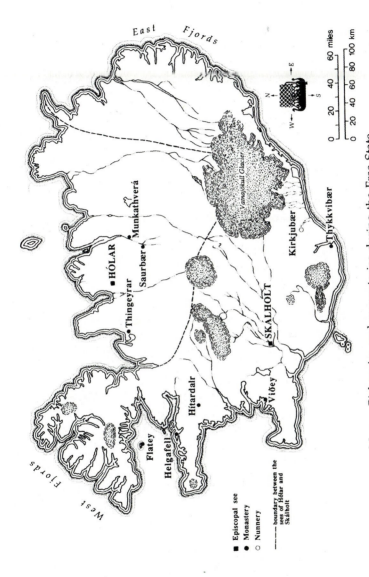

Map 4. Bishoprics and monasteries during the Free State.

them. The factor of size, however, seems to be clearly understood. Einar Ól. Sveinsson notes that "the monastic population was, to be sure, not large, from five to ten members to a house, and we have no information that before 1300 there were in any Icelandic monastery more than five monks at one time."[16] Communities of monks in Iceland followed the rules of either the Benedictine or the Augustinian order, but were not branches of specific international houses. Instead they seem to have relied heavily on native cultural traditions. This reliance was perhaps owing to the Icelandic custom whereby monasteries were often founded and maintained through the participation of *goðar* and prominent *bændr*, a number of whom retired to these communities at the end of their lives.

Icelandic monasteries served as centers of learning and probably of instruction, although information about the latter is scant. We probably know most about the Benedictine monastery at Thingeyrar in the northern diocese. It was Iceland's first monastery to survive and it was perhaps the most scholarly. Its monks were particularly interested in hagiographical works. They wrote early sagas of Norway's missionary kings, Óláfr Tryggvason and Óláfr the Saint, and promoted the saintly reputation of the northern diocese's first bishop, Jón Ögmundarson. In 1185-1188 Karl Jónsson, Thingeyrar's abbot, visited Norway. There, with the participation of King Sverrir, he wrote the beginning of *Sverris saga*, a biography of the king, telling of the struggles of this Faroese claimant who after years of civil war came to rule all Norway. No one knows who wrote the rest of *Sverris saga*, but it is possible that this and a few family sagas were written at Thingeyrar. The scholarly production of Thingeyrar's monks was aided by their monastery's exceptional prosperity. At the founding of this first religious community, Bishop

16. Einar Ól. Sveinsson, *The Age of the Sturlungs: Icelandic Civilization in the Thirteenth Century*, trans. Jóhann S. Hannesson, Islandica 36 (Ithaca: Cornell University Press, 1953), p. 112. See esp. n. 1.

Jón Ögmundarson granted Thingeyrar a portion of Hólar's tithes. Thingeyrar's own property provided good trout and salmon fishing, fertile pasturage, and an abundant supply of seabirds' eggs. The monastery also held valuable rights to the gathering of driftwood.

Despite Thingeyrar's prosperity, few Icelandic monasteries could be considered rich and, with only a handful of members in each, these tiny communities faced grave difficulties in keeping their doors open. Those that failed early left almost no trace. The late start and slow growth of the monastic movement during the life of the Free State contributed to the limited role of Icelandic monasteries in noncultural spheres. Thingeyrar may have been started in 1112, but it was not formally established until 1133.[17] The second one, also in the northern diocese of Hólar, was founded at Munkathverá in 1155. A third monastery, established in the north at Saurbær, lasted only from 1200 to 1212. In the Skálholt diocese the first monastery was founded at Hítardalr about 1166 and lasted to approximately 1200. Within the diocese other monasteries were established at Thykkvibær in 1168, on the island of Flatey in 1172 (moved to Helgafell in 1184), and on Viðey in 1226.[18]

The only nunnery to operate during the period of Free State was founded at Kirkjubær in 1186. Probably because of inadequate financial resources, this establishment was placed under the control of Skálholt in 1218 and apparently was soon disbanded.[19]

---

17. Magnús Már Lárusson, "Kloster: Island," *KLNM* 8, cols. 544-546; Hermann Pálsson, "Stofnun Þingeyraklausturs," in his *Tólfta öldin: Þættir um menn og málefni* (Reykjavik: Prentsmiðja Jóns Helgasonar, 1970), pp. 92-102. The official date for the opening of the Thingeyrar monastery is 1133; the earlier date is more hypothesis than fact (Magnús Stefánsson, "Kirkjuvald eflist," pp. 82-83).

18. The establishments of Thingeyrar, Munkathverá, and Kirkjubær followed the Benedictine Rule; Thykkvibær, Flatey, Viðey, and probably Saurbær belonged to the Augustinian Order.

19. This nunnery was revived toward the end of the thirteenth century.

BISHOPS AND PRIESTS

The position of the Icelandic bishops has parallels in de-centralized societies in which feuding plays a large role. Consider, for example, the ambiguous role of the bishop, the *vladika*, in Montenegrin society:

> The vladika in Cetinje himself had to earn most of the respect he received as bishop. He found himself in a curious position: he was a political leader without any real coercive power who was also the chief representative of a religious ideology that the tribesmen resisted in many of its facets. In trying to resolve blood feuds, a vladika had to work against the indigenous Montenegrin code of honor, as he upheld the specific values of the church. From an outside perspective this was useful, in that the feuding tribesmen themselves were virtually prisoners of their own warlike secular moral code, and therefore needed the moral leverage of a milder, competing set of values in trying to settle their feuds. Indeed, tribesmen who were not directly involved in the feud saw their vladika as someone who, through force of persuasion, might be able to help a tribal community out of these difficulties. But pacification was made very difficult by the fact that the participants themselves were at best extremely ambivalent about setting aside their feuds and frequently would ignore supernaturally based threats made by their vladika.[20]

Like the Christian Montenegrins, the Icelanders accepted the primacy of their religion, but they faced a dilemma. Participation in feud was a way of life in Iceland. Feuding regulated wealth and status, a situation reinforced by the courts and the focus on law. Advocacy, brokerage, *vinfengi*, and arbitration were the accepted ways that people implemented their social and political relationships. The Icelandic church evolved in a way that complemented what already existed rather than setting itself at odds with expected social behavior. The role of peacemaker was an integral part in the operation of Icelandic consensual governance, and bishops often participated in arranging settlements. Just as some

---

20. Christopher Boehm, *Blood Revenge: The Anthropology of Feuding in Montenegro and Other Tribal Societies* (Kansas: University Press of Kansas, 1984), p. 68.

chieftains were adept at this role, so too were some bishops. Brandr Sæmundarson of Hólar (1163-1201) was such a leader and many turned to him for advice.

From the days of Bishop Gizurr in the eleventh century, the office of bishop was highly prestigious. The two bishops sat in the *lögréttu* where they enjoyed full voting rights and where, we may guess, their views were respected. In spiritual matters the bishops possessed great authority. Although we do not have much information on the subject, it is reasonable to assume that as mediators between the corporeal world and eternal life, the clergy in general enjoyed strong spiritual influence. In cultural matters the Icelandic church was also highly influential. Clerics played an important role in introducing educational and literary concepts. Both sees maintained schools where the sons of chieftains and farmers were educated. These schools, together with other centers of learning such as those maintained in the homes of prominent chieftain families (for example, the Haukdælir from Haukadalr and the Oddaverjar from Oddi), enlarged the intellectual world of twelfth- and thirteenth-century Icelanders.

Even though the *bændr* respected their bishops they seem to have been careful not to surrender to them too much authority, especially when potential patronage was involved. The *bændr* did not grant their bishops the opportunity to engage themselves in the regular payment of alms, an otherwise traditional function of the Roman church. Instead the farmers, through their self-governing *hreppar*, retained for themselves the right to collect and to disburse locally the *thurfamannatíund*. This part of the tithe, which was designated for the poor, was substantial, amounting to a quarter of the tithe collected locally. In retaining control over the distribution of poor relief, the *bændr* seem to have been reinforcing their status.

The episcopal seats at Hólar and Skálholt were often filled by members of the most powerful families, especially by the Haukdælir and the Oddaverjar in the south. But only on a very few occasions were the elections sources of major controversy, and almost never of feud or other violence. For example, by 1174 Bishop Klængr of Skálholt, having become old and sickly, received permission from Archbishop Eysteinn Erlendsson (1161-1188) in Norway to arrange for a successor. The subsequent selection in 1174 of the new Skálholt bishop was carried out in a highly political manner.[21] Klængr went to the Althing where, after consultations, three candidates were selected. Each of the three regions that together formed the diocese, the west, the south, and the east, put forward an aspirant. After further negotiations the old bishop was asked to choose from among the nominees. Klængr selected Thorlákr Thórhallsson, a priest noted for his virtue and financial acumen. A good business sense was a helpful quality since the see of Skálholt was in poor financial condition as the result of Klængr's having built at Skálholt a large cathedral using imported timber. Thorlákr, who had been a founder and abbot of the first Augustinian monastery in the country at Thykkvibær, was the candidate of the Oddaverjar, led by the chieftain Jón Loftsson. Klængr died in 1176, and in accordance with the normal procedure, the candidate-elect went abroad for consecration.

The consistent lack of conflict in the filling of high Icelandic church positions is a factor that may help us evaluate the relative political and economic importance of the Icelandic bishops. We may postulate that had the office been one of significant power, the choice of a new bishop would have led to fierce contention among leading families, ever on the lookout for more authority. The Christian Law Section of *Grágás* gives no rules as to how Icelandic bishops were to be elected. Until 1237, when the archbishop and the cathedral chapter at Niðaróss finally refused to consecrate the two Icelandic candidates, one because he was a *goði* and the other because he was illegitimate, the Icelanders elected their

---

21. *Þorláks biskups saga hin elzta,* ch. 9, pp. 98-99; *Þorláks biskups saga hin yngri,* ch. 10, pp. 272-273 (*Biskupa sögur,* vol. 1, ed. Hið íslenzka bókmentafélag [Copenhagen: S. L. Möllers, 1858]). See also *Byskupa sögur,* ed. Guðni Jónsson, vol. 1, pp. 49-51.

own church leaders according to their own criteria. When one of Iceland's two bishops died or became too infirm to carry out his functions, the normal procedure was for the other bishop to suggest a politically acceptable candidate to the chieftains assembled at the Althing, a practice of secular interference which would have been generally unacceptable on the European mainland even before the Second Lateran Council in 1139. Guðmundr Arason's election to the seat at Hólar in 1201 by an assembly of laymen and clergy from the Northern Quarter was one of the most controversial during the life of the Free State, yet even in that instance the open competition for the office caused no violence.

The lack of confrontation over the control of Iceland's two bishoprics stands in contrast to the fierce rivalries that otherwise characterized power struggles among Icelandic leaders. With so much of the church's wealth in secular hands, and thus already committed to the political process, there was little inducement for leaders to fight over control of the possible remaining resources of the church. Whatever the reasons, conditions in Iceland were at variance with those in many parts of Europe, where the elaborate political machinations often preceding the selection of high churchmen underscored the political, economic, and governmental role of the church. Icelandic bishops were handicapped by the nature of Icelandic diocesan administration. At least until 1267 neither Hólar nor Skálholt had a cathedral chapter of canons (the *kórsbræðr*, choir brethren, of Norwegian cathedrals).[22] Thus during the life of the Free State, that is, after the Second Lateran Council, the Icelandic episcopal centers operated not only differently from but also less effectively than most of their European counterparts. Probably no chapters existed because the bishops lacked the economic means to support them.

The first Icelandic bishop who tried to lessen secular in-

22. In 1267 after the end of the Free State, Bishop Jörundr of Hólar (1267-1313) received permission to institute a chapter, but it is not clear how quickly the chapter came into being.

fluence on his diocese was Thorlákr Thórhallsson of Skálholt (1178-1193, later canonized). Thorlákr attempted to gain control over church property and to enforce on the laity the church's views on the sanctity of marriage, demanding that laymen give up their concubines and end marriages to which he found impediments.[23] During his contests with the chieftains of his diocese, he received no assistance from his colleague, Bishop Brandr Sæmundarson of Hólar. When Thorlákr died after years of bitter disputes with various *goðar*, most of which he lost, the chieftains at the Althing displayed their power over the governance of the church by electing as his successor the *goði* Páll Jónsson (1195-1211). Páll was the illegitimate son of the *goði* Jón Loftsson and Thorlákr's sister, Ragnheiðr. Jón, who first seems to have been a strong supporter of Thorlákr, became the bishop's chief opponent and, in spite of the bishop's vehement objection, he had for years kept Ragnheiðr as his concubine. Jón had also successfully refused to relinquish to the bishop control over his church property.

In keeping with the long-standing custom by which temporal Icelandic leaders took church orders, both Jón Loftsson and Páll Jónsson were deacons. Páll was a learned man and, although a reasonable Icelandic choice for bishop, he was a highly unusual candidate for high church office in light of the standards of the Roman church.[24] Contrary to Roman procedure, he was not elected by the "greater and sounder part" of a cathedral chapter because there were no such

---

23. Marriage and the sexual behavior of laity and clergy are discussed by Jenny M. Jochens, "The Church and Sexuality in Medieval Iceland," *Journal of Medieval History* 6(1980):377-392, and by Frank, "Marriage," 474-484.

24. See, for example, Pope Innocent III's decretal, "Innotuit nobis," written in 1200 to the archbishop of Canterbury, in which Innocent states the recognized procedure and established standards for ecclesiastical election (*Liber extra* 1.6.20, in Emil Friedberg, ed., *Corpus iuris canonici*, vol. 2 [Leipzig: B. Tauchnitz, 1881], cols. 61-63). An excellent account on the procedure of ecclesiastic election from the eleventh to the thirteenth century is Robert L. Benson, "Election by Community and Chapter: Reflections on Co-Responsibility in the Historical Church," *The Jurist* 31(1971):54-80.

chapters in Iceland, and his illegitimate birth was an irregularity that, under standard church rules, could be remedied only by a papal dispensation. Further, Páll was married. His wife was the daughter of a priest, and the couple had four children. Páll's marriage was another irregularity that should have been remedied by consultation with church authorities before his election. Technically, in fact, because he was ineligible on at least two counts, he should have been "requested" (*postulatus*) rather than "elected" (*electus*).[25] Nevertheless, the Norwegians were accustomed to the practices of the Icelanders. According to his saga (*Páls saga biskups*, chs. 3-4), when Páll came to Norway King Sverrir, who had enemies among his own churchmen, treated him with manifest friendship. After Páll's ordination by Bishop Thórir, he returned home and ended his Uncle Thorlákr's experiments with church reform. He returned the diocese of Skálholt to the older insular traditions of the Icelandic church.

Reform of the Icelandic church was difficult because it was not a semi-independent state-within-a-state. It was a not clearly defined organization that was, from the start, largely subject to lay supervision. The church's acceptance of the norms of the secular community was formalized in the period 1122-1133 when the laws governing Christian observances, including those modified for Icelandic conditions, were written down.[26] These laws, contained in *Kristinna laga þáttr*, the Christian Law Section of *Grágás*, together with the separate tithe entries,[27] served to define the relations between church and temporal society. As noted above (see chapter 2), *Kristinna laga þáttr* remained in force in Skálholt until 1275 and in Hólar until at least 1354. Beyond governing the internal life of the church and supervising the moral and

25. See *Liber extra* 1.5, containing six decretals "De postulatione praelatorum," in Friedberg, ed., *Corpus*, vol. 2, cols. 41-48.

26. There is an irony in the date: in 1122 the papacy concluded an agreement—the Concordat of Worms—with the Holy Roman Emperor Charles V. The concordat guaranteed a degree of autonomy to the church in the elevation of bishops within Germany and, especially, Italy.

27. *GG* Ib, pp. 205-218 (chs. 255-268).

marriage practices of their flocks, the Icelandic bishops had relatively little legal authority. Even when laws from the Christian Law Section of *Grágás* were broken, the bishop had little direct control. Judicial matters stemming from breaches of Christian laws or cases involving a cleric were handled by secular courts. The bishops exercised judicial authority only when a priest was disobedient to his superior. Even in such instances the church's inability to execute one of its judgments made it advisable, at times, to turn the matter over to the secular courts.

The demand that the bishop be given independent judicial power over his clergy and control over church property was taken up by Iceland's other reform bishop, Guðmundr Arason of Hólar (1203-1237). Like Thorlákr, Guðmundr was in the end unsuccessful in achieving his goals. Also like Thorlákr, he was not the leader of a united church party. During Guðmundr's long conflict with secular leaders, he received no support from Skálholt, either during the episcopate of Páll Jónsson or during that of Magnús Gizurarson (1216-1237). Unlike Bishop Thorlákr's contest, however, Guðmundr's turned violent. Guðmundr early showed a predilection toward gathering unruly men about him. In the fall of 1208 some of the bishop's followers killed Kolbeinn Tumason, Guðmundr's main opponent, in a skirmish. Kolbeinn had been the most prominent chieftain in the north, and he was the man responsible for Guðmundr's election.

Guðmundr's victory was short-lived, for after the spring of 1209 his efforts were continually blocked by a series of alliances among chieftains living in many parts of the country. On several occasions the bishop was driven from Hólar and forced to wander about the countryside. The situation did not please churchmen in Norway, and twice Guðmundr obeyed summonses by the archbishop to come to Norway. Although he spent a total of eight winters there, he seems to have received little support. When he returned to Iceland in 1218 after his first stay, his goals had changed. He no longer advanced his earlier claim for increased judicial authority; instead he became a champion of the poor.

Guðmundr's episcopate came during a period when the ideals of poverty and humility had gained popularity in medieval Europe. Among the ideas circulating which may have influenced him were those that motivated the mendicant friars and inspired the rebellious Waldensian movement. Guðmundr now lived in poverty, often surrounded by a following of men and women, including clergy, weapon-bearing men, vagrants, beggars, and thieves. According to Jón Jóhannesson, the years around the beginning of the thirteenth century were times of famine, and "the great number of beggars in Bishop Guðmundr's day has no parallel in Icelandic history, either before or after."[28] When he was able to do so, Guðmundr allowed most of the revenues of his diocese to go to charitable causes. Here again he clashed with *goðar* and *bændr* who saw the depletion of the episcopal treasury as a demonstration of the bishop's irresponsibility.

Secular leaders repeatedly dispersed Guðmundr's following, and at times he was held in confinement. The struggle, which continued for well over a decade, helped some *stórgoðar* to increase their authority at the expense of the farmers' traditional independence. Many *bændr* opposed the bishop; they seem to have particularly disliked his demand that they provide hospitality for his following. *Íslendinga saga* (ch. 37) tells us that Guðmundr, accompanied by 120 followers, spent the summer of 1220 moving about in Reykjadalr, a region east of Eyjafjörðr. When Guðmundr came for the second time to the farm called Múli, the local *bændr*, forty strong, barred the way. After declaring that the *bóndi* at Múli was possesed by an unclean spirit, the bishop moved on without a fight. The farmers, nevertheless, must have felt threatened. They sent for assistance from two *stórgoðar* who lived outside the region, Sighvatr Sturluson from Eyjafjörðr and Arnórr Tumason from Skagafjörðr. Seizing the opportunity, Sighvatr and Arnórr quickly gathered men and came east to Reykjadalr; eventually they came to blows with the bishop's followers.

28. Jón Jóhannesson, *History*, p. 212.

Although Guðmundr did not win any lasting victories for the church, his stormy three decades as bishop of Hólar marked a turning point in Icelandic affairs. The controversy that surrounded Guðmundr's actions gave the archbishop and later the Norwegian king their first prolonged opportunity to intervene in Icelandic affairs. At different times during the controversy, these foreign lords summoned both Icelandic bishops and many chieftains to their presence. Although the bishops and chieftains chose frequently to ignore the summonses, the door for interference from abroad had been opened. From the 1240s to the 1260s the king increasingly intervened in Iceland's internal affairs, undermining Icelandic autonomy. The turmoil that surrounded Thorlákr's and Guðmundr's attempts to institute in Iceland the claims of the Universal Church tends to overshadow the otherwise peaceful role the bishops assumed in Icelandic society.

The Icelandic priesthood was a major impediment to more centralized church control, in part because the priests did not form a united religious caste. Some were loyal followers of their bishops while others, perhaps the majority, participated as self-interested freemen in the acquisitive maneuverings that characterized Icelandic life. Most priests married, saw to their children's inheritances, and adapted their responsibilities as churchmen to the dominant codes of the society. With regularity they took part in the incessant disputes and feuds as partisan advocates, arbitrators, and supporters of kinsmen and political allies. When in 1208 Bishop Guðmundr Arason of Hólar placed the chieftains opposing him under an interdict, his position was undermined by the lack of support from the Skálholt episcopacy but also from many priests of his own diocese who continued to associate with the excommunicates. These priests held religious services for Guðmundr's enemies and continued to do so after they themselves had been placed under the ban. This state of affairs continued for many years.

The situation of the Icelandic clergy had already, by the late twelfth century, troubled the Norwegian archbishop in Niðarós. In 1173 Archbishop Eysteinn Erlendsson (1161-

1188) wrote in a letter "to the Bishops in Iceland, the Chieftains, and all the people":

> Now, all those clergymen from the lowest orders to the highest, those who have killed men, to them I forbid the performing of religious services. And, from this time on, I forbid all clerics to undertake the role of prosecutor in lawsuits except when they act on the behalf of disabled relatives, fatherless children, or defenseless poverty-stricken women. These prosecutions must be assumed for God's sake and for no other reason irrespective of any recompense.[29]

In 1180 Archbishop Eysteinn, who was having his own troubles with King Sverrir of Norway, was forced by the king to leave Niðaróss. His injunction against Icelandic priests participating in lawsuits apparently was not heeded. In 1190 Archbishop Eiríkr Ívarsson wrote to the Icelanders reminding those in orders, beginning with subdeacons, "not to undertake prosecutions that would have to be pursued with valor and weapons."[30]

The participation of Icelandic priests in legal disputes is confirmed by *Sturlunga saga*, which shows many priests taking part in feuds. A detailed example of the manner in which a decidedly peaceful cleric was drawn into a feud is found in *The Saga of Hvamm-Sturla* (*Sturlu saga* [*Sturl.* 1], chs. 30-36). One of the conflicts the saga narrates was a large feud from the last part of the twelfth century whose action swirls around Páll Sölvason, a wealthy priest and *goði* from Reykjaholt in the Western Quarter. According to *The Saga of Bishop Thorlákr* (ch. 9), Páll was famed for his skill in managing his property; he was also one of the three candidates considered at the Althing in 1176 for the office of bishop of Skálholt. The feud, called the *Deildartungumál* (the Tunga affair) after one of the main properties, started when someone contested Páll's, and hence his legitimate sons', right to inherit all the

---

29. *DI*, vol. 1, pt. 1, p. 222.
30. *DI*, vol. 1, pt. 1, p. 291.

valuable property claimed by Páll after the death of his widowed and childless daughter.[31]

Two other examples from *Sturlunga saga* of priests actively engaged in lawsuits and feuds are considered in this book. One (chapter 6) concerns Guðmundr Arason, who in the early thirteenth century became bishop of Hólar. At the time of the saga account, Guðmundr was a priest of illegitimate parentage who took on the prosecution of a killer. The other example (chapter 8) concerns the turmoil resulting from attempts by the priest Eyjólfr Hallsson to acquire additional inheritances for his legitimate sons. For a short time he was an unsuccessful candidate for bishop of Hólar when Guðmundr Arason was elected to that position in 1201. A few years later, in 1206, Eyjólfr became abbot of the short-lived monastery of Saurbær.

In summary, although the church was a catalyst for numerous changes in Iceland, it did not uproot earlier social and political processes but adjusted to them. In the centuries after the conversion Icelandic society maintained its rural social context, dominated by law and feud, while integrating roles and demands of the church.

---

31. For a summary of the Tunga affair see Jesse L. Byock, *Feud in the Icelandic Saga* (Berkeley, Los Angeles, London: University of California Press, 1982), pp. 154-160.

8

Farmers Under Duress:
A Lucrative Source of Wealth

In a certain sense it may be said that feuds play the same role in family sagas as love plays in novels. But a very essential difference between the role of feuds in family sagas and the role of love in novels lies in the fact that feuds really were the most important happenings of that time in Iceland—content dictated by life itself—while romantic emotions have hardly been the most important occurrences in Europe since the novel became predominant in European literatures.

—M. I. Steblin-Kamenskij

Important as it is to say that land was the basic constituent of wealth, this statement does not tell us how chieftains acquired it. Certainly a chieftain could inherit or obtain by marriage parcels of land, but neither of these possibilities explains how leaders, such as Snorri goði around the year 1000 and Hvamm-Sturla in the mid-twelfth century, obtained the wealth necessary to exercise power.

In Iceland's settled agrarian society, land was difficult to obtain, whatever its use or value. By the end of the tenth-century settlement period, all usable free land had been claimed, and in the later centuries much of the island's valuable property remained under family ownership. The *bændr* were never a servile peasant class. On the contrary, they owned property, valued it, and guarded it carefully. In a society that never saw the introduction of town life, land remained a cherished family possession, one that determined the owner's status. How, then, did chieftains as the governing group profit from this state of affairs? The answer is found in the ties of mutual interdependence which bound together chieftains and farmers.[1] In this and following chapters the link between *goðar* and *bændr*—especially as it influenced the transfer of wealth—is examined in the light of narrative examples taken from the family and Sturlunga sagas and from references in *Grágás*.

The essential problem a farmer faced, either in defending or in pushing for his rights, was his exclusion from legal privileges enjoyed by the chieftains. Individually or in a band, the farmers may have had the physical ability to defend their rights or even to kill their opponents (including chieftains), but when such action was undertaken without a chieftain's protection a farmer exposed himself and his family to potentially devastating consequences. The *bóndi* might lose both status and land. In important matters, law in medieval Iceland operated principally on the *goði* level. If a *goði* brought or supported a case against a farmer, the farmer could hardly defend himself without the aid of another chieftain.

Something more than simple strength was at issue. The presence of chieftains was indispensable to the negotiations and compromises that characterized the settlement of disputes and the judicial process in early Iceland. Although the law gave farmers the right as individuals to bring cases before the courts, custom and procedure placed restrictions in their way. Note the parallel with our theoretically more equitable modern societies. Today any citizen may bring a case

1. Sigurður Nordal eloquently sums up the complex and unusual character of the Icelandic arrangement, conceiving of the interplay between *goði* and *bóndi* as analogous to the finesse involved in salmon fishing. The Icelandic farmer, like the strong and agile salmon, fights the fisherman's line, while the *goði* uses the skills of a sport fisherman in knowing when to play out the line. In mainland Europe, by contrast, Nordal sees the relationship between lord and follower as less subtle: he describes the vassal as similar to a heavy cod, easily caught in a net (*Íslenzk menning* [Reykjavik: Mál og menning, 1942], p. 120).

to court, just as any medieval Icelander could. If a modern lawsuit is complex, the claimant's action will almost certainly be fruitless without the guidance of a specialist. So it was in medieval Iceland, especially with issues serious enough to merit consideration in the courts of the national assembly. Once disputes had been turned over to advocates, especially *goðar*, each side built a case within the parameters of legally acceptable action, whether the intention was to settle in or out of court.

In Iceland's world of confrontation, of claim and counterclaim, the resolution of a dispute depended not only on the strength and justice of the case but also on the power and prestige of the *goði* who was presenting it. A freeman who could not resolve a dispute by himself approached a chieftain, just as a disputant today might enlist the services of a lawyer. In the modern judicial system, it is the attorney who decides whether or not he will take a case and what his fee will be. As in medieval Iceland, the modern claimant may win his point, but his legal advocate often reaps a significant financial benefit.

After the verdict is given, a modern attorney's task is usually finished; in medieval Iceland a chieftain's responsibility did not necessarily end at that point. Without executive structures, the courts had no mandate to carry out a sentence. Because there was no apparatus to enforce a judicial decision, the plaintiff had to see to it that the legal victory became an actual victory. If the plaintiff was strong enough, or if he could count on friends or kin, he might try to carry out the sentence on his own. Most freemen, however, turned to chieftains for this service, a service that reinforced the need for advocates. At times a chieftain's task may have been the easy collection of a few farm animals; on other occasions he may have had to enforce a judgment of outlawry. Such a job, requiring manpower and time, may have exposed the *goði* to attacks from either the defendant or his kin group.

ACQUISITION OF PROPERTY IN THE
FAMILY SAGAS

Disputed Property in the East Fjords

An incident like the one described below is familiar to any reader of the sagas. Taken from *Vápnfirðinga saga* (*ÍF* 11, ch. 7), it has to do with local feuds in the East Fjords. The conflict, beginning over a piece of wooded land owned jointly by neighboring farmers, is one in a series of disputes that originated among *bændr* but in the end involved chieftains. The next few pages trace the evolution of this seemingly trivial incident up to the point at which two rival local chieftains confront each other.[2]

The incident begins when Thórðr and Thormóðr, each the thingman of a different local chieftain, quarrel over grazing and tree-cutting rights in a forest they own jointly. Forests were a rare and coveted commodity in Iceland. Thórðr, threatened by his more aggressive neighbor Thormóðr, goes to his chieftain Brodd-Helgi, tells him about the problem, and asks him for aid. But Brodd-Helgi, an overbearing man, drives a hard bargain. He refuses to help his thingman unless the latter hands over his wealth and land and comes to live on Brodd-Helgi's farm: "Brodd-Helgi said he didn't have a mind to quarrel over his [Thórðr's] property and would have no part of it unless he assigned him all his property by *handsal* and moved to Hof with all his possessions." In a tight spot, Thórðr accepts Brodd-Helgi's offer; by *handsal* he legally assigns his patrimony to his *goði*, thus increasing Brodd-Helgi's wealth and power in the area.

Of importance in this exchange is the use of the term *handsal* (verb *at handsala*). The word refers to a handshake that formalized or sealed an agreement. To be recognized as legally binding, a *handsal* had to be witnessed. *Handsal* agreements could be entered into for many reasons: to arrange a marriage and dowry, to transfer land, to bind a resolution

---

2. In chapter 10 the importance of this incident is examined within the larger context of the power struggle described in the saga.

of a feud. A transfer of land by *handsal*, in which one man gave over his land, perhaps to a *goði* in return for protection, sometimes violated Iceland's inheritance laws. It may seem farfetched that a farmer would deed his land away just because he was threatened by his neighbor, but Thórðr has very few options: he can stay on his farm and risk losing his life to his bullying neighbor, or he can secure the protection of a powerful man. By handing over his land, Thórðr gains security and, perhaps, peace of mind for himself and his family; on the other hand, he loses both for himself and his heirs the autonomy and the status that go with being a *bóndi*. Brodd-Helgi also has choices. As a *goði* he wants to increase his wealth and power, and thus his influence, but he must weigh against those advantages the costs of taking the farmer's case. Geitir, Thormóðr's chieftain and a more peaceful man than Brodd-Helgi, is already embroiled in a feud with Brodd-Helgi. Local farmers will watch carefully to see which chieftain gains the prestige of keeping Thórðr's land and the advantage over his rival.

Of significance in the relationship between Brodd-Helgi and Thórðr is the clear awareness of the difference in power between *goði* and *bóndi*. Each man has something that the other desires. The farmer has a sound claim to half ownership in a parcel of disputed land, but he lacks the strength to support his claim. The chieftain has no valid right to the land but does have the power to assert a claim because of his role as supporter of his thingman; each has something of value with which he can bargain. The freeman receives a service and the chieftain receives a payment that benefits him financially or politically or both. Integral to the exchange is the fact that the chieftain, Brodd-Helgi, is in the right place at the right time and has enough power to act both in his own and in Thórðr's interest.

After the negotiations between Brodd-Helgi and Thórðr are completed and the claim to the land is transferred, Thórðr and his family go to live on Brodd-Helgi's farm. Having given up his rights to the land, the most Thórðr can hope for is that Brodd-Helgi will protect him for life and that his enemy Thormóðr will also lose his right to the land. We never learn of Thóróðr's fate; after this incident he disappears from the saga. Thóróðr's opponent Thormóðr soon finds Brodd-Helgi to be a difficult man with whom to share land. Thormóðr in his turn loses the use of the forest and calls on his *goði*, Geitir Lýtingsson, for aid. This incident is one of a larger series of events (discussed in chapter 10). Decisions like the one facing Brodd-Helgi have much to do with a chieftain's ultimate success or failure. If a chieftain presses his thingmen too hard he loses their support, which is vital to his position. If he misjudges his power and abuses his position too often, his thingmen seek other means of maintaining themselves and protecting their families and property. If he is not aggressive enough in supporting his thingmen, he may similarly lose vital support.

Disputed Property in the Salmon River Valley

Another example of a farmer calling upon a *goði* to act as his advocate and paying the chieftain generously for the service is found in *Laxdæla saga* (ch. 16). In this instance, however, a feud is cut off before it can escalate because the advocates engaged settle the case quickly out of court (ch. 16). A farmer, Thórðr goddi, has an argument with his wife, the strong-willed Vigdís. The wife wants Thórðr to harbor her outlawed distant kinsman, a vagrant. When Thórðr betrays the outlaw, Vigdís declares herself divorced. She goes to her kinsman, the powerful chieftain Thórðr gellir (the Bellower), and together they plan to claim half of the farmer's estate. Thórðr goddi, who is described as rich though ineffectual, turns for support to the local chieftain, Höskuldr Dala-Kollsson.

Again, as in *Vápnfirðinga saga*, the meeting between *goði* and *bóndi* becomes a business negotiation. Farmer Thórðr goddi is in a weak position. In order to face Thórðr gellir, he needs the support of an equally powerful chieftain. But Höskuldr is in no rush to offer his protection. In fact, he taunts the *bóndi* with the seriousness of his position: "You have often been scared before but never with better reason." In this incident Höskuldr is in a position similar to that of Brodd-Helgi in *Vápnfirðinga saga*, although the motivation and the fate of these two leaders are quite different. Known as an upright and proud man, Höskuldr is presented in *Laxdæla saga* and in other sagas as intelligent, capable, and successful. He is almost the exact opposite of the brash and violent Brodd-Helgi. *Laxdæla saga* makes it clear that Höskuldr's success is attributable in large part to his restraint and sagacity (ch. 7).

Thórðr goddi, realizing that Höskuldr wants something in return for his aid, offers to pay handsomely: "Thórðr then offered Höskuldr money for his support and said he would not be stingy with it." Still Höskuldr is reluctant to help. Thórðr goddi is known to be tight with his money, and both parties are aware that the *bóndi* is in a very precarious position. Faced with this reality, farmer Thórðr sweetens the offer: "I would like you to manage all the property through a *handsal* agreement. Then I would offer to foster your son Óláfr and leave it all to him when I'm gone, as I have no heirs here in Iceland." Childless, Thórðr does not have close relatives in Iceland. Thus the farmer's land is especially valuable to the chieftain, as it is not subject to possible counterclaims by Icelandic heirs; Höskuldr will have to contest only the wife's claim. The proposition is so advantageous that Höskuldr decides to support Thórðr, and the two men enter into a binding agreement.

Höskuldr is certain to reap a windfall profit without having to scheme for it. Moreover, the fee will include an inheritance for his illegitimate and favorite son Óláfr, later called pái (the Peacock). Thus far Höskuldr's major contribution to the deal has been his potential as an advocate. He assesses the plight of the farmer and bases his fee on the depth of Thórðr goddi's desperation.

Ironically, the *bóndi* has from the start a strong legal case, but it is the chieftain who profits. Once Höskuldr is in charge of the defense, he seeks to placate the opposing chieftain with handsome gifts; at the same time he tells Thórðr gellir that Vigdís has brought no charges that would legally justify her leaving her husband. Further, as Höskuldr points out, Thórðr goddi's actions that prompted the marital split were reasonable, since the farmer was attempting to rid himself of his wife's outlawed relative. Although this effort had aroused Vigdís's ire and scorn, it was entirely legal. In a succinctly narrated passage (ch. 16), Höskuldr shows his skill as a broker by defending his bastard son's promised inheritance through a knowledge of law and an understanding of men:

> Höskuldr sent handsome gifts to Thórðr gellir and asked him not to take offense at what had happened, for he and Vigdís had no legal claim on Thórðr goddi for the money. He pointed out that Vigdís had not brought any valid charges against her husband which could justify her desertion: "Thórðr was none the worse a man for seeking some means of ridding himself of someone who had been thrust upon him and was as prickly with guilt as a juniper bush."

This incident from *Laxdæla saga* has a thematic purpose beyond the problem of farmer Thórðr. Höskuldr is aware that legitimate sons seldom appreciate their father's love for the offspring of a concubine, and that Óláfr's legitimate half brothers will probably try to stop the boy (as they do) from inheriting a substantial share of Höskuldr's property. Whether a traditional tale or a pure invention of the sagaman, Thórðr goddi's story offers a reasonable explanation of how Höskuldr causes valuable lands to come into Óláfr's possession.[3] Thórðr goddi emerges from his trials much better off than Thórðr in *Vápnfirðinga saga*. Thórðr goddi fosters the son of an important figure and thereby acquires a chieftain's protection. Unlike farmer Thórðr in *Vápnfirðinga saga*, Thórðr goddi lives out his life on his own land.

In *Laxdæla saga* the narrative section on Höskuldr and his sons is a lengthy introduction to the core of the saga: the famous love triangle of Kjartan, Guðrún, and Bolli. Before

---

3. A similar arrangement, though one not involving the complication of illegitimacy, is found in *Hænsa-Þóris saga* (ÍF 3, ch. 2).

the tale reaches that point, however, sufficient background must be presented. Not only does the sagaman unravel the genealogy of the families, both legitimate and illegitimate; he also thoroughly catalogs the passage of property through generations. In this story of people and land, Óláfr the Peacock and his property play an important role. Kjartan is Óláfr's son and Höskuldr's grandson. The land deal made with Thórðr goddi forms the initial underpinning of the fortune of a great family stemming from Höskuldr's illegitimate line. This wealth plays a significant part in the later tragic killing of Kjartan.

Farmer Thórðr goddi in *Laxdæla saga* and farmer Thórðr in *Vápnfirðinga saga* both provide opportunities for chieftains to profit quickly and bloodlessly from their service as advocates. This practice, which has its roots in the political and economic realities that shaped Iceland's early development, was not always so painless, as we shall see.

INHERITANCE CLAIMS IN *STURLUNGA SAGA*

Over the centuries, the *goðar* consistently managed to win out over other farmers in gaining control of valuable lands, prizes that within the spirit of Icelandic law were available to all freemen. The family sagas portray the *goðar* as advocates who frequently profited from the troubles of others. The early sagas in the Sturlunga compilation present a similar picture. In particular, they repeatedly show leaders maneuvering to obtain the property of farmers, behavior familiar from the family sagas. The following pages present examples taken from three sagas of the Sturlunga compilation: *The Saga of Hvamm-Sturla*, *The Saga of Guðmundr Dýri*, and *The Saga of the Icelanders*. These three sagas recount events from the late twelfth century, and all three examples concern valuable land. In one instance the property in question, Helgastaðir, is a church farmstead (a *staðr*). As frequently happened in Iceland, disputes over these properties begin with contentions among farmers. Again we see chieftains maneuvering to gain a foothold on someone else's land by acquiring a legal claim, often of a tenuous nature. Once that has been done, the determination of ownership becomes a matter of political negotiation, dependent more on power than on the justness of the claim. The detail with which the saga authors describe these instances may reflect the concern of the contemporary twelfth- and thirteenth-century audiences over the increasing wealth of successful leaders.

In the give-and-take of the Icelandic court system, a compromise solution was the usual outcome of a lawsuit. This reality made the advancement of a questionable legal claim a potentially profitable venture. It gave an ambitious individual, even one who had no previous claim to another's property, reasonable hopes for at least some success in acquiring a part of the wealth. In some instances, as in the maneuver employed by the chieftain Einarr Thorgilsson in his efforts to gain possession of the farm Heinaberg, an aggressor might allege an infraction of the law by the property owner and begin a prosecution. The lawsuit might cause the defendant not only to lose his property but also to be made an outlaw, a judgment that could cost him his life.

The Struggle to Inherit Helgastaðir

The Saga of Guðmundr Dýri, which is set in the Eyjafjörðr region (map 3a), opens with a dispute over land. Members of the family of Guðmundr Eyjólfsson, a wealthy farmer, are in disagreement as to who will inherit his property, Helgastaðir, in Reykjadalr. Guðmundr had willed the land to his son before retiring to a monastery, but unexpectedly the son predeceases the father. The son's wife prudently leaves Helgastaðir after recovering her dowry and agreeing to a settlement that divides her property from that of her dead husband.

The young man's early death raises a difficult question of inheritance within the family. Guðmundr has two poor brothers who want to inherit their nephew's property. "It was the opinion of many men," according to the saga, "that his [the son's] father should be his heir and receive the inheritance, but Guðmundr's brothers, Björn and Halldórr, said that Guðmundr could neither inherit the property nor take care of it because he was a monk. Then men divided into opposing groups, and there were many on each side" (ch. 1).

As the debate about inheritance continues, another farmer, the priest Eyjólfr Hallsson, begins to scheme on his own behalf. He has two sons and wants to set each one up independently. The acquisition of Helgastaðir would provide Eyjólfr with the additional inheritance he needs to achieve his goal. Although he is an outsider, Eyjólfr rides over to the monastery at Thverá to bargain with Guðmundr. As a result, he buys the land and the inheritance for little more than half the market value, with the proviso that he will be "answerable himself, if it should come before the law" (ch. 1). By doing so, Eyjólfr gains a presumption of ownership in the tangled negotiations that follow. The brothers Halldórr and Björn, who deem the property to be their own, are angry when they hear the news. They swear that Eyjólfr will not be permitted to benefit from his deal while they themselves are in need. Carrying out their oaths will not be easy for the brothers, as Eyjólfr is a strong opponent. Descended from several lawspeakers, he is a man who has many friends and kinsmen.

The account of Eyjólfr's actions gives an insight into the manner in which important churchmen were integrated into Iceland's operating systems of wealth and power, for after the events described here this same Eyjólfr Hallsson was, as noted earlier, a candidate for bishop of Hólar and from 1206 to 1212 was abbot of the monastery of Saurbær. Here he is the owner (warden) of Grenjaðarstaðir, one of the richest *staðir* in the country. Like the brothers, he is a *bóndi*, and as a father he is on the lookout for the welfare of his son. Now that Eyjólfr has a claim to Helgastaðir, the issue is no longer who ought to inherit the land but which contestant—he or the blood heirs—is more powerful.

In their claim to ownership, the brothers are supported by the law; *Grágás* specifies that land may not be transferred without consent of the heirs; to do so is *arfskot*, cheating on an inheritance.[4] Guðmundr failed to consult the brothers when he sold the property to Eyjólfr. According to *Grágás* the brothers have the right to prosecute Guðmundr, the testator, who is liable to a sentence of three years' outlawry or to lose control of his property. Such a prosecution would be fruitless, however, for Guðmundr no longer has possession of the property.

Violence is an option. The brothers might simply try to kill Eyjólfr, who is clearly interfering with their rights to family land. There is no suggestion, however, that they ever seriously consider taking so drastic an action, which would be dangerous and probably self-defeating. They might get themselves killed in the attempt, or, if they did succeed in killing Eyjólfr, they would probably be outlawed and hunted down by Eyjólfr's sons or kinsmen. The brothers' decision to shun violence follows a perceived pattern of behavior: restraint, that is, action in accordance with the principle of *hóf*, gains the upper hand. It is a socially conditioned response of men who understand their society well enough not to overextend their reach.

The angry brothers seek support of their rights through the advocacy of their *goðar*. Each brother is the thingman of a different *goði*, and when the brothers turn to their respective chieftains for support, it is not hard to guess the result. The chieftains are apparently unsympathetic, and the saga laconically tells us that each *bóndi* by *handsal* makes over to his *goði* his entire claim to the "wealth": "hvárr handsalaði sínum goðorðsmanni heimting fjárins" (ch. 1). In return, the powerless *bændr* get only the satisfaction of seeing their position vindicated by Eyjólfr's being denied the use of the land. After they have transferred their legal claims, the brothers drop out of the saga. Their *goðar*, Önundr Thor-

---

4. GG Ia, pp. 247, 249 (ch. 127); II, p. 84 (ch. 66), p. 100 (ch. 76), p. 127 (ch. 95). *Arfskot* is discussed in more detail in chapter 9.

kelsson and Thorvarðr Thorgeirsson, if successful, will keep all the fruits of the coming legal action. The contest over Helgastaðir is now between Eyjólfr, backed by his powerful family and friends, and the allied chieftains of the two brothers.

Before it is brought to an end, the dispute over Helgastaðir develops into a major confrontation.[5] The process of settlement begins when the *goði* Guðmundr dýri enters the case as a *góðviljamaðr*, separating the threatening sides. As neither party is able to force its rival to withdraw or is willing to risk an all-out attack, a stalemate ensues. Having succeeded in keeping the two sides apart, Guðmundr becomes a neutral arbitrator of the opposing claims. In the end, through arbitration, the property is awarded to a father and son who are closely related to both sides by alliance, kinship, or marriage. This compromise solution is agreeable to everyone, as it gives all parties a future interest in the land. Each claimant can assume that the property may eventually come into his family.

Inheritance Rights to Heinaberg

The second Sturlunga example of property changing hands between farmers and leaders is of special interest because it concerns two well-known and powerful *goðar*. One is Hvamm-Sturla, the progenitor of the Sturlungs; the other is Einarr Thorgilsson (1121?-1185) from Staðarhóll, one of Sturla's major rivals. The incident from *The Saga of Hvamm-Sturla* (ch. 28) takes place in western Iceland and begins in the 1170s. A wealthy *bóndi* named Birningr Steinarsson lives on a small farm called Heinaberg on Skarðsströnd. Birningr is married and has a daughter named Sigríðr. The marriage is not happy. The *bóndi* and his wife divorce and each sub-

5. At least four local chieftains, Thorvarðr Thorgeirsson, Önundr Thorkelsson, Einarr Hallsson, and Guðmundr dýri become involved in the contest. Map 3a in chapter 6 shows the locations of these chieftains and some of their thingmen. The saga does not indicate the exact site of the two brothers' farms, but it tells us they lived in this region.

sequently remarries. By his new marriage Birningr has a son, Thorleikr, whom he now names as his heir. He neglects his daughter from the first marriage, and she fares poorly. Eventually she becomes the mistress of a Shetlander. Even though she has no power or position and is ignored by her father, Sigríðr does possess one valuable attribute: an inheritance claim that can and will undermine Birningr's control of his farm.

Why did important leaders like Sturla and Einarr contend over Birningr's small property? The farm of Heinaberg, only a narrow strip of land along the coast and with cliffs at its back, is itself of little value. In terms of ecology, however, the reason for Einarr's and Sturla's keen interest becomes clearer. A few meters off the coast below the farm buildings lie several tiny, flat islands which appear only on detailed local maps. Because of their size these islands would have been relatively valueless if they had not been, as they remain in modern times, one of the best seal-hunting spots along that stretch of coast.[6] As this information would have been well known to the local audience, it did not need to be included in the saga narrative.

Perceiving a way to gain possession of Birningr's valuable property, Einarr buys from Sigríðr the expectation of her inheritance. Without the purchase, the *goði* would have been guilty of robbery if he had seized Birningr's land; now its ownership is a legal matter. As a person with an interest in the disposition of the property, Einarr accuses Birningr of having contracted an unlawful second marriage. He intimates that Birningr can escape the repercussions of this legal infraction by moving over to Einarr's estate with his goods, though he does agree to share the rest of Birningr's property with the second wife and her son "according to what he finds advisable."

Einarr, an overbearing and sometimes violent man, is thus threatening Birningr, but the *bóndi*, faced with so ruinous a

6. I appreciate Björn Thorsteinsson's good company on our trip to Heinaberg.

demand, refuses to yield. In an effort at further intimidation, Einarr responds to Birningr's intransigence by sending one of his men to collect Birningr's geldings from the heath. When the man returns to Einarr's farm with seventy beasts, Einarr has them slaughtered. Although he has not yet taken Birningr's land, Einarr's first move has been highly profitable. When cured, the meat from seventy geldings will go a long way toward providing for the large winter establishment of a wealthy and generous *goði;* alternately, it can be sold or given away.

Birningr, however, chooses not to buckle under. Instead, he seeks aid from Einarr's rival, Hvamm-Sturla, a *goði* who has an interest in checking the growth of Einarr's wealth and power. In addition, Sturla and Birningr are members of the Snorrungar family; they trace their descent back to a common ancestor, the crafty chieftain Snorri goði (d. 1031). If Birningr expects preferential treatment from Sturla because of kinship ties, enabling him to emerge from this affair unscathed, he is mistaken. Sturla does agree to help Birningr, but he arranges matters to his own advantage; the two men make a *handsal* agreement whereby Birningr conveys all his property to Sturla. The agreement also specifies that Birningr is to live out his life on Sturla's farm at Hvammr and that Birningr's wife, Guðbjörg, is to remain at Heinaberg.

For the moment at least, a stalemate has been reached. Neither Einarr nor Sturla wants openly to confront the other over the land. Each *goði* has gained from the property of a farmer, and for a while they are content to let the matter drop. Sturla will not prosecute Einarr for the robbery "as long as Einarr voices no displeasure with Sturla's and Birningr's *handsal*." Each chieftain settles for what he has received and the matter remains uncontested for a number of years. *Sturlu saga* ends with the dispute over Heinaberg unresolved.

Resurgence of the Dispute over Heinaberg

The status of Birningr's property, Heinaberg, turns up again at the opening of *Íslendinga saga* after Sturla dies of old age. At the time of Sturla's death in 1183, Birningr is living on Sturla's farm. His second wife Guðbjörg and their young son Thorleikr have, under Sturla's watchful eye, continued to live at Heinaberg. In 1185 Einarr rides to Heinaberg with seven men and, in the presence of Guðbjörg, lays claim to Birningr's property. When Guðbjörg refuses to give up the land, Einarr and his men ride off to round up the livestock on the farm and drive the animals away with them. Seeing what the men are doing, Guðbjörg and the other women rush out of the house, followed by Birningr's son Thorleikr and his foster brother Snorri.

Einarr must feel that he and his men are in complete control of the situation, as only women and boys are living at Heinaberg. Guðbjörg's son Thorleikr is described as still not quite twenty years old and "slight of stature," and Snorri, the foster brother, is even younger. But these young farmers have been pushed to their limit, and Einarr is about to receive the surprise of his life.

While her women chase the cattle away from Einarr's men, Guðbjörg and the boys turn on Einarr: "Guðbjörg grabbed his cloak with both hands and held it behind him, and both boys struck him at the same time" (ch. 2). After inflicting a severe wound on Einarr, the boys run away before the chieftain's men can get at them, and "Einarr and his followers went home but left the animals behind." The boys make good their escape and take shelter with Sturla's family at Hvammr. Einarr lies ill with his wounds for a while and then dies. The killing of a *goði* by farmers without the aid or sanction of chieftains was an unusual event. Einarr, who was not noted for his political acumen, was killed because he miscalculated in his dealings with farmers. This saga portrays the checks and balances of the social order functioning in such a way that everyone faced some kind of danger. Birningr's son has vindicated his father's honor, but his deed will eventually cost him the property.

Birningr's son Thorleikr and his foster brother Snorri remain with Sturla's family until the case comes to trial at the thing. In the meantime Einarr's sisters, who are his heirs, settle his estate and then prepare a lawsuit against the killers and those who have aided them. A relative of Einarr's, Thorvaldr Gizurarson, takes charge of the case. He seeks out the advice and help of Jón Loftsson, the most powerful chieftain of his day. Jón was known as a wise and just man; his words carried weight and his views elicited respect throughout Iceland. As Einar Ól. Sveinsson has noted, "For all his [Jón's] ambition he was a man of moderation, and as he was also the most equitable of men, he was the greatest peacemaker in the country in his time."[7]

It is interesting, then, to note the reason given in the saga for Jón's decision to come to the aid of the prosecution against Einarr's young killers. The saga makes clear that in their lifetimes Jón and Einarr had little in common and did not like each other. With Einarr's death, however, the issue is not friendship but the guarding of privilege. In reply to the request for aid in the prosecution, Jón states that he was not in a *vinfengi* relationship with Einarr which would make him feel any obligation in this case. Nevertheless, it seems to Jón that "things have come to a dangerous pass if there is no attempt to right matters when men of little regard strike down chieftains." Therefore Jón pledges his word to support the prosecution.

When the case comes to court at the Althing, both Thorleikr and Snorri are outlawed. Rather than allowing them to be hunted down as outlaws, members of Sturla's family arrange passage out of the country for their young kinsmen. Although he has saved his life and upheld his personal honor, Birningr's son has lost all claim to his land. An example to other farmers, the outcome of the case satisfies Jón Loftsson. As to the final ownership of Heinaberg, *Sturlunga saga* gives no indication. The story of the feud over Heinaberg was apparently included in the sagas because it explained the death of Einarr Thorgilsson. With the political

7. Einar Ól. Sveinsson, *The Age of the Sturlungs: Icelandic Civilization in the Thirteenth Century*, trans. Jóhann S. Hannesson, Islandica 36 (Ithaca: Cornell University Press, 1953), p. 25.

connection gone, the disposition of this property is not of importance to the author of *Íslendinga saga*, Sturla Thórðarson, Hvamm-Sturla's grandson and namesake.

The ambitions of chieftains such as Einarr Thorgilsson called for aggressive tactics. Such tactics, including the use of trumped-up legal claims to acquire property, by their very nature alienated farmers and chieftains whose property rights were being challenged. Set in the historical context of the late twelfth century, Einarr's death is an example of how acquisitive actions could produce a deadly reaction.

9

Limitations on a Chieftain's Ambitions

Revenge is a dish best served cold.

—Old Sicilian adage

In exacting payment for his services a *goði* was subject to restraints. Such limitations are particularly evident in a feud related in *Eyrbyggja saga* between two strong chieftains whose contest over power and land polarized the local community. The prospect of arousing the vengefulness of local farmers often frustrated the ambitions of a chieftain. In *Eyrbyggja saga*, Arnkell goði chooses to ignore this risk. In return for his services he acquires by *handsal* the rights to properties to which he had no prior claim. By this action, involving *arfskot* (cheating of heirs, or transferring land without the heirs' consent), Arnkell arouses the animosity of neighboring farmers who are willing to fight to maintain their claims to the lands. The story of Arnkell marks the limits that a chieftain, greedy for wealth, exceeded at peril to his life. Set within the context of a long-standing rivalry between Snorri goði and Arnkell goði, the events that develop from the machinations of a *bóndi* named Thórólfr bægifótr (Lamefoot) form a narrative unit (chs. 30-34) with ramifications immediately following (chs. 35-38).[1] The story frequently turns on

1. Further ramifications are described in ch. 63, when Thórólfr returns from the grave to take vengeance on Thóroddr, one of the sons of Thorbrandr (Vésteinn Ólason,"Nokkrar athugasemdir um Eyrbyggja sögu,"

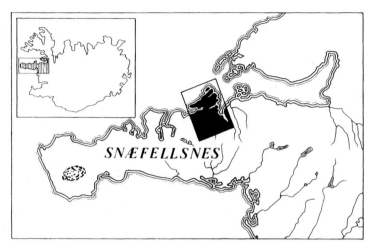

Map 5. Snæfellsnes. The blackened area extends from the outermost point of Thórsnes, facing the sea, to the innermost point of Álptafjörðr (Swans' Fjord). The blackened area is detailed in maps 6 and 7.

actions that stem from greed, fear, ambition, or downright meanness, as it describes coldhearted bargaining between farmers and chieftains.[2]

All the events take place in one small region of Snæfellsnes, shifting between Álptafjörðr,[3] a fjord that cuts into the northern shore of the peninsula, and Helgafell, the farmstead on Thórsnes where Snorri goði lives. The legal case arising from Thórólfr's actions is settled at the local Thórsnes Thing. The action is limited to disputes that em-

---

Skírnir 145[1971]:11; see also Jesse L. Byock, *Feud in the Icelandic Saga* [Berkeley, Los Angeles, London: University of California Press, 1982], pp. 131-133).

2. Sections of this chapter appeared in Jesse L. Byock,"Inheritance and Ambition in *Eyrbyggja saga*," in *The Sagas of the Icelanders: Essays in Criticsm*, ed. John Tucker (New York: Garland Press, 1987).

3. Álptafjörðr ("Swans' Fjord") is named for the large number of swans that to this day congregate there.

broil the two chieftains and the owners of four farms that lie near Bólstaðr, Arnkell's farm at the inland end of the fjord. The main characters are known from *Landnámabók*, where the events are sketchily outlined (S86, H74). In 1931 the archaeologist Matthías Thórðarson conducted an excavation at Arnkell's farm.[4] Because Bólstaðr had so little surrounding land, it had previously been doubted that a chieftain of Arnkell's stature would have lived there. At Bólstaðr, the excavation uncovered the remains of a small habitation that had been replaced in the early period of the Free State by a much larger and better-equipped house, well worthy of a chieftain. As the water of the fjord has claimed much of the farmstead land, all that remains is an outline of stones marking the house. The farms of the two freedmen in the saga, Úlfarr and Örlygr, are still marked by distinct square patches of green grass where their fields once lay.

Along with knowing that Álptafjörðr is very small, a local audience would have been aware of several other basic facts. First, as the eastern side of the fjord is too steep to provide good farmland, no habitations of consequence were located there. Second, because Bólstaðr, Arnkell's farm, was too small to support the needs of so ambitious a chieftain, one would expect him to be land-hungry. Third, Kár]sstaðir at the innermost point of the fjord was the real prize. Its low-lying, broad hayfields were the most extensive in the area, and through the middle of the farm ran one of the best salmon and trout rivers in the region. The surrounding mountains, by keeping out the harshest winter winds and in the summer retaining the heat from the sun, contributed to the productivity of Kársstaðir's rich grasslands. As testimony to its inherent value, Kársstaðir is the only farm in Álptafjörðr which is still inhabited today.[5]

4. Matthías Thórðarson,"Bólstaðr við Álftafjörð: Skýrsla um rannsókn 1931," *Árbók hins íslenzka fornleifafélags*, 1932, 1-28.
5. My thanks to Gísli Gíslason, the *bóndi* at Kársstaðir, for discussing with me the relative merits of the lands and streams in Álptafjörðr.

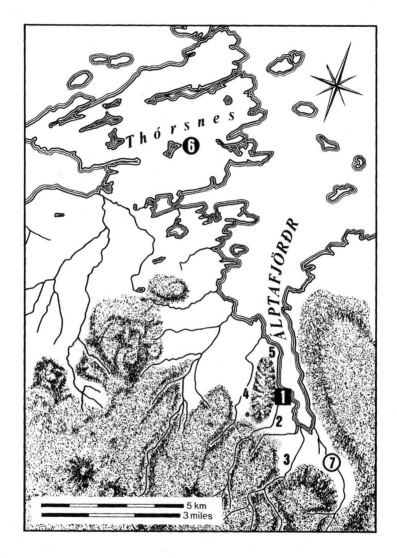

Map 6. Landownership in Álptafjörðr at the start of the incidents
described in this chapter. 1. Bólstaðr (Arnkell goði); 2. Úlfarsfell
(Úlfarr the freedman); 3. Örlygsstaðir (Örlygr the freedman); 4.
Hvammr (Thórólfr Lamefoot); 5. Krákunes (the woodland); 6.
Helgafell (Snorri goði); 7. Kársstaðir (the six sons of Thorbrandr).
The circled numbers designate land owned by the chieftain Snorri
or by his thingmen, the sons of Thorbrandr. The square designates
the property of the chieftain Arnkell.

ARNKELL'S QUEST FOR WEALTH AND POWER

The danger inherent in Arnkell's territorial ambitions is sensed by the sons of Thorbrandr, who live at Kársstaðir in the inner fjord. With impassable mountains at their backs, these farmers need a safe route to Helgafell, where their chieftain Snorri goði lives, as well as free access to the Thórsnes thing. As the story progresses, their adversary Arnkell is claiming the properties on the western side and at the mouth of the fjord, thus cutting off their lifeline. Arnkell is also interfering with their expected inheritance of some of these properties.

The sons of Thorbrandr are determined to retain their freedom of movement, property rights, and local status. Their frustrations illustrate the limitations of Iceland's system of consensual order. Thórólfr, Arnkell goði's father and a viking in his youth, is an unjust and overbearing man (*mjök ójafnaðarfullr*). Arriving in Iceland late in the settlement period, he acquired a sizable piece of land by challenging an elderly *landnámsmaðr* to a duel and killing him. Wounded in the duel, Thórólfr became known as Lamefoot. Later he sold part of his land to Úlfarr and to Úlfarr's brother Örlygr, two slaves freed by Thorbrandr of Kársstaðir.

Úlfarr leysingi (freedman) has prospered on his farm, called Úlfarsfell, and Thórólfr, who lives at Hvammr, resents the freedman's skill at farming and weather forecasting. Now an old man himself, Thórólfr is increasingly difficult to deal with, and he wants to hurt Úlfarr. On the ridge that separates the farms, the two men jointly own a mountain meadow. One summer day Thórólfr goes with a few slaves and gathers in all the hay, even though part of it clearly belongs to Úlfarr. The latter, who is younger than Thórólfr, confronts the old man in the act of stealing the hay, but Thórólfr refuses to listen to reason. Rather than come to blows, Úlfarr chooses to take the matter to his neighbor and

goði, Arnkell, son of Thórólfr. Thórólfr has no share in Arnkell's chieftaincy. Though reluctant to take part in the dispute, Arnkell does
ask his father to pay Úlfarr for the hay, but Thórólfr refuses.
His refusal strains the relationship between father and son
and puts Arnkell in a difficult position. When his friend and
follower Úlfarr chides him for not acting more decisively on
his behalf, Arnkell himself pays Úlfarr for the hay and seeks
reimbursement by slaughtering some of his father's oxen.
Thórólfr, who does not approve of Arnkell's solution, swears
that he will make Úlfarr pay for the loss of his livestock.[6]

Úlfarr's Land Shifts to Arnkell

The conflict, which hitherto has been a neighbors' squab-
ble over hay, becomes more serious. Thórólfr, though taking
no immediate action, continues to brood over the wrong
done him. At his Yule feast he serves his slaves strong drink
and incites them to burn Úlfarr in his house, but the plot
fails when Arnkell sees the fire and puts it out. The next
day Arnkell has Thórólfr's slaves led to a promontory and
hanged.

Frightened by the attempt on his life, Úlfarr places himself under the protection of his chieftain Arnkell (ch. 31):
"After that [the attempted murder and the hanging of the
slaves], Úlfarr transferred to Arnkell by *handsal* agreement
all his property, and Arnkell became his guardian [*varn-
aðarmaðr*]." Arnkell's acceptance of the burden of guardianship is not gratuitous. In return for Arnkell's protection,
Úlfarr assigns all his wealth (*fé sitt allt*)[7] to the chieftain in a

6. For a discussion of the narrative progression in chs. 30-31 of *Eyrbyggja
saga*, see Byock, *Feud*, pp. 152-154; see also William Ian Miller, "Avoiding
Legal Judgment: The Submission of Disputes to Arbitration in Medieval
Iceland," *American Journal of Legal History* 28(1984):126-130.
7. *Fé* in this instance has the legal meaning of both land and chattels,
as in GG Ia, p. 15 (ch. 4): "Þar er maþr leggr fe til kirkio. hvartz þat er i
londom eþa bv fe. eþa lausom avrom . . . ." See also GG II, p. 17 (ch. 13);
III, p. 15 (*Skálholtsbók*, ch. 5).

formal agreement (*handsal*) which we later learn was duly witnessed. With one variation, the transaction between Úlfarr and Arnkell is, according to the lawbooks, an example of *arfsal*, cession of the right of inheritance. *Arfsal*, a binding agreement, differs from *arfskot*, fraud or cheating in matters of inheritance.[8] In *arfsal*, one of the two parties agrees to take the other into his household and care for him in return for an assignment of inheritance rights. The variation in this instance is that Úlfarr continues to live on the property he is relinquishing instead of moving to Arnkell's farm.

The *handsal* between Úlfarr and Arnkell especially affects a group of neighboring farmers, the six sons of Thorbrandr, who are the foster brothers of Arnkell's rival Snorri goði. Úlfarr had been freed by Thorbrandr, who is now an old man and whose sons have taken over his property and rights. Thorbrandr's sons feel they have been cheated by Arnkell's transaction with Úlfarr: "The Thorbrandssons did not like this *handsal* because they had thought themselves owners of Úlfarr's wealth, as he was their freedman." In accordance with the laws on *arfsal*, those who originally stood to inherit land may nullify a transaction if they are not in agreement with the assignment. In the instance of a freedman without children, *Grágás* is very precise: the manumitter (*frjálsgjafi*) is the heir.[9] If a freedman such as Úlfarr signs away the rights of his manumitter, he can be accused of *arfskot*, according to *Grágás*.[10]

Icelandic law assumed that a freedman (*leysingi*) might have difficulty earning his living. *Grágás* specifies that if a freedman could not maintain himself and did not have a son or daughter to look after him, then his manumitter was required to support him.[11] The manumitter was compensated

---

8. *GG* Ia, pp. 247-249 (ch. 127).

9. *GG* Ia, p. 227 (ch. 119); II, p. 72 (ch. 60). An apparent exception occurs when the manumitter is himself the freedman's slayer. See Lúðvík Ingvarsson, *Refsingar á Íslandi á þjóðveldistímanum* (Reykjavik: Bókaútgáfa Menningarsjóðs, 1970), p. 316; *GG* Ia, p. 172 (ch. 96).

10. *GG* Ia, p. 247 (ch. 127); II, p. 85 (ch. 66).

11. *GG* Ib, p. 17 (ch. 134); II, p. 126 (ch. 93).

by becoming the legal heir if his freedman died childless. Freedmen (*leysingjar*) were in this respect a single generation of former slaves who were not completely free from their manumitters. They remained united to manumitters by bonds of quasi-kinship, remaining dependent on them as minor children were on their fathers.[12]

Úlfarr has done well for himself; far from having difficulty earning his living, he has accumulated enough wealth to arouse the greed of those around him. Because he has presumably never looked for support to his manumitters, the Thorbrandssons, he may well think that he owes them nothing, that his self-earned property is his to dispose of as he pleases, without recognizing their claims. The Thorbrandssons, on the other hand, are within the letter of the law in considering themselves heirs of the childless Úlfarr, even if they never maintained him in his lifetime.

By promising protection to a farmer in need of support, Arnkell has, through the legality of *handsal*, taken possession of a valuable piece of property. In establishing a claim to the land by means of Úlfarr's *arfsal*, Arnkell has ignored the inheritance rights held by the wellborn sons of Thorbrandr. Nevertheless, he is still maneuvering within legal limits. Úlfarr, for his part, is considered to have committed *arfskot* and is stirring up animosity in the district by selecting Arnkell as his protector. Yet few other viable options are available to him. Consider Úlfarr's position. His most direct procedure would be to attack and kill Thórólfr, but he wisely refrains from choosing a solution that would be foolhardy for a simple farmer (a freedman) whose opponent is kin to a chieftain. By killing Thórólfr, Úlfarr would force Arnkell to seek redress, perhaps even blood vengeance. Possibly Úlfarr fears that he would be injured in a confrontation with the tough old viking. Another choice open to Úlfarr is to seek protection from the sons of Thorbrandr, who are his legal heirs.

---

12. Kirsten Hastrup, *Culture and History in Medieval Iceland: An Anthropological Analysis of Structure and Change* (Oxford: Clarendon Press, 1985), p. 116.

As powerful warriors they would be dangerous enemies to any opponent. Because they do not possess a *goðorð*, however, they cannot exercise the full power of the law in Úlfarr's favor. Further, their chieftain lives much farther away from Úlfarr than does Arnkell, whose land is no more than a long arrow shot away.

The Thorbrandssons also have options. They can attack Arnkell with the intention of killing him. Although in the end the Thorbrandssons do just that, at this stage they are not willing to go that far. As Arnkell is a skillful opponent and a powerful chieftain, these farmers choose to handle the dispute through the proper legal channels. Their next move is to seek the advocacy of their *goði*. Úlfarr's, and initially the Thorbrandssons', rejection of a violent solution is reminiscent of farmers' restraint in similar situations in other family and Sturlunga sagas; under duress, farmers consciously avoid initiating action against their chieftains. As the *goðar* guard the privilege of their official position, so, too, the *bændr* keep their conduct within the limits imposed by that position.

The sons of Thorbrandr choose not to act alone, even legally. Theoretically they could have summoned Arnkell either to the local thing or to the Althing. In the reality of Icelandic legal procedures, however, an armed following was a prerequisite for success. These *bændr*, lacking the position in society to command such a following, would stand little chance against Arnkell goði and his thingmen. Indeed, the saga does not suggest that Thorbrandr's sons even consider taking independent court action. Instead, they turn to Snorri goði.

Snorri, apparently seeing little opportunity for self-aggrandizement in taking on a case against Arnkell, refuses to support the Thorbrandssons. Snorri was an astute power broker who was revered as an ancestor by many of the prominent people of the thirteenth century, including the Sturlungs. As the present example reveals, Snorri's reputation was based on shrewdness rather than on physical prowess. In view of Arnkell's clear intention to push his claim, a confrontation at the courts on behalf of Thorbrandr's sons would be dangerous for Snorri. On the other hand, what has Snorri to gain by supporting his foster brothers? If Arnkell wins the case, he keeps the rights to the land. But if Snorri wins, he would be expected to turn the rights over to the Thorbrandssons. If Snorri exacts from them a price commensurate with the risks involved, such as Úlfarr's property, he would himself arouse the hostility of these potentially dangerous men. Snorri, who is not a rash man, chooses not to put himself in a precarious position. Snorri's refusal to support his thingmen makes them legally impotent. Even though they are powerful and wellborn farmers with clearly established rights, they are helpless without an advocate.

Theoretically, Úlfarr might turn to Snorri goði for assistance, but that option is not realistic. Snorri, who lives at a distance out on Thórsnes, could not effectively aid Úlfarr if Arnkell or Thórólfr should harass him. Furthermore, an agreement with Úlfarr would probably be counterproductive for Snorri. By accepting what Úlfarr has to offer (assignment of his land) in return for protection, Snorri would probably anger the sons of Thorbrandr. Such action might even force them to unite with Arnkell against Úlfarr. Given the choices, Arnkell is really the only suitable advocate for Úlfarr, though it is questionable what advantage Arnkell would have in seeing Úlfarr enjoy a long life.

Thórólfr's Land Shifts to Snorri Goði

Financial considerations again enter into the continuing legal process when a bargain is struck between Thórólfr Lamefoot and Snorri goði. Once more, a farmer requests the support of a chieftain in return for a specific payment. As the details are different from Úlfarr's transfer of his land to Arnkell, however, the situations of Úlfarr and Thórólfr present a notable contrast. Úlfarr is a freedman who desperately needs protection; Thórólfr is a wellborn man under no physical duress. Thórólfr's intention is to exercise his rights in order to obtain personal revenge against Arnkell. He is prepared to go to Snorri and to contract for the support of his son's chief enemy, a man with whom he has no ties of friendship or kinship. Presented in unusually sharp detail, the scenes are tightly narrated examples of how a clever leader bargains with a determined *bóndi* and gains land in return for his advocacy.

Thórólfr is especially irked by Arnkell's refusal to pay compensation for the hanging of his slaves after the failed attempt to burn Úlfarr to death. According to two complicated entries in *Grágás*,[13] Thórólfr's claim for compensation is probably justified. A master whose slaves have been killed has the right to demand that the issue be settled in court. Here is another example of a *bóndi* who knows his legal rights but lacks the strength to uphold them. Thórólfr needs an advocate.

Determined to seek vengeance, Thórólfr swallows his pride and solicits support from the other local broker, Snorri goði. As the meeting begins, the *goði* offers food to his unexpected guest, but Thórólfr refuses it, saying that "he has no need to eat his host's food." Thórólfr informs Snorri that, as a major leader in the district (*héraðshöfðingi*), the chieftain is obligated to support those who have suffered injury. The appeal to Snorri's sense of justice or duty is a waste of time. When he hears that Thórólfr wants to prosecute his own son, Arnkell, Snorri viciously humbles the old man. Reminding Thórólfr of his family ties, Snorri declares that Arnkell is a better man than his father.

The positions of the two men are clear. Neither likes the other, and Snorri, who is in complete control of the situation, sees no reason even to be civil to the father of his rival. If Thórólfr wants Snorri to use his power, he will have to appeal to an interest other than the chieftain's sense of duty. Thórólfr, aware that something more is required, offers to give Snorri some of the compensation for the slaves if Snorri will take the case. Snorri flatly refuses his support, saying

13. GG Ia, pp. 190-191 (ch. 111); II, pp. 395-397 (ch. 379).

that he will not interject himself into the dispute between father and son.

Thórólfr then realizes that if he wants to uphold his rights he will have to offer Snorri something of real value. And Thórólfr does indeed possess a worthwhile bargaining unit, a property in Álptafjörðr called Krákunes, on which stands a valuable forest. He offers Snorri a *handsal* of this property, "the greatest treasure in the region," if Snorri will prosecute Arnkell. With all the power of understatement the saga author lets us know that Snorri feels a "great need" to possess the forest. So in return for taking on the case of Thórólfr's loss of his slaves, Snorri accepts a *handsal* of the land.

At the local spring assembly, the Thórsnes Thing, Snorri brings the case against Arnkell for the killing of the two slaves. When the two chieftains arrive at the thing, each has a large following. After the accusation has been made before the court, Arnkell calls witnesses to prove that he caught the slaves in the act of burning a farmstead. Snorri replies that Arnkell could have killed the slaves with impunity if he had done so at the scene of the burning. *Grágás* supports Snorri's contention, specifying that men may be struck down as being outside the law when caught in the act of setting a fire ("með ellde tecnom til breno").[14] According to Snorri, Arnkell forfeited his right to kill the slaves when he did not act immediately but later had them taken to a promontory to be executed. Therefore, Snorri claims, Arnkell has failed to observe the law and thus is unable to use it in his own defense.

After a discussion of legal points, the arbitration process begins. Men come forward offering to help in the resolution of the dispute. Two brothers, who have connections with the opposing parties, are chosen to arbitrate, and they arrange a settlement. Arnkell pays a modest sum to Snorri, who in turn passes the pouch to Thórólfr; Snorri has already been paid in land. But Thórólfr, who expended so much energy in bringing about this confrontation between Arnkell

14. *GG* Ia, p. 185 (ch. 109).

and Snorri, feels cheated: "I did not expect, when I gave you my land, that you would pursue this case in so petty a manner, and I know that Arnkell would not have denied me such compensation for my slaves if I had left it up to him." Apparently it does not occur to him that Snorri is less concerned with discrediting Arnkell and getting a large sum for the slaves than in winning his legal point in order to keep Krákunes.

The forest acquired by Snorri carries a price beyond the aid promised to Thórólfr. As the saga makes clear, Arnkell believes that Snorri has unlawfully acquired title to the Krákunes woods. Arnkell's view is that his father Thórólfr "committed *arfskot* when he transferred the forest to Snorri goði." Here Arnkell seems to be in the right: Thórólfr's transfer of the forest to Snorri is an instance of *arfskot* in that the title was conveyed without the prior agreement of Arnkell, Thórólfr's rightful heir. According to *Grágás*,[15] Arnkell, as the heir, has the right to bring an action to remove the testator, in this case Thórólfr, from control of the property. Arnkell, however, has little to gain from such an action, as Thórólfr is no longer in control of the forest and as he himself will inherit his father's other property. Arnkell therefore waits until he thinks the time is ripe; then he rides over to Krákunes and kills a man named Haukr, one of Snorri's freeborn followers, who is transporting wood from the forest to Helgafell. By killing Haukr, Arnkell is openly claiming that Snorri has no right to take wood from Krákunes. At the same time he is asserting his own control over the forest.

Úlfarr Claims Örlygr's Land

By becoming Úlfarr's guardian, Arnkell had acquired control of a property at the expense of the sons of Thorbrandr. The transaction brings still other advantages to Arnkell. Not only is Úlfarr a childless landowner, but his brother Örlygr also has no children. When Örlygr dies, Úlfarr, backed up

15. GG Ia, p. 247 (ch. 127); II, p. 84 (ch. 66).

by Arnkell, claims that he is his brother's heir and takes possession of all of Örlygr's property, including his farm Örlygsstaðir. In doing so he is once again openly thwarting Thorbrandr's sons, who had expected to inherit because Örlygr, like Úlfarr, was their father's freed slave. Although Úlfarr's and Örlygr's farms are both small, together they make up a substantial portion of the usable land within the fjord. Furthermore, Örlygsstaðir borders on Kársstaðir, the farm of the Thorbrandssons. By acquiring control first of Úlfarsfell and then of Örlygsstaðir, Arnkell has extended his property to the borders of Kársstaðir. The question of what he intends to do next makes the situation dangerous for the sons of Thorbrandr. Their confrontation with Arnkell over Örlygr's property clearly shows that the owners of Kársstaðir feel cheated (ch. 32):

> And when Örlygr died, Úlfarr sent immediately for Arnkell, who came quickly to Örlygsstaðir. Together Úlfarr and Arnkell took into their possession all of Örlygr's property. When the Thorbrandssons learned of the death of Örlygr they went to Örlygsstaðir and laid claim to all the property there. They declared that whatever their freedman had owned was their property. Úlfarr, however, said that he held the right to his brother's inheritance. The sons of Thorbrandr asked Arnkell what he intended to do. Arnkell replied that if he had a say in the matter Úlfarr would not be robbed by any man as long as they were partners. Then the sons of Thorbrandr left and went immediately out to Helgafell [Snorri goði's farmstead].

As noted earlier, *Grágás* clearly stipulates that the manumitter is the rightful heir of a childless freedman. (Again the sons of the manumitter, Thorbrandr, are concerned with protecting their inheritance.) As the law, to our knowledge, does not allow a brother's claim in such a situation, Arnkell is acting illegally in asserting his right to Örlygr's property. Although the law explicitly upholds the sons of Thorbrandr as Örlygr's heirs, Arnkell through his previous experience knows that they will not act without the backing of their chieftain Snorri.

By taking the property Arnkell is humiliating Snorri; he seems convinced that Snorri will back down in the face of an open challenge, and that is exactly what happens. When the sons of Thorbrandr go to Helgafell to seek Snorri's aid, the chieftain again refuses to support his thingmen and foster brothers. He even manages to blame them for the dispute, stating that he "would not quarrel over this issue with Arnkell because they [the Thorbrandssons] had been so careless as to let Arnkell and Úlfarr arrive at the property first and take it into their possession." Without the support of their *goði*, Thorbrandr's sons again find themselves outmaneuvered. As in the earlier exchange with Arnkell over Úlfarr's property, they back down and do not openly contest their neighbor's seizure of their inheritance. Snorri, however, cannot fail to understand the threat made by his foster brothers when they remark, as they leave Helgafell, that their chieftain "would not long retain his authority if he did not concern himself with a matter such as this."

Úlfarr's Demise

Úlfarr does not enjoy for long the use of Örlygr's property, for old Thórólfr Lamefoot is still plotting. While returning home with gifts from Arnkell's autumn feast, Úlfarr is ambushed and killed by a man sent by Thórólfr. By chance Arnkell is standing outside his house and sees the killer running across a field. Now, though his protection has proved ineffectual in keeping Úlfarr alive, he acts quickly in his own interest. Sending some of his followers to kill the runner,[16] he immediately rides to Úlfarr's farmstead where he claims that as Úlfarr's protector he should inherit the property.

Meanwhile, Thorbrandr's sons, having learned of Úlfarr's death, set out to claim the property of their freedman for themselves. When they reach the farmstead they find Arnkell, supported by a following, already there. Arnkell, deny-

---

16. To kill so quickly a man whom he only suspects to be an assassin is curious. Very few details would need to be changed in the story to implicate Arnkell in the killing. Certainly Úlfarr's death was to his advantage. The few sentences toward the end of ch. 37 eulogizing Arnkell may be a later interpolation.

ing the precedence of their claim (*tilkall*), supports his own by bringing forward witnesses who were present when Úlfarr assigned his property to Arnkell by *handsal*. Displaying an intense interest in legal maneuverings, the sagaman has Arnkell declare that "he would hold firm to his right to the property since the original agreement had not been challenged at law. Arnkell warned them [Thorbrandr's sons] not to encumber the property with a legal claim because he intended to hold onto it as though it were his patrimony." Again Arnkell is master of the situation, both legally and physically.[17]

Outmaneuvered and overpowered, the sons of Thorbrandr leave the farmstead and once again seek the help of their chieftain, Snorri. As before, Snorri refuses to support his thingmen. He does, however, point out to the Thorbrandssons that, although Arnkell has established a legal claim to the lands and has taken possession of the chattels, the property lies equidistant between them and in the end "will fall to the stronger." Snorri reminds his foster brothers that they "will have to put up with the situation as others do, since Arnkell now stands above all men's rights here in the district. And that will continue as long as he lives, whether it is longer or shorter" (ch. 32). In this way Snorri incites his followers to violence.

Snorri's prediction that the lands will fall to the stronger party is an accurate assessment, for in the end Arnkell does not realize his ambitions. Yet before he meets a violent death at the hands of Snorri and the Thorbrandssons (ch. 37), he gains control of almost all of Álptafjörðr. After Thórólfr Lamefoot dies (ch. 33), Arnkell acquires his father's farm at Hvammr (4 on maps 6 and 7). This acquisition further reduces the Thorbrandssons' freedom of movement. Both sides of the ridge between Úlfarsfell and Hvammr, site of the meadow where Úlfarr and Thórólfr first came into conflict,

---

17. The laws apparently imposed a time limit on challenges to the transfer of inheritance rights, although the exact provisions are unclear. See *GG* Ia, p. 249 (ch. 127).

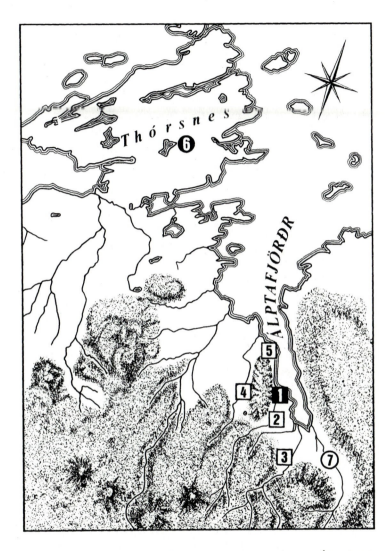

Map 7. The effect of Arnkell's actions on land claims in Álptafjörðr immediately before Arnkell's death. The squares indicate land that Arnkell [1] has acquired or land that he claims. A circle designates land owned by Snorri goði [6] or by his thingmen, the sons of Thorbrandr [7].

are now controlled by Arnkell, hemming in the sons of Thorbrandr whose property is the only one in the fjord still outside Arnkell's control (see map 5).

In considering their position the sons of Thorbrandr may
have been aware of stories recounting the limitations of independent action by *bændr* when asserting their rights. The
tragedy of Gísli Súrsson, as told in *Gísla saga Súrssonar*,[18] is
an example. Gísli becomes embroiled in a personal dispute
with his chieftain, who is also his neighbor and his brother-
in-law. Gísli, who is physically a match for his opponent,
attacks and kills him. Legally Gísli is in no position to survive the consequences of his act. By killing the chieftain with
whom he has been allied, he has at one stroke removed the
most logical person to whom he could turn and has also
signaled people with political clout that he is untrustworthy.
As Gísli finds out, no matter how honorably motivated his
action, there is little willingness to defend him or to seek a
settlement for him in the courts. The disaffected include the
members of Gísli's family, who give him very little support.
His sister becomes a determined enemy and his brother is
angered because of Gísli's violent act. In killing a chieftain
to whom he is related by marriage, Gísli has lowered his
relatives' status and undermined their political strength. The
brother of the chieftain whom Gísli has killed, after assuming
the vacant *goðorð*, now seeks vengeance. Against the physical might of a chieftain with his followers at the thing, Gísli
is virtually powerless in the court system, and he is declared
a full outlaw.

The End of Arnkell's Ambitions

The story of the conflicting claims in Álptafjörðr reveals
the profits accruing to an ambitious leader, as well as the
dangers and the choices he faces. Arnkell repeatedly manip-
ulates the law to gain possession of new and valuable properties while abusing the rights of freeborn farmers. Arnkell,

18. ÍF 6, pp. 1-118.

however, miscalculates. The sons of Thorbrandr can be cheated, but they cannot be ignored. Snorri, at his own autumn feast, is finally shamed into supporting his thingmen, and he agrees to take part in an attack on Arnkell. In response to their taunts, Snorri gives one of them an axe, remarking that it would be a suitable weapon with which to kill Arnkell. The farmer Thorleifr kimbi, who is equally hard-nosed, replies: "Don't think that I will hesitate to swing this axe at Arnkell once you are ready" (ch. 37).

Once they are assured of a chieftain's backing, the sons of Thorbrandr become a serious threat to Arnkell. Events move quickly. Snorri and Thorbrandr's sons await the right opportunity. One night they learn that Arnkell has gone alone with only a few slaves to tend to the hay on his newly acquired lands. At a distance from his men at Bólstaðr, Arnkell is an easy target. Although he defends himself courageously, the sons of Thorbrandr, with Snorri in command, kill him.

Details of the ensuing court case are sketchy, but the outcome is clearly a success for Snorri. The only sentence of outlawry—banishment for three winters—for the killing of Arnkell falls on Thorleifr kimbi, the son of Thorbrandr who had publicly taken responsibility for administering the deathblow. As to the lands, the saga later tells that Bólstaðr, Arnkell's farm, is deserted while Örlygsstaðir and Úlfarsfell return to the possession of Thorbrandr's sons.

For all his local wealth and power, Arnkell seems not to have made many friends among his fellow chieftains. Nor has he created a successful system of family or political alliances, and no competent advocate steps forward to prosecute his killers. Perhaps what is not said but understood is that Snorri, a master politician in other tales such as *Njáls saga* and *Laxdæla saga*, was not sitting idle during the time that he was suffering abuse from Arnkell. Instead, he was quietly gathering assurances from other *goðar* that when the moment came, he and his followers would not be attacked in the courts for the killing. Left on their own, Arnkell's female heirs take over the responsibility of bringing a court case, and they mishandle the suit. According to the laconic description in *Eyrbyggja saga*, the result of the suit was "not as honorable as one might have expected for so important a leader as Arnkell. The leading men of the country then made it law that never afterward should a woman or a youth less than sixteen winters be the chief prosecutor in a case of manslaughter; and this law has held ever since."[19]

In its story of Arnkell, *Eyrbyggja saga* shows that within Iceland's system of order, the ambitions of a chieftain could be frustrated by *bændr* who know how to assert their rights.

19. This passage agrees with entries in *GG* Ia, pp. 167-169 (ch. 94); II, pp. 334-336 (ch. 297).

10

Vinfengi: A Mechanism of Power

Each of the wise should wield his power in moderation;
He will find that no one is foremost when bold men
gather.
—*The Sayings of the High One (Hávamál)*

Consensual order worked in Iceland because the country
was not burdened with a complex political or social hierarchy. *Vápnfirðinga saga*, a tale set in the eastern part of the
island, gives a detailed picture of the means by which power
was regulated and political ambition was contained. The
saga focuses on a power struggle between two young chieftains, Brodd-Helgi Thorgilsson, who lived at Hof, and Geitir
Lýtingsson, whose farm was at Krossavík, and follows the
feud until it is finally resolved by the succeeding generation.
The contest, which begins in Vápnafjörðr (Weapons' Fjord),
a series of low-lying green valleys, eventually engages people spread widely throughout the East Fjords as well as leaders from the Northern Quarter. As the feud progresses it
touches the political nerve of a large area, and additional
farmers and chieftains are frequently drawn into the conflict
through contractual friendship arrangements, i.e., *vinfengi*.
Both Brodd-Helgi and Geitir rely on *vinfengi*, and ultimately
their survival depends on their skill in establishing new ties
of friendship and maintaining old ones. Through *vinfengi* arrangements Geitir and Brodd-Helgi, who themselves were
fast friends in the beginning, acquire the supplementary
power necessary to influence court decisions.

Like Arnkell goði in *Eyrbyggja saga*, Brodd-Helgi is a man who wins most of the lesser engagements along the way but loses the larger contest. Geitir, like Snorri goði, typifies the Icelandic hero who not only succeeds in destroying an overbearing rival but also manages to survive with his power intact. Indicative of the interests of saga author and audience, accounts of such rivalries detail the political behavior of the opponents. The relative merits of moderation (*hóf*) are weighed against lack of restraint (*ójafnaðr*).

Although he is aggressive, Brodd-Helgi is careful to remain within the law. His well-controlled offensive actions and Geitir's defensive responses show that both individuals understand and abide by the rules of a sophisticated political game. To his own disadvantage, however, Brodd-Helgi does not maintain his restraint. Just as he has nearly succeeded in destroying Geitir's authority he loses his self-control. His conduct becomes so immoderate and overbearing that chieftains and farmers in other regions adopt a more friendly attitude toward Geitir. Brodd-Helgi's ultimate failure and death are attributable in part to his abuse of *vinfengi* in his relations with farmers and with other chieftains. For his part Geitir, in a display of political acumen, establishes a network of *vinfengi* ties that protect him from disastrous legal consequences.

Geitir and Brodd-Helgi are both capable leaders, but they differ widely in their approach to problems. Brodd-Helgi, with marked skill at arms, is courageous and willing to expose himself to danger. Early in the saga he is described as "a tall man, strong, and early matured, handsome and imposing, not talkative in his youth, stubborn and harsh from an early age. He was cunning and capricious" (ch. 1). In contrast, Geitir is not a fighter, and as he ages he becomes "a man of great wisdom" (ch. 3). As their feud progresses, Brodd-Helgi acknowledges the difference between the two men and characterizes his opponent: "It has always been true that Geitir is the wiser of us, though he has time and again been overcome by sheer force" (ch. 8).

Two distinct types of chieftain and two distinct operational methods are presented. Brodd-Helgi, like Arnkell, assails his rival openly and is a dangerous opponent. Geitir, like Snorri goði, avoids fighting back until he feels that local *bændr* and more distant *goðar* have reached a consensus that his opponent must be stopped. Geitir, as the defensive type of *goði* who publicly displays moderation, displays his acuity in choosing the decisive moment to strike back. A chieftain like Geitir or Snorri goði can turn another chieftain's abuse of privilege to his own advantage, but he must be subtle about it. The defensive leader must maintain his composure over long periods of time until his rival becomes overconfident and extends himself too far. He plays on the fears of *bændr* whose lands and lives have been jeopardized by his more aggressive opponent. Despite desertions as the feud wears on, Geitir's strength becomes concentrated in a small band of trusted followers. These faithful thingmen are aware of their own self-interest and, like their chieftain, fear the rise of an openly aggressive local leader. They know that concentration of power and wealth in the hands of one chieftain, if not counterbalanced, will erode the status of landowners like themselves.

The points of contention between the two *goðar* govern the progression of the saga and serve as the framework for the following discussion. The first incident between the chieftains concerns a foreign trader's goods. In the second, the foreigner's Icelandic partner is persecuted by Brodd-Helgi; the third incident deals with the dowry of Brodd-Helgi's wife, who is also Geitir's sister; the fourth is a clash over land between two farmers, Þórðr and Þormóðr Steinbjarnarson (see chapter 8); the fifth concerns Brodd-Helgi's attempt to buy the allegiance of one of Geitir's *bændr*; and the sixth catalogs Brodd-Helgi's breach of *vinfengi* with Guðmundr the Powerful, a power broker from the Northern Quarter. The threads of *vinfengi* relationships that both Brodd-Helgi and Geitir establish with Guðmundr run through the whole story of the feud.

More so than the feud between Arnkell goði and Snorri goði, which concentrates on the control of land, the contest between Geitir and Brodd-Helgi focuses on the control of allies, especially through *vinfengi*. Again the differences between the two *goðar* become apparent. Brodd-Helgi, unlike Geitir, is careless with his power. He shows a self-destructive need to avenge insults, real or perceived. As the dispute between the two *goðar* develops, the affairs of secondary characters become increasingly involved in it.

Inheriting a Foreigner's Goods

Brodd-Helgi's and Geitir's first quarrel concerns a wealthy Norwegian merchant called Hrafn who arrives in Vápnafjörðr with an Icelandic partner who goes to his own farm at Krossavík in Reyðarfjörðr, farther down the coast.[1] Hrafn takes lodgings with Geitir for a winter. Apparently (the saga is not explicit) Brodd-Helgi and Geitir plot to kill Hrafn because, as is all too clear, they covet the foreigner's wealth.

Besides his supply of trade goods stored at Geitir's farm, the Norwegian has other valuable possessions. He always wears a gold arm ring and always carries with him a small strongbox, reputedly filled with gold and silver. Because Hrafn presses people hard on their debts, he is soon unpopular. Without Icelandic family and with no alliance such as *vinfengi* or sworn brotherhood, he is virtually unprotected. During a feast in the winter, he is found dead outside the farmhouse. No one takes responsibility for the killing, which thus becomes murder. The Norwegian's gold arm ring and strongbox are not found with the body. None of the local *goðar* shows any inclination to search out the killer or to prosecute the case. As no other Icelanders have a claim to Hrafn's possessions, conveniently secure in Geitir's storehouse, Brodd-Helgi and Geitir agree to split them equally. The two *goðar*, however, decide to wait out the winter and to legalize their agreement at the local spring assembly. Then a dispute arises to disturb the *vinfengi* between the

---

1. Thorleifr's farm at Krossavík in Reyðarfjörðr is not to be confused with Geitir's farm at Krossavík in Vápnafjörðr. See map 8.

chieftains. Both of them are privy to some secret information about the murder and are concerned about the disappearance of Hrafn's valuables. Brodd-Helgi suggests that Geitir made off with the dead merchant's strongbox, and Geitir asks Brodd-Helgi about the arm ring. Meanwhile, there is a new development which the *goðar* had not counted on. Hrafn's partner, Thorleifr inn kristni (the Christian), determines that Hrafn's family in Norway shall inherit his goods. Thorleifr is an unusually honest and courageous man whose moral stature is understood to be connected with his religion.[2] The story is set in the period before the conversion but was written several centuries after it.

While the two chieftains are away at the local Sunnudalr *várthing*, Thorleifr removes the goods from Geitir's storehouse, loads them on his ship, and waits off the coast for a favorable wind to take him to Norway. The chieftains discover their loss when they return from the assembly. Although they have only small boats, Brodd-Helgi pushes for an immediate attack on Thorleifr's ship. Geitir, however, sees the danger in this venture and suggests that they wait and let the wind drive the ship onto the shore. When the winds shift and Thorleifr escapes to the open sea, Brodd-Helgi blames Geitir for their tactical error. The trust between the two leaders diminishes and their friendship cools. In Norway Thorleifr gives Hrafn's goods to the merchant's heirs, thus vitiating any accusation of robbery the chieftains might make against him.

Brodd-Helgi's Revenge against Thorleifr

When Thorleifr returns to Iceland, Brodd-Helgi desires revenge, pure and simple, without any obvious gain in

2. For a discussion of Thorleifr's Christianity, see Ernst Walter, *Studien zur Vápnfirðinga saga* (Halle [Saale]: Max Niemeyer Verlag, 1956), pp. 44-50. Alan Berger ("Lawyers in the Old Icelandic Family Sagas: Heroes, Villains, and Authors," *Saga-Book of the Viking Society for Northern Research* 20[1978-1979]:72-75) also discusses this episode in light of the saga author's use of the law.

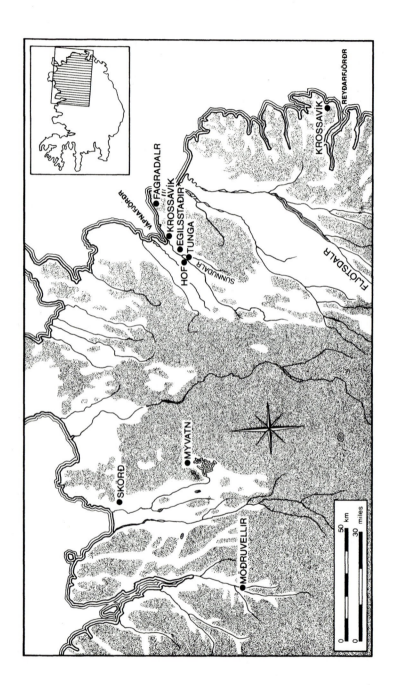

REYDARFJÖRDR

KROSSAVIK

KROSSAVIK

FAGRADALR

VAPNAFJÖRDR

KROSSAVIK

EGILSSTADIR

TUNGA

HOF

SUNNUDALR

FLJOTSDALR

MYVATN

SKÖRD

MÖDRUVELLIR

50 km

30 miles

Map 8. The arena of conflict in the contest between Geitir and Brodd-Helgi from *Vápnfirðinga saga*, showing locations of the participants. The exact sites of the farms at Fljótsdalr, Mývatn, and Tunga are not known. The site of the spring assembly in Sunnudalr was probably close to the farms of Hof and Tunga.

Brodd-Helgi Thorgilsson (chieftain)	Hof
Stout Ketill	Fljótsdalr
Egill Steinbjarnarson	Egilsstaðir
Geitir Lýtingsson (chieftain)	(1) Krossavík in Vápnafjörðr
	(2) Fagradalr
Guðmundr the Powerful (chieftain)	Möðruvellir
Ófeigr Járngerðarson	Skörð
Thórðr	Tunga
Thorleifr the Christian	Krossavík in Reyðarfjörðr
Thormóðr Steinbjarnarson	In Sunnudalr
Ölvir the Wise	Mývatn

wealth or power. Although lacking grounds for prosecution, he patiently waits for an opportunity to lay a claim against Thorleifr. The outlook is not promising, for Thorleifr's farm Krossavík, unlike the holdings of Brodd-Helgi and Geitir, is not in Vápnafjörðr but in Reyðarfjörðr, farther to the south and down the coast. Moreover, Thorleifr is not a rash man and seems to have no obvious enemies. If Brodd-Helgi is to seek vengeance, he must operate at a considerable distance from home and devise a means of attack.

Thorleifr is in a much better position than Hrafn had been. As an Icelandic *bóndi* he enjoys the full rights and prerogatives of his socially defined position. Should Brodd-Helgi kill a *bóndi* without cause, it would be difficult and expensive for him to defend himself in the courts against an alliance of enemies. A skillfully handled prosecution would certainly set him back and perhaps even destroy him.

Despite his rash temper and overbearing manner, Brodd-Helgi funnels his animosity into socially acceptable channels. His determination to keep his thirst for vengeance within lawful bounds is demonstrated in his attempt to entrap Thorleifr, for which an opportunity soon opens up. Steinvör, a priestess in charge of collecting dues for a local temple, complains to her relative Brodd-Helgi that Thorleifr has, as a Christian, refused to pay the temple tax. Brodd-Helgi, hoping to escalate this refusal into an adjudication, initiates a series of complicated maneuvers, described by the saga author with seeming relish.

Our understanding of this new cluster of events would be clearer if we knew whose thingman Thorleifr was. Jón Jóhannesson suggests that Thorleifr may have been a thingman of Steinvör, the temple priestess.[3] At that time a woman could inherit a *goðorð*, although she had to empower a man to act on her behalf. Because Thorleifr is known from other extant sources, among them *Kristni þáttr* in *Óláfs saga Tryggvasonar en mesta*, it is possible that the author left out this in-

3. *ÍF* 11, p. 33, n. 1.

formation on the assumption that his audience had prior knowledge of the *bóndi*.

Brodd-Helgi's first tactic is to form an alliance with a farmer living closer to Thorleifr. Traveling inland to Fljótsdalr (River Valley), he pays an unexpected visit to Digr-Ketill (Stout Ketill), a *bóndi* described as a most worthy person. Although the two men hardly know each other, they soon swear *vinfengi*. Brodd-Helgi then asks the unsuspecting Ketill to implement their new agreement by prosecuting Thorleifr for failing to pay his temple tax. Brodd-Helgi has devised a clever scheme: once he is summoned by Ketill, Thorleifr will think he is merely facing another *bóndi*. Put off his guard by this ruse, Thorleifr will be unprepared in the court when he suddenly finds himself confronted by a powerful chieftain with his armed thingmen.

Surprised and perhaps angered by Brodd-Helgi's devious request, Ketill protests, but nevertheless he honors the agreement: "I would not have sworn *vinfengi* with you, had I known what was at the bottom of it, for Thorleifr is a man with many friends [*maðr vinsæll*]. Still, I won't refuse you this first time" (ch. 5). Ketill rides to Krossavík in Reyðarfjörðr and at first tries to persuade Thorleifr to pay the nominal temple fee. When Thorleifr flatly refuses, Ketill summons him, probably to the Fljótsdalr district spring assembly.

After the summons is issued a violent storm prevents Ketill from leaving; Thorleifr offers him and his men hospitality for several days. As he leaves, Ketill gratefully pledges his friendship to Thorleifr and promises to invalidate the case against him. Thorleifr tells Ketill that "your *vinfengi* is of great value to me, but it does not matter to me whether or not the case holds up" (ch. 5).

Brodd-Helgi arrives at the thing with a large following, but Ketill keeps his promise and the case against Thorleifr comes to nothing. Finding his plans frustrated, Brodd-Helgi reproaches Ketill for deceiving him and announces that "our *vinfengi* is over." The saga tells us that Brodd-Helgi is unable to get a "hold on Thorleifr, and he [Thorleifr] is now out of this saga" (ch. 5).

After leaving the thing Brodd-Helgi bitterly reproaches Geitir for the humiliation of the failed legal suit, although it is by no means certain that Geitir had anything to do with the fiasco. At this point the rift between the two chieftains widens into feud; the sagaman has been preparing his audience for this development by relating the events that have gradually been alienating the former friends. The prelude to the wider conflict could have been far simpler, but saga narrative is distinguished by complicated machinations just like these. Brodd-Helgi's quarrel with Geitir escalates from a simple difference between two friends to a fierce struggle for power. Brodd-Helgi's actions against the more passive Geitir proceed in the manner prescribed by the guidelines of Icelandic feud.

Struggle to Claim a Dowry

Just as Brodd-Helgi earlier avoided committing a random act of violence against Thorleifr, he now adopts the same cautious approach to Geitir. As the tale develops Brodd-Helgi is guided not only by malice toward Geitir but also by his desire for political gain. To achieve his end Brodd-Helgi uses the law at every opportunity. He seizes on any claim, however spurious, to entrap his enemy and backs it with all his strength. In aiming for the destruction of Geitir, Brodd-Helgi, like Arnkell goði in *Eyrbyggja saga*, is challenging the tradition of consensual order. If Geitir is eliminated as a viable force, Brodd-Helgi will dominate the area and might be able to destroy the system of nonterritorial leadership which protects the rights of the farmers. On a wider scale, by disturbing the balance on which the Icelandic political system rests, he might pose a threat even to other, more distant, chieftains.

A new point of contention arises when both chieftains lay claim to the dowry of Halla, Geitir's sister and Brodd-Helgi's wife. Halla, dying of a lingering illness, has graciously allowed her husband to replace her in the household, but she is humiliated by Brodd-Helgi's immediate engagement to a young widow. This act, the saga tells us, is widely condemned in the district, as Halla is well liked.

At first Brodd-Helgi persuades Halla to remain at Hof until his new wife arrives, but Geitir and his brother send men to bring her home to Krossavík. The separation raises a series of questions. As a party to the dissolved marriage Halla has the right to repossess her dowry, perhaps adding to it a share of the profit that has accrued from its use during the union. Brodd-Helgi, however, has no intention of dividing up the property. His plan shows how cunning he is: he simply ignores Halla's intention to separate from him before her death. As she is removing her personal possessions, "Helgi stood outside the doorway and acted as if he did not know that Halla was leaving" (ch. 6). When Brodd-Helgi refuses to honor Geitir's demand that he pay Halla a sum equal to the value of her remaining property, Geitir regards the refusal as an insult.

Geitir's subsequent attempts to obtain a money payment (*penninga*) for the value of his sister's property are equally fruitless. Brodd-Helgi refuses to relinquish his control of Halla's property, saying that he hopes she will yet return to Hof. As a negotiated settlement is not possible the next step would be a legal case, but here too Brodd-Helgi shows his ability to thwart Geitir. Brodd-Helgi's reasoning is simple: he is in possession of the lands, and he thus will be taking a chance of losing the property if he allows the issue to go to court. Geitir, on the other hand, has a strong legal case when, and if, he can get to court.

To block Geitir, Brodd-Helgi seeks to deny him access to legal process. In the spring, when Geitir summons Brodd-Helgi to the local Sunnudalr Thing, he has the ablest men on his side. But Brodd-Helgi, with a larger group of thing-men, manages to bar Geitir from the site of the court. When Geitir summons his adversary to the Althing, Brodd-Helgi, backed by Guðmundr the Powerful, is once again successful in having Geitir's case voided. The dispute has still not been resolved[4] after two attempts. As the conflict continues, the animosity between the two *goðar* understandably deepens. The contention over Halla's dowry is more serious than the earlier disputes between the two leaders. Dowries consisted of heirlooms, farm implements, livestock, land, and perhaps a portion of a family's known monetary wealth. In the social context of a family's control over its destiny, the dowry had a value higher than its monetary worth. Seizing on the importance of the issue, Brodd-Helgi has chosen to make the retention of Halla's dowry a test of his ability to humiliate his opponent and to ignore due process. In the eyes of the community, Brodd-Helgi's refusal to accept the customary way of settling disputes is a signal that reveals his intention to strip Geitir of his authority and gain control over the local region for himself.

Skirmishes over a Woodland

Brodd-Helgi, having thwarted Geitir's efforts to settle the dowry issue legally, now seeks to end Geitir's role as a leader of local *bændr*. His opportunity comes in a dispute between two neighboring farmers, Thórðr from Tunga in Sunnudalr and Thormóðr Steinbjarnarson, one of Geitir's thingmen. Brodd-Helgi assumes Thórðr's part ownership of the woodland (see chapter 8), then ruthlessly harasses and finally kills Thormóðr. Geitir again loses face when he is unable to bury his thingman or to exact compensation from Brodd-Helgi for the killing.

Seeking a Thingman's Allegiance

The saga next tells us that a ship skippered by Thórarinn Egilsson arrives in Vápnafjörðr. At this point some of the genealogical information supplied by the sagaman at the start of his story becomes significant. Thórarinn is one of

---

4. For narrative and social aspects of resolutions, see Jesse L. Byock, "Dispute Resolution in the Sagas," *Gripla* 6(1984):86-100.

the promising younger members of a prominent family of local *bændr* who are Geitir's thingmen. Thórarinn's father, Egill from Egilsstaðir, is the brother of Thormóðr from Sunnudalr, the farmer whom Brodd-Helgi killed in the dispute over the woodland at Tunga and for whom he never paid compensation. Thórarinn is the brother of Hallfríðr, the first wife of Geitir's son Thorkell.

Brodd-Helgi now directs his attention to the newly returned trader Thórarinn. Should Brodd-Helgi succeed in entering into a *vinfengi* relationship with Thórarinn, he might be able to detach Thórarinn and perhaps other members of his family from Geitir. Such a shift in allegiance would endanger Geitir, for these *bændr* are among his most able thingmen. In describing the contest for Thórarinn's allegiance the sagaman plays on divisions in the community caused by a competition between chieftains (ch. 11):

> Brodd-Helgi rode to the ship and invited Thórarinn, and as many of his men as he wanted to bring along, to lodge at his farm. When Thórarinn said that he would accept the invitation, Helgi went home to announce that his household should expect Captain Thórarinn as their guest.
>
> Geitir also went to the ship to meet Thórarinn, and asked if he intended to go to Hof. Thórarinn said that the matter had been spoken of but had not been decided upon. Geitir told Thórarinn that it would be better for him to come to Krossavík "because, as I see it, few of my men do well for themselves in accepting Helgi's hospitality." The result was that Thórarinn decided to go to Krossavík.
>
> Brodd-Helgi, hearing of this arrangement, immediately rode to the ship with horses already saddled, intending to take Thórarinn home with him. Thórarinn told Helgi that things had now been decided differently. And Helgi replied, "I wish to show you that I invited you to my house without deceit and that I will bear you no animosity if you go to Krossavík." The next day Helgi rode to the ship again and gave Thórarinn five stud horses, all dandelion yellow, for the sake of his *vinfengi*.
>
> Geitir went to fetch Thórarinn and asked the trader whether he had received the stud horses from Brodd-Helgi. Thórarinn said that he had. "Then I counsel you," said Geitir, "to return those stud horses." Thórarinn did so, and Helgi took back the stud horses.

Thórarinn stayed with Geitir through the winter and went abroad the following summer.

Brodd-Helgi Breaks Vinfengi

Beginning with the death of a foreigner and continuing through a quarrel between two local farmers, the saga has chronicled the growing feud between the two *goðar*. With each stage the story has come closer to disturbing the fragile relationship between *goðar* and *bændr*. From this point on the quarrel penetrates more deeply into the community, forcing local farmers and also distant chieftains to take sides.

The saga suggests that Brodd-Helgi is disadvantaged not so much by his basic greed as by the method that he chooses to satisfy it. As the story progresses he ignores the norms of reciprocity which govern relationships between chieftains. Arrogantly disregarding the danger inherent in provocative conduct, Brodd-Helgi breaks *vinfengi* agreements and makes new enemies. On one occasion at the Althing, he refuses to keep a bargain made with his "friend" Guðmundr inn ríki (ch. 10):

> One summer Brodd-Helgi lacked support at the Althing, and he asked Guðmundr the Powerful for assistance. But Guðmundr said he was not inclined to help Helgi at every thing meeting, thereby putting himself on unfriendly terms [*óvinsæla sik*] with other chieftains and getting no benefit from Helgi in return. Whereupon they settled the matter, Guðmundr promising to aid Helgi in return for half a hundred of silver.[5] When the court was dismissed and Helgi's case had gone well he and Guðmundr met at the booths, and Guðmundr claimed the payment from Helgi. But Helgi said that he had no obligation to pay; moreover, he added, he did not see why he should have to pay within their *vinfengi* relationship. Guðmundr answered, "It is poorly done on your part always to be in need of others, but not to pay what you have promised. And your *vinfengi* seems worth little to me. I will never ask for this money again; nor will I ever help you again." Then they parted, with their *vinfengi* at an end.

5. "Hálft hundrað silfrs." A "hundred" was actually 120, so Brodd-Helgi is offering 60 aurar of silver.

When Geitir heard about this dispute he went to meet with Guðmundr, offering him payment in return for his *vinfengi*. Guðmundr refused to take Geitir's money, saying that he had little desire to help men who always accepted the meaner lot in all their dealings with Helgi.

Although less violent than Brodd Helgi, Geitir is not averse to scheming to increase his own wealth and power. He shows no remorse for having helped to kill the Norwegian; indeed, his desire to acquire Hrafn's goods was obvious. But as a leader Geitir avoids bullying tactics. And, in contrast with Brodd-Helgi, he is not willing to risk his life in violent confrontation, whatever its guise of legality. Geitir's strength lies in his ability to manipulate the defensive aspects of the legal system. Each of the two rival leaders, in his own way, pushes the definition of acceptable action to its limits. The struggle between them reveals the faults and the dangers in their respective positions.

By his aggressiveness in his feud with Geitir, Brodd-Helgi forces the local *bændr* to divide into two camps. Whether enticed or threatened, many of Geitir's thingmen desert their leader and align themselves with Brodd-Helgi. Geitir's remaining thingmen are in an increasingly difficult position. They are like Snorri goði's faithful followers, the sons of Thorbrandr in *Eyrbyggja saga*, in that they must make their *goði* act or seek other alliances.

Geitir Establishes Vinfengi

In *Vápnfirðinga saga* Geitir's loyal followers also choose to protect their rights and property by inciting their defensive leader to act. Upon his return from his voyage Thórarinn Egilsson finds that Geitir has timidly moved from Krossavík to a farm called Fagradalr, farther away from Brodd-Helgi. Many thingmen have left Geitir, and the region is almost completely under the fist of Brodd-Helgi. The only hope is inciting Geitir to act. As spokesman for Geitir's thingmen, the trader Thórarinn Egilsson presents Geitir with an ultimatum (ch. 11):

The thingmen of Geitir took counsel together and decided they could no longer tolerate Brodd-Helgi's *ójafnaðr*. They traveled to meet with Geitir. Thórarinn asked, "How long is it going to go on like this? Until everything comes to a bad end? Many men are leaving you now, and they all attach themselves to Helgi. We consider your timidity the sole reason you hold back from going against Helgi. You are the more clever of the two and, moreover, you have no fewer brave men with you than he has with him. And now, for our part, there are two choices: either you travel home to your farm at Krossavík, never move from it again, and take action against Helgi should he henceforth do you any dishonor, or we will sell our farms and move away, some from the country, and some from the district."

The thingmen of Geitir have the courage and the motivation to attack and kill an aggressive *goði*. They are unwilling, however, to become tragic characters in the manner of Gísli Súrsson, who acted intemperately and killed a chieftain when his sense of honor was violated. Recognizing their legal impotence, the few farmers who remain loyal to Geitir force the burden of action to shift from the aggressive Brodd-Helgi to their defensive leader. It is the latter who must seize an opportunity to attack and kill his rival and yet avoid disaster in the courts. The attack, to be successful, must catch the rival off guard.

In their ability to blunt the legal counterclaim after killing a fellow chieftain, Geitir and Snorri goði show their astuteness. They play a waiting game. Both manage to convince their peers that the killing was the best alternative for them and for their district. In *Eyrbyggja saga* Snorri's precourt political dealings are not detailed. Instead, the sagaman simply recounts Snorri's success in defending himself and his thingmen after the killing of Arnkell. *Vápnfirðinga saga* describes Geitir's journey through the northeastern part of the country before he moves back to Krossavík. The journey enables Geitir to test the waters and to see whether there is enough support from the other *goðar* for the killing of Brodd-Helgi. One result of Geitir's new offensive posture is that Guðmundr inn ríki from Möðruvellir is now willing to support him. Another factor in Geitir's favor is Brodd-Helgi's repeated lack of *hóf* (ch. 12):

Geitir prepared for a trip and went north to Skarð in Ljósavatn[6] to Ófeigr Járngerðarson. Guðmundr the Powerful came [to Ófeigr's farm] to meet Geitir and the two sat the whole day in conversation. Later they parted, and Geitir took lodging with Ölvir inn spaki [the Wise] at his farm in Mývatn. Ölvir questioned Geitir carefully about Brodd-Helgi. Geitir spoke well of him, saying that Brodd-Helgi was a most important person, stubborn and harsh but a good man in many ways. "Is he not a great *ójafnaðarmaðr?*" asked Ölvir. "Helgi's *ójafnaðr,*" Geitir answered, "affects me most in that Helgi finds it disagreeable to have the same sky over me as over him." Ölvir responded, "Shall all this, then, be tolerated?" "It has been until now," said Geitir. Thus they ended their talk, and Geitir traveled home. Now all was quiet for the rest of the winter.

The saga moves quickly to a resolution of the contest. Although the manuscript of the saga is damaged at this spot, the outlines of the action seem clear. Geitir, with his trusted thingmen, ambushes and kills Brodd-Helgi while the latter is on his way to the thing with only a few men. In the ensuing court case Geitir, supported by his new friend Guðmundr the Powerful, reaches an advantageous settlement with Brodd-Helgi's son Bjarni.[7] By its terms Geitir retains his *goðorð*. He pays Bjarni an honorable compensation and a few of his followers are banished for a time—a small price to pay for the demise of Brodd-Helgi. Geitir resumes his position as a respected *goði* of the district and treats his nephew Bjarni well. Eventually Bjarni's stepmother incites him to kill Geitir, an act which he regrets immediately and which causes him to be pursued by Geitir's inept son Thorkell. In the end the two cousins resolve their differences honorably.

6. Skörð is the plural of Skarð (a mountain pass), and both words are place names. The saga says Skarð, but Ófeigr lived at Skörð in Reykjahverfi (see map 6). Skarð in Ljósavatn (Ljósavatnsskarð) is the name of a wide gap in the mountains about midway between the farms Skörð and Möðruvellir.

7. Bjarni was the son of Brodd-Helgi and Halla, Geitir's sister.

SUMMARY

Like *Eyrbyggja saga*, *Vápnfirðinga saga* illustrates ways in which wealth changes hands and in which power is dependent upon networks of kin, thingmen, advocacy, and *vinfengi* ties. When a single leader attains hegemony in a region, it causes farmers in this lateral society more unease than a similar situation might in European societies dominated by territorial lordship, where loyalty and control were often defined by the location of one's land. It would seem that the farmers in Iceland often had more alternative courses of action than did farmers elsewhere in northern Europe because the shifting intrigues of power were not bound by territorial constraints. As seen in *Eyrbyggja saga* and *Vápnfirðinga saga*, however, Icelandic *bændr* also had the responsibility to find their own solutions when faced with an *ójafnaðarmaðr*'s infringement of their rights.

11

Conclusion

The family and Sturlunga sagas are a rich source of information on wealth and power in medieval Iceland. These stories are based on patterns and structures that reflect the functioning of a centuries-old system of consensual order. Along with references to the laws and to the known history of Iceland, I have relied on saga narrative to explore the dynamic of power operative in the early centuries of the Icelandic Free State. I have also used these narrative sources to explore the ways in which the chieftains acquired wealth, primarily land, from the more vulnerable *bændr*.

In the tenth century the settlers of Iceland developed a system of government which differed from those the immigrants left behind in their European homelands. Even the church, after the conversion to Christianity in 1000, was less an independent power to be reckoned with than in contemporaneous Western societies. Only toward the end of the Free State did a small group of powerful chieftains, the *stór-goðar*, come close to gaining centralized executive authority. This study distinguishes between the governmental order operating in Norse societies closer to the European mainland and the unusual structure that emerged in Free State Iceland. Throughout I have sought to determine the underlying patterns and systems of exchange which enabled a headless society with a cultural focus on law to function as a cohesive body politic. At the core of Iceland's consensual order was a highly developed system of reciprocity among landowning farmers and chieftains. Especially significant were the ties of mutual obligation between *goði* and thingman and advocacy relationships.

The *goðar* derived some advantage over prosperous farmers from taxes, certain aspects of trade, and the revenue generated by governmental duties. The exercise of such exclusive rights, however, did not consistently bring to these leaders incomes large enough to offset the costs of leadership. Instead, the wealth of the *goðar*, like that of the *bændr*, was based primarily on ownership of productive lands, including church farmsteads (*staðir*). But land, because it was scarce in Iceland and often subject to family inheritance rights, was difficult to acquire.

How, then, did some chieftains maintain their prominence and others increase their wealth and power? Scholars have chosen to skirt this central question by assuming, or even asserting, that chieftains did not reap significant profits from their position of leadership. This long-accepted view (discussed in chapter 5) has prevented a clear understanding of the ties of interdependence which united chieftains and farmers. In fact, a *goði* did have the opportunity to derive a substantial income from control of a chieftaincy. Because of the manner in which advocacy arrangements dominated the exercise of authority, chieftains were in a uniquely advantageous position to acquire property from *bændr*. These freemen, when threatened by violence, an encroaching claim, or the ramifications of feud, sought the services and the protection that *goðar* were best able to provide. As the examples taken from the family and early Sturlunga sagas illustrate, the chieftain's price was sometimes so high as to ruin the farmer. At other times the outcome did not favor the *goði*, as Iceland's consensual system was not one-sided. Ambition and greed in Icelandic leaders often led to aggression, and aggression triggered a host of countermeasures allowing the system to remain in balance for several centuries.

Sources of Epigraphs

Dedication page.
Jónas Kristjánsson, "The Roots of the Sagas." In *Sagnaskemmtun: Studies in Honour of Hermann Pálsson on his 65th Birthday, 26th May 1986*, ed. Rudolf Simek, Jónas Kristjánsson, and Hans Bekker-Nielsen, Philologica Germanica 8 (Vienna: Hermann Böhlaus Nachf., 1986), p. 187.

Chapter 1.
Landnámabók, ed. Jakob Benediktsson, ÍF 1 (S2), pp. 32, 34.

Chapter 2.
Landnámabók, ed. Jakob Benediktsson, ÍF 1, cii (*Thórðarbók*).
Richard F. Tomasson, *Iceland: The First New Society* (Minneapolis: University of Minnesota Press, 1980), p. 4.

Chapter 3.
W. P. Ker, *Epic and Romance: Essays on Medieval Literature* (London 1896; New York: Dover, 1957), pp. 200-201.
Victor W. Turner, "An Anthropological Approach to the Icelandic Saga," in *The Translation of Culture: Essays to E. E. Evans-Pritchard*, ed. T. O. Beidelman (London: Tavistock Publications, 1971), p. 352.

Chapter 4.
History of the Archbishops of Hamburg-Bremen, by Adam of Bremen, trans. Francis J. Tschan, Columbia University Records of Civilization 53 (New York: Columbia University Press, 1959), p. 217 (Book 4, ch. 36).

Hákonar saga Hákonarsonar, ed. Marina Mundt, Norrøne tekster 2 (Oslo: Norsk historisk kjeldeskrift-institutt, 1977), p. 144.

Chapter 5.
James Bryce, *Studies in History and Jurisprudence*, vol. 1 (Freeport, N.Y.: Books for Libraries Press, 1968), p. 280.

Chapter 6.
Robert A. LeVine, "The Internalization of Political Values in Stateless Societies," *Human Organization* 19(1960):58.
James Bryce, *Studies in History and Jurisprudence*, vol. 1 (Freeport, N.Y.: Books for Libraries Press, 1968), p. 285.

Chapter 7.
Guðmundar saga dýra, ch. 4, in *Sturlunga saga*, ed. Jón Jóhannesson, Magnús Finnbogason, and Kristján Eldjárn, vol. 1 (Reykjavik: Sturlunguútgáfan, 1946), p. 168.

Chapter 8.
M. I. Steblin-Kamenskij, *The Saga Mind*, trans. Kenneth H. Ober (Odense: Odense University Press, 1973), p. 94.

Chapter 10.
Hávamál, stanza 64, in Hans Kuhn, ed., *Edda: Die Lieder des Codex Regius nebst verwandten Denkmälern* (Heidelberg: Carl Winter Universitätsverlag, 1962), p. 27.

Abbreviations

DI   *Diplomatarium Islandicum: Íslenzkt fornbréfasafn.*
16 vols. Copenhagen and Reykjavik: S. L.
Möller and Hið íslenzka bókmentafélag, 1857-
1952.

GG   *Grágás.* Ed. Vilhjálmur Finsen. 3 vols. Vol. I
a-b, *Grágás: Islændernes Lovbog i Fristatens Tid,*
udgivet efter det kongelige Bibliotheks Haandskrift.
Copenhagen: Brødrene Berlings Bogtrykkeri,
1852. Vol. II: *Grágás efter det Arnamagnæanske*
Haandskrift Nr. 334 fol., Staðarhólsbók. Copenhagen: Gyldendalske Boghandel, 1879. Vol.
III: *Grágás: Stykker, som findes i det Arna-*
magnæanske Haandskrift Nr. 351 fol. Skálholtsbók
og en Række andre Haandskrifter. Copenhagen:
Gyldendalske Boghandel, 1883.

ÍF   *Íslenzk fornrit.* Reykjavik: Hið íslenzka fornritafélag, 1933-.

KLNM   *Kulturhistoriskt lexikon för nordisk medeltid.* 22
vols. Malmö: Allhems förlag, 1956-1978.

Saga Íslands   Sigurður Líndal, ed. *Saga Íslands.* 3 vols.
Reykjavik: Hið íslenzka bókmenntafélag,
Sögufélagið, 1974-1978.

Sturl.   *Sturlunga saga.* Ed. Jón Jóhannesson, Magnús
Finnbogason, and Kristján Eldjárn. 2 vols.
Reykjavik: Sturlunguútgáfan, 1946.

Bibliography

Abel, Richard L. "A Comparative Theory of Dispute Institutions in Society." *Law and Society Review* 8(1973):216-347.

Aðalsteinsson, Jón Hnefill. *Under the Cloak: The Acceptance of Christianity in Iceland with Particular Reference to the Religious Attitudes Prevailing at the Time.* Acta Universitatis Upsaliensis, Studia Ethnologica Upsaliensia 4. Stockholm: Almqvist and Wiksell, 1978.

Adam of Bremen. *History of the Archbishops of Hamburg-Bremen.* Trans. Francis J. Tschan. Columbia University Records of Civilization 53. New York: Columbia University Press, 1959.

Agnarsdóttir, Anna, and Árnason, Ragnar. "Þrælahald á þjóðveldisöld." *Saga* 21(1983):5-26.

Amory, Frederic. "Narrative Syntax in the Typical Saga Scene." *Journal of English and Germanic Philology* 79(1980):390-407.

Andersen, Per Sveaas. *Samlingen av Norge og kristningen av landet 800-1130.* Handbok i Norges historie 2. Bergen: Universitetsforlaget, 1977.

Andersson, Theodore M. *The Problem of Icelandic Saga Origins: A Historical Survey.* Yale Germanic Studies 1. New Haven: Yale University Press, 1964.

Árnason, Vilhjálmur. "Saga og siðferði: Hugleiðingar um túlkun á siðfræði Íslendingasagna." *Tímarit Máls og menningar* 46(1985):21-37.

Arnórsson, Einar. "Alþingi árið 930." *Skírnir* 104(1930):6-48.

―――. "Alþingi árið 1000." *Skírnir* 104(1930):68-106.

―――. "Alþingi árið 1262." *Skírnir* 104(1930):116-134.

―――. *Réttarsaga Alþingis.* Reykjavik: Alþingissögunefnd, 1945.

Arvidsson, Rolf. "Source-Criticism and Literary History: Lauritz Weibull, Henrik Schück and Joseph Bédier: A Discussion." *Mediaeval Scandinavia* 5(1972):96-138.

Baetke, Walter, ed. *Die Isländersaga.* Wege der Forschung 151. Darmstadt: Wissenschaftliche Buchgesellschaft, 1974.

Bagge, Sverre. "Borgerkrig og statsutvikling i Norge i middelalderen." *Historisk tidsskrift* 65(1986):145-197.

―――. "The Formation of the State and Concepts of Society in 13th Century Norway." In *Continuity and Change: Political Institu-*

tions and Literature in the Middle Ages, ed. Elisabeth Vestergaard, pp. 43-59. Proceedings of the Tenth International Symposium Organized by the Center for the Study of Vernacular Literature in the Middle Ages. Odense: Odense University Press, 1986.

Bandamanna saga. Ed. Guðni Jónsson. ÍF 7, pp. 291-363. 1936.

Bauman, Richard. "Performance and Honor in 13th-Century Iceland." *Journal of American Folklore* 99(1986):131-150.

Beck, Heinrich. "*Laxdæla saga*—A Structural Approach." *Saga-Book of the Viking Society for Northern Research* 19(1977):383-402.

Bekker-Nielsen, Hans. "Frode mænd og tradition." In *Norrøn fortællekunst: kapitler af den norsk-islandske middelalderlitteraturs historie*, ed. Hans Bekker-Nielsen, Thorkil Damsgaard Olsen, and Ole Widding, pp. 35-41. Copenhagen: Akademisk forlag, 1965.

Benediktsson, Jakob. "Landnámabók: Some Remarks on Its Value as a Historical Source." *Saga-Book of the Viking Society for Northern Research* 17(1969):275-292.

————. "Landnám og upphaf allsherjarríkis." In *Saga Íslands* 1:153-196.

————. "Markmið Landnámabókar: Nýjar rannsóknir." *Skírnir* 148(1974):207-215.

Benediktsson, Jakob, ed. *Hugtök og heiti í bókmenntafræði.* Reykjavik: Mál og menning, 1983.

Benson, Robert L. "Election by Community and Chapter: Reflections on Co-Responsibility in the Historical Church." *The Jurist* 31(1971):54-80.

————. "The Gelasian Doctrine: Uses and Transformations." In *La notion de l'authorité au moyen âge: Islam, Byzance, Occident*, ed. George Makdisi, Dominique Sourdel, and Janine Sourdel-Thomine, pp. 1-44. Paris: Presses Universitaires de France, 1982.

Berger, Alan. "Lawyers in the Old Icelandic Family Sagas: Heroes, Villains, and Authors." *Saga-Book of the Viking Society for Northern Research* 20(1978-79):70-79.

Bergthórsson, Páll. "Kuldaskeið um 1300?" *Veðrið* 12(1967):55-58.

————. "Þroskalíkur byggs á Íslandi." *Veðrið* 10(1965):48-56.

Berman, Melissa A. "*Egils saga* and *Heimskringla*." *Scandinavian Studies* 54(1982):21-50.

Bibire, Paul. "Verses in the Íslendingasögur." In *Alþjóðlegt fornsagnaþing, Reykjavík, 1973.* Reykjavik: International Association for Scandinavian Studies, 1973.

Biskupa sögur. Ed. Hið íslenzka bókmentafélag. 2 vols. Copenhagen: S. L. Möllers, 1858-1878. See also *Byskupa sögur.*

Black-Michaud, Jacob. *Cohesive Force: Feud in the Mediterranean and the Middle East.* Oxford: Basil Blackwell, 1975.

Bloch, Marc. *Feudal Society.* Trans. L. A. Manyon. 2 vols. Chicago: University of Chicago Press, 1961.

Bloch, R. Howard. *Medieval French Literature and Law.* Berkeley, Los Angeles, and London: University of California Press, 1977.

Bø, Olav. "Hólmganga and Einvígi: Scandinavian Forms of the Duel." *Mediaeval Scandinavia* 2(1969):132-148.

Bøe, Arne. "Hauld." In *KLNM* 6, cols. 251-254.

Boehm, Christopher. *Blood Revenge: The Anthropology of Feuding in Montenegro and other Tribal Societies.* Lawrence. University Press of Kansas, 1984.

Bongert, Yvonne. *Cours d'histoire du droit pénal français: de la second moitié du XIIIᵉ siècle à l'ordonnance de 1493.* Paris: Cours de droit, 1970.

_____. *Recherches sur les cours laïques du Xᵉ au XIIIᵉ siècle.* Paris: Picard, 1948.

Boyer, Régis. *La Saga de Snorri le Godi (Eyrbyggja Saga).* Paris: Aubier Montaigne, 1973.

_____. "L'évêque Gudmundr Arason, témoin de son temps." *Études Germaniques* 3(1967):427-444

_____. *Les sagas islandaises.* Paris: Payot, 1978.

Bryce, James. *Studies in History and Jurisprudence.* 2 vols. 1901. Freeport, N.Y.: Books for Libraries Press, 1968.

Byock, Jesse L. "The Age of the Sturlungs." In *Continuity and Change: Political Institutions and Literary Monuments in the Middle Ages,* ed. Elisabeth Vestergaard, pp. 27-42. Proceedings of the Tenth International Symposium Organized by the Center for the Study of Vernacular Literature in the Middle Ages. Odense: Odense University Press, 1986.

_____. "Cultural Continuity, the Church, and the Concept of Independent Ages in Medieval Iceland." *Skandinavistik* 15/1(1985):1-14.

_____. "The Dark Figure as Survivor in an Icelandic Saga." In *The Dark Figure in Medieval German and Germanic Literature,* ed. Edward R. Haymes and Stephanie Cain Van D'Elden, pp. 151-163. Göppinger Arbeiten zur Germanistik 448. Göppingen: Kümmerle Verlag, 1986.

_____. "Dispute Resolution in the Sagas." *Gripla* 6(1984):86-100.

_____. *Feud in the Icelandic Saga.* Berkeley, Los Angeles, and London: University of California Press, 1982.

_____. "Governmental Order in Early Medieval Iceland." *Viator* 17(1986):19-34.

_____. "'Milliganga': Félagslegar rætur Íslendingasagna." *Tímarit Máls og menningar* 47(1986):96-104.

_____. "The Narrative Strategy of Small Feud Stories." In *Les Sagas de Chevaliers (Riddarasögur),* ed. Régis Boyer, pp. 405-415. Civilisations 10. Paris: Presses de l'Université de Paris-Sorbonne, 1985.

————. "The Power and Wealth of the Icelandic Church: Some Talking Points." In *The Sixth International Saga Conference 1985*, vol. 1, pp. 89-101. Copenhagen: Det arnamagnæanske Institut, 1985.

————. "Saga Form, Oral Prehistory, and the Icelandic Social Context." *New Literary History* 16(1984-85):153-173.

Byskupa sögur. Ed. Guðni Jónsson. 3 vols. [Akureyri]: Íslendingasagnaútgáfan, Haukadalsútgáfan, 1953. See also *Biskupa sögur*.

Byskupa sögur. Ed. Jón Helgason for Det kongelige nordiske oldskriftselskap. Copenhagen: Munksgaard, 1938. (Now considered as Editiones Arnamagnæanæ, ser. A, 13, pt. 1.)

Byskupa sögur. Ed. Jón Helgason. Editiones Arnamagnæanæ, ser. A, 13, pt. 2. Copenhagen: Reitzel, 1978.

Chaney, William A. *The Cult of Kingship in Anglo-Saxon England: The Transition from Paganism to Christianity.* Berkeley, Los Angeles, and London: University of California Press, 1970.

Chestnutt, Michael. "Popular and Learned Elements in the Icelandic Saga Tradition." In *Proceedings of the First International Saga Conference, University of Edinburgh, 1971*, ed. Peter Foote, Hermann Pálsson, and Desmond Slay, pp. 28-65. London: Viking Society for Northern Research, 1973.

————. "An Unsolved Problem in Old Norse-Icelandic History." *Mediaeval Scandinavia* 1(1968):122-137.

Ciklamini, Marlene. "The Old Icelandic Duel." *Scandinavian Studies* 35(1963):175-194.

Cleasby-Vigfusson. See *Icelandic-English Dictionary*.

Clover, Carol J. *The Medieval Saga.* Ithaca and London: Cornell University Press, 1982.

Conroy, Patricia. "*Laxdæla saga* and *Eiríks saga rauða*: Narrative Structure." *Arkiv för nordisk filologi* 95(1980):116-125.

Dennis, Andrew. "*Grágás*: An Examination of the Content and Technique of the Old Icelandic Law Books, Focused on Þingskapaþáttr (the 'Assembly Section')." Ph.D. dissertation, Cambridge University, 1973.

Dillmann, François-Xavier. *Culture & Civilisation vikings.* Caen: Publications du Centre de Recherches sur les Pays du Nord et du Nord-Ouest de l'Université de Caen, 1975.

Diplomatarium Islandicum: Íslenzkt fornbréfasafn. 16 vols. Copenhagen and Reykjavik: S. L. Möller and Hið íslenzka bókmentafélag, 1857-1952. Abbreviated *DI*.

Dronke, Ursula. *The Role of Sexual Themes in Njáls Saga.* The Dorothea Coke Memorial Lecture in Northern Studies, University College, London, 27 May 1980. London: Viking Society for Northern Research, 1980.

Duby, Georges. *The Early Growth of the European Economy: Warriors and Peasants from the Seventh to the Twelfth Century.* Trans. Howard B. Clarke. Ithaca: Cornell University Press, 1974.

_____. *Rural Economy and Country Life in the Medieval West.* Trans. Cynthia Postan. Columbia: University of South Carolina Press, 1968.

_____. *La société aux XIe et XIIe siècles dans la région mâconnaise.* Paris: Armand Colin, 1953.

_____. *The Three Orders: Feudal Society Imagined.* Trans. Arthur Goldhammer. Chicago: University of Chicago Press, 1980.

Durrenberger, E. Paul. "Sagas, Totems, and History." *Samfélagstíðindi* 5(1985):51-81.

Edda: Die Lieder des Codex Regius nebst verwandten Denkmälern. Ed. Gustav Neckel. 4th ed. Revised by Hans Kuhn. 2 vols. Heidelberg: Carl Winter Universitätsverlag, 1962.

Egils saga Skalla-Grímssonar. Ed. Sigurður Nordal. ÍF 2. 1933.

Einarsdóttir, Ólafía. *Studier i kronologisk metode i tidlig islandsk historieskrivning.* Bibliotheca historica Lundensis 13. Stockholm: Natur och kultur, 1964.

Einarsson, Bjarni. "On the Status of Free Men in Society and Saga." *Mediaeval Scandinavia* 7(1974):45-55.

_____. *To skjaldesagaer: En analyse af Kormáks saga og Hallfreðar saga.* Bergen: Universitetsforlaget, 1976.

Einarsson, Stefán. *A History of Icelandic Literature.* Baltimore: Johns Hopkins University Press, 1957.

_____. *Íslenzk bókmenntasaga 874-1960.* Reykjavik: Snæbjörn Jónsson, 1961.

Ellehøj, Svend. *Studier over den ældste norrøne historieskrivning.* Bibliotheca Arnamagnæana 26. Copenhagen: Munksgaard, 1965.

Evans-Pritchard, Edward Evans. *Kinship and Marriage among the Nuer.* London: Oxford University Press, 1953.

_____. *The Nuer.* London: Oxford University Press, 1940.

Eyrbyggja saga. Ed. Einar Ól. Sveinsson and Matthías Thórðarson. ÍF 4, pp. 1-191. 1935.

Fichtner, Edward G. "Gift Exchange and Initiation in the *Auðunar þáttr vestfirzka.*" *Scandinavian Studies* 51(1979):249-272.

Fidjestøl, Bjarne, et al., eds. *Festskrift til Ludvig Holm-Olsen på hans 70-årsdag den 9. juni 1984.* Øvre Ervik: Alvheim & Eide, 1984.

Finnbogason, Guðmundur. "Alþingi árið 1117." *Skírnir* 104 (1930):107-115.

Finsen, Vilhjálmur. "Om de islandske love i fristatstiden." *Aarbøger for nordisk oldkyndighed og historie,* 1873, pp. 101-250.

_____. *Om den oprindelige ordning af nogle af den islandske fristats institutioner.* Copenhagen: Bianco Lunos Kgl. Hof-Bogtrykkeri, 1888.

The First Grammatical Treatise. Ed. Hreinn Benediktsson. University of Iceland Publications in Linguistics 1. Reykjavik: Institute for Nordic Linguistics, 1972.

Foote, Peter G. "The Audience and Vogue of the Sagas of Icelanders—Some Talking Points." In his *Aurvandilstá: Norse Studies*, pp. 47-55. Odense: Odense University Press, 1984.

_____. "Observations on 'Syncretism' in Early Icelandic Christianity." *Árbók Vísindafélags Íslendinga*, 1974, pp. 69-86.

_____. "On the Conversion of the Icelanders." In his *Aurvandilstá: Norse Studies*, pp. 56-64. Odense: Odense University Press, 1984.

_____. "Oral and Literary Tradition in Early Scandinavian Law: Aspects of a Problem." In *Oral Tradition—Literary Tradition: A Symposium*, ed. Hans Bekker-Nielsen, Peter Foote, Andreas Haarder, and Hans Frede Nielsen, pp. 47-55. Odense: Odense University Press, 1977.

_____. "Secular Attitudes in Early Iceland." *Mediaeval Scandinavia* 7(1974):31-44.

_____. "Some Lines in Lögréttuþáttr." In *Sjötíu ritgerðir helgaðar Jakobi Benediktssyni 20. júlí 1977*, ed. Einar G. Pétursson and Jónas Kristjánsson, pt. 1, pp. 198-207. Reykjavik: Stofnun Árna Magnússonar, 1977.

_____. "Sturlusaga and Its Background." *Saga-Book of the Viking Society for Northern Research* 13(1946-1953):207-237.

_____. "Things in Early Norse Verse." In *Festskrift til Ludvig Holm-Olsen på hans 70-årsdag den 9. juni 1984*, pp. 74-83. Øvre Ervik: Alvheim & Eide, 1984.

_____. "Þrælahald á Íslandi." *Saga* 15(1977):41-74.

Foote, Peter G., and Wilson, David M. *The Viking Achievement: The Society and Culture of Early Medieval Scandinavia*. London: Sidgwick and Jackson, 1970.

Frank, Roberta. "Marriage in Twelfth- and Thirteenth-Century Iceland." *Viator* 4(1973):473-484.

Fried, Morton H. *The Evolution of Political Society*. New York: Random House, 1967.

_____. "On the Evolution of Social Stratification and the State." In *Readings in Anthropology*. Vol. II: *Cultural Anthropology*, ed. Morton H. Fried, pp. 462-478. New York: Thomas Y. Crowell, 1968.

Friedberg, Emil, ed. *Corpus iuris canonici*. 2 vols. Leipzig: B. Tauchnitz, 1879-1881.

Friedman, David. "Private Creation and Enforcement of Law: A Historical Case." *Journal of Legal Studies* 8(1979):399-415.

Fritzner, Johan. *Ordbog over det gamle norske sprog*. Ed. Didrik A. Seip and Trygve Knudsen. 4 vols. Oslo: Tryggve Juul Møller Forlag, 1883-1954.

Fry, Donald K. *Norse Sagas Translated into English: A Bibliography*. AMS Studies in the Middle Ages 3. New York: AMS Press, 1980.

Gade, Kari Ellen. "Hanging in Northern Law and Literature." *Maal og Minne* (1985):159-183.

Gelsinger, Bruce E. *Icelandic Enterprise: Commerce and Economy in the Middle Ages.* Columbia: University of South Carolina Press, 1981.

Gísla saga Súrssonar. Ed. Björn K. Thórólfsson and Guðni Jónsson. ÍF 6, Vestfirðinga sǫgur, pp. 1-118. 1943.

Gluckman, Max. "The Peace in the Feud." *Past and Present* 8(1955):1-14.

Grágás. Ed. Vilhjálmur Finsen. 3 vols. Vol. I a-b: *Grágás: Islændernes Lovbog i Fristatens Tid, udgivet efter det kongelige Bibliotheks Haandskrift.* Copenhagen: Brødrene Berlings Bogtrykkeri, 1852. Vol. II: *Grágás efter det Arnamagnæanske Haandskrift Nr. 334 fol., Staðarhólsbók.* Copenhagen: Gyldendalske Boghandel, 1879. Vol. III: *Grágás: Stykker, som findes i det Arnamagnæanske Haandskrift Nr. 351 fol. Skálholtsbók og en Række andre Haandskrifter.* Copenhagen: Gyldendalske Boghandel, 1883. Abbreviated GG.

[*Grágás*] *Laws of Early Iceland: Grágás I.* Trans. Andrew Dennis, Peter Foote, and Richard Perkins. University of Manitoba Icelandic Studies 3. Winnipeg: University of Manitoba Press, 1980.

Grímsdóttir, Guðrún Ása. "Um afskipti erkibiskupa af íslenzkum málefnum á 12. og 13. öld." *Saga* 20(1982):28-62.

Grimstad, Kaaren. "A Comic Role of the Viking in the Family Sagas." In *Studies for Einar Haugen Presented by Friends and Colleagues*, ed. Evelyn Firchow et al., pp. 243-252. Janua Linguarum Series Maior 59. The Hague: Mouton, 1972.

Guðmundar saga dýra. Sturl. 1, pp. 160-212.

Guðnason, Bjarni. "Theodoricus og íslenskir sagnaritarar." In *Sjötíu ritgerðir helgaðar Jakobi Benediktssyni 20. júlí 1977*, ed. Einar G. Pétursson and Jónas Kristjánsson, pt. 1, pp. 107-120. Reykjavik: Stofnun Árna Magnússonar, 1977.

[*Gulathing Law*] "Den ældre Gulathings-Lov." In *Norges gamle love* 1:1-118.

Gunnarsson, Gísli. *Monopoly Trade and Economic Stagnation: Studies in the Foreign Trade of Iceland, 1602-1787.* Skrifter utgivna av ekonomisk-historiska föreningen i Lund 38. Lund: Studentlitteratur, 1983.

Gurevich [Gurevitj], Aaron J. [Aron Ya.]. "Edda and Law: Commentary upon Hyndlolióð." *Arkiv för nordisk filologi* 88(1973):72-84.

——. *Feodalismens uppkomst i västeuropa.* Trans. Marie-Anne Sahlin. Stockholm: Tidens förlag, 1979.

——. "Representations of Property during the High Middle Ages." *Economy and Society* 6(1977):1-30.

——. "Saga and History: The 'Historical Conception' of Snorri Sturluson." *Mediaeval Scandinavia* 4(1971):42-53.

————. "Wealth and Gift-Bestowal among the Ancient Scandinavians." *Scandinavica* 7(1968):126-138.

Hænsa-Þóris saga. Ed. Sigurður Nordal and Guðni Jónsson. *ÍF* 3, pp. 1-47. 1938.

Hákonar saga Hákonarsonar etter Sth. 8 fol., *AM 325 VIII, 4to og AM 304, 4to*. Ed. Marina Mundt. Norrøne tekster 2. Oslo: Norsk historisk kjeldeskrift-institutt, 1977.

Hallberg, Peter. "The Concept of gipta-gæfa-hamingja in Old Norse Literature." In *Proceedings of the First International Saga Conference, University of Edinburgh, 1971*, ed. Peter Foote, Hermann Pálsson, and Desmond Slay, pp. 143-183. London: Viking Society for Northern Research, 1973.

————. "Forskningsöversikt: Från den norröna forskningsfronten." *Samlaren* 106(1985):67-79.

————. *The Icelandic Saga*. Trans. Paul Schach. Lincoln: University of Nebraska Press, 1962.

————. "Nyare studier i isländsk sagalitteratur." *Samlaren* 93(1972):211-237.

Halldórsson, Ólafur. *Grænland í miðaldaritum*. Reykjavik: Sögufélag, 1978.

Halldórsson, Óskar. "Sögusamúð og stéttir." *Gripla* 1(1975):92-104.

————. *Uppruni og þema Hrafnkels sögu*. Rannsóknastofnun í bókmenntafræði við Háskóla Íslands, Fræðirit 3. Reykjavik: Hið íslenska bókmenntafélag, 1976.

Halvorsen, Eyvind Fjeld. "Dómr: Island." In *KLNM* 3, cols. 217-218.

Harding, Alan. *The Law Courts of Medieval England*. Historical Problems: Studies and Documents 18. London: George Allen & Unwin, 1973.

Harris, Joseph C. "Genre and Narrative Structure in Some Íslendinga Þættir." *Scandinavian Studies* 44(1972):1-27.

Hartz, Louis. *The Founding of New Societies*. New York: Harcourt, Brace, and World, 1964.

Hastrup, Kirsten. "Classification and Demography in Medieval Iceland." *Ethnos* 44(1979):182-191.

————. "Cosmology and Society in Medieval Iceland: A Social Anthropological Perspective on World-View." *Ethnologia Scandinavica*, 1981, pp. 63-78.

————. *Culture and History in Medieval Iceland: An Anthropological Analysis of Structure and Change*. Oxford: Clarendon Press, 1985.

————. "Kinship in Medieval Iceland." *Folk* 23(1981):331-344.

————. "Text and Context: Continuity and Change in Medieval Icelandic History as 'said' and 'laid down.' " In *Continuity and Change: Political Institutions and Literary Monuments in the Middle Ages*, ed.

Elisabeth Vestergaard, pp. 9-25. Proceedings of the Tenth Inter-
national Symposium Organized by the Center for the Study of
Vernacular Literature in the Middle Ages. Odense: Odense Uni-
versity Press, 1986.
Haugen, Einar. *The Scandinavian Languages*. Cambridge: Harvard
University Press, 1976.
Heimskringla, by Snorri Sturluson. Ed. Djarni Aðalbjarnarson. ÍF 26
28. 1941-1951.
Heimskringla: History of the Kings of Norway, trans. Lee M. Hollander.
Austin: University of Texas Press, 1964.
Heinrichs, Anne. "Über Blutrache auf Island in der Sagazeit." *Kurz
und Gut* 4(1970):20-23, 30-32.
Heinrichs, H. M. "Mündlichkeit und Schriftlichkeit: Ein Problem
der Sagaforschung." In *Akten des V. internationalen Germanisten-
Kongresses, Cambridge 1975*, ed. Leonard Forster and Hans-Gert
Roloff, pp. 114-133. Bern: Herbert Lang, 1976.
Helgason, Jón. *Handritaspjall*. Reykjavik: Mál og menning, 1958.
————. *Jón Ólafsson frá Grunnavík*. Safn Fræðafjelagsins um Ísland
og Íslendinga 5. Copenhagen: S. L. Möller, 1926.
————. *Norrøn litteraturhistorie*. Copenhagen: Levin and Munks-
gaard, 1934.
Helle, Knut. *Norge blir en stat 1130-1319*. Handbok i Norges historie
1/3. Bergen: Universitetsforlaget, 1964.
Heller, Rolf. "Das Alter der Eyrbyggja saga im Licht der Sprach-
statistik." *Acta Philologica Scandinavica* 32(1978):53-66.
————. *Die literarische Darstellung der Frau in den Isländersagas*. Saga
2. Halle (Saale): Max Niemeyer Verlag, 1958.
————. "Studien zu Aufbau und Stil der *Vápnfirðinga saga*." *Arkiv
för nordisk filologi* 78(1963):170-189.
Hermannsdóttir, Margrét. "Fornleifarannsóknir í Herjólfsdal-Vest-
mannaeyjum 1971-1981." *Eyjaskinna: Rit Sögufélags Vestmannaeyja*
1(1982):83-127.
Herskovits, Melville J. *Man and His Works: The Science of Cultural
Anthropology*. 12th ptg. New York: Alfred A. Knopf, 1970.
Heusler, Andreas. *Das Strafrecht der Isländersagas*. Leipzig: Duncker
and Humblot, 1911.
————. *Zum isländischen Fehdewesen in der Sturlungenzeit*. Abhandlun-
gen der königlich-preussischen Akademie der Wissenschaften,
Phil.-hist. Klasse 4. Berlin: Verlag der königlichen Akademie der
Wissenschaften, in Kommission bei Georg Reimer, 1912.
Historia de antiquitate regum Norwagiensium, by Theodoricus mona-
chus. In *Monumenta Historica Norvegiae*, ed. Gustav Storm, pp. 1-
68. Christiania: A. W. Brøgger, 1880.
Hoebel, E. Adamson. "Feud: Concept, Reality, and Method in the

Study of Primitive Law." In *Essays on Modernization of Underdeveloped Societies*, ed. A. R. Desai, vol. 1, pp. 500-513. Bombay: Thacker & Co., 1971.

Hofmann, Dietrich. "Die Bedeutung mündlicher Erzählvarianten für die altisländische Sagaliteratur." In *Sjötíu ritgerðir helgaðar Jakobi Benediktssyni 20. júlí 1977*, ed. Einar G. Pétursson and Jónas Kristjánsson, pt. 1, pp. 344-358. Reykjavik: Stofnun Árna Magnússonar, 1977.

————. "Die mündliche Sagaerzählkunst aus pragmatischer Sicht." *Skandinavistik* 12(1982):12-21.

————. "Reykdoela saga und mündliche Überlieferung." *Skandinavistik* 2(1972):1-26.

Holm-Olsen, Ludwig. "Sverris saga." In *KLNM* 17, cols. 551-558.

Holtsmark, Anne. "Det nye syn på sagaene." *Nordisk tidskrift för vetenskap, konst, och industri* 35(1959):511-523.

Hrafns saga Sveinbjarnarsonar. Sturl. 1, pp. 213-228. Also in *Biskupa sögur.*

Hughes, Shaun F. D. "The Last Frontier: The Renaissance in Iceland, 1550-1750." *Parergon: Bulletin of the Australian and New Zealand Association for Medieval and Renaissance Studies* 12(1975):20-31.

————. Review of Óskar Halldórsson, *Uppruni og þema Hrafnkels sögu*. *Scandinavian Studies* 52(1980):300-308.

Hungrvaka. Ed. Guðni Jónsson. *Byskupa sögur*, vol. 1, pp. 1-31.

An Icelandic-English Dictionary. Ed. Richard Cleasby and Gudbrand Vigfusson. 2d ed., with suppl. by William A. Craigie. Oxford: Clarendon Press, 1957.

Ingvarsson, Lúðvík. *Refsingar á Íslandi á þjóðveldistímanum.* Reykjavik: Bókaútgáfa Menningarsjóðs, 1970.

Íslendingabók, by Ari Thorgilsson. Ed. Jakob Benediktsson. ÍF 1. 1968.

[*Íslendingabók*] *The Book of the Icelanders (Íslendingabók) by Ari Thorgilsson.* Ed. and trans. Halldór Hermannsson. Islandica 20. Ithaca: Cornell University Library, 1930.

Íslendinga saga. Sturl. 1, pp. 229-534.

Íslenzk orðabók. Ed. Árni Böðvarsson. 2d ed. Reykjavik: Bókaútgáfa Menningarsjóðs, 1983.

Íslenzk fornrit. Reykjavik: Hið íslenzka fornritafélag, 1933-. Abbreviated ÍF.

[*Járnsíða*] "Kong Haakon Haakonssøns islandske Lov." In *Norges gamle love* 5:13-15. *Grágás* III, pp. 467-473.

Jesch, Judith. "Some Early Christians in Landnámabók." In *The Sixth International Saga Conference 1985*, vol. 1, pp. 513-529. Copenhagen: Det arnamagnæanske Institut, 1985.

Jochens, Jenny M. "The Church and Sexuality in Medieval Iceland." *Journal of Medieval History* 6(1980):377-392.

_____. "Consent in Marriage: Old Norse Law, Life, and Literature." *Scandinavian Studies* 58(1986):142-176.

_____. "The Impact of Christianity on Sexuality and Marriage in the King's Sagas." In *The Sixth International Saga Conference 1985,* vol. 1, pp. 531-550. Copenhagen: Det arnamagnæanske Institut, 1985.

_____. "En Islande médiévale. Á la recherche de la famille nu cléaire." *Annales: Économies, Sociétés, Civilisations* (1985):95-112.

_____. "The Medieval Icelandic Heroine: Fact or Fiction?" *Viator* 17(1986):35-50.

Jóhannesson, Jón. *Gerðir Landnámabókar.* Reykjavik: Félagsprent-smiðjan, 1941.

_____. *A History of the Old Icelandic Commonwealth: Íslendinga saga.* Trans. Haraldur Bessason. University of Manitoba Icelandic Studies 2. Winnipeg: University of Manitoba Press, 1974.

_____. *Íslendinga saga.* Vol. 2: *Fyrirlestrar og ritgerðir um tímabilið 1262-1550.* Reykjavik: Almenna bókafélagið, 1958.

Jónsbók. Ed. Ólafur Halldórsson. Copenhagen, 1904. Repr. Odense: Odense Universitetsforlag, 1970.

Jónsson, Finnur. "Islands mønt, mål og vægt." In *Mål och vikt,* ed. Svend Aakjær, pp. 155-161. Nordisk kultur 30. Stockholm: Albert Bonniers förlag, 1936.

_____. *Norsk-islandske kultur- og sprogforhold i 9. og 10. årh.* Det Kgl. Danske Videnskabernes Selskab. Historisk-filologiske Meddelser 3, pt. 2. Copenhagen: A. F. Høst, 1921.

_____. "Tilnavne i den islandske oldlitteratur." *Aarbøger for nordisk oldkyndighed og historie,* 2d ser., 22(1907):161-381.

Karlsson, Gunnar. "Dyggðir og lestir í þjóðfélagi Íslendingasagna." *Tímarit Máls og menningar* 46(1985):9-19.

_____. "Frá þjóðveldi til konungsríkis." In *Saga Íslands* 2:1-54.

_____. "Goðar and Höfðingjar in Medieval Iceland." *Saga-Book of the Viking Society for Northern Research* 19(1977):358-370.

_____. "Goðar og bændur." *Saga* 10(1972):5-57.

_____. *Hvarstæða: Leiðbeiningar um bókanotkun í sagnfræði.* Reykjavik: Sagnfræðistofnun Háskóla Íslands, 1981.

_____. "Icelandic Nationalism and the Inspiration of History." In *The Roots of Nationalism: Studies in Northern Europe,* ed. Rosalind Mitchison, pp. 77-89. Edinburgh: John Donald Publishers, 1980.

_____. "Stjórnmálamaðurinn Snorri." In *Snorri: Átta alda minning,* ed. Gunnar Karlsson and Helgi Thorláksson, pp. 23-51. Reykjavik: Sögufélag, 1979.

_____. "Völd og auður á 13. öld." *Saga* 18(1980):5-30.

Karlsson, Gunnar, and Thorláksson, Helgi, eds. *Snorri: Átta alda minning.* Reykjavik: Sögufélag, 1979.

Karlsson, Stefán. " 'Bóklausir menn': A Note on Two Versions of

Guðmundar saga." In Sagnaskemmtun: Studies in Honour of Hermann Pálsson on his 65th Birthday, 26th May 1986, ed. Rudolf Simek, Jónas Kristjánsson, and Hans Bekker-Nielsen, pp. 277-286. Philologica Germanica 8. Vienna: Hermann Böhlaus Nachf., 1986.

——. "Guðmundar sögur biskups: Authorial Viewpoints and Methods." In The Sixth International Saga Conference 1985, vol. 2, pp. 983-1005. Copenhagen: Det arnamagnæanske Institut, 1985.

——. "Islandsk bogeksport til Norge i middelalderen." Maal og Minne (1979):1-17.

Katalog over de oldnorsk-islandske håndskrifter i det Store Kongelige Bibliotek og i Universitetsbiblioteket samt den Arnamagnæanske Samlings tilvækst 1894-1900. Ed. Kommissionen for det Arnamagnæanske Legat. Copenhagen: Gyldendalske Boghandel, 1900.

Kellogg, Robert. "Sex and the Vernacular in Medieval Iceland." In Proceedings of the First International Saga Conference, University of Edinburgh, 1971, ed. Peter Foote, Hermann Pálsson, and Desmond Slay, pp. 244-257. London: Viking Society for Northern Research, 1973.

Ker, W. P. Epic and Romance: Essays on Medieval Literature. London, 1896. Repr. New York: Dover, 1957.

Kern, Fritz. Kingship and Law in the Middle Ages. Trans. S. B. Chrimes. Oxford: Blackwell, 1939.

Knirk, James. Oratory in the Kings' Sagas. Oslo: Universitetsforlaget, 1981.

Koefoed-Petersen, Otto. "La royauté dans les pays scandinaves aux époques des sagas et des vikings." In La Monocratie, pt. 1, pp. 107-118. Recueils de la Société Jean Bodin pour l'Histoire Comparative des Institutions 21. Brussels: Éditions de la Librarie Encyclopédique, 1969.

Kress, Helga. "Ekki höfu vér kvennaskap: Nokkrar laustengdar athuganir um karlmennsku og kvenhatur í Njálu." In Sjötíu ritgerðir helgaðar Jakobi Benediktssyni 20. júlí 1977, ed. Einar G. Pétursson and Jónas Kristjánsson, pt. 1, pp. 293-313. Reykjavik: Stofnun Árna Magnússonar, 1977.

Kristjánsson, Jónas. "Annálar og íslendingasögur." Gripla 4(1980):295-319.

——. "Bókmenntasaga." In Saga Íslands 2:147-258.

——. "Bókmenntasaga." In Saga Íslands 3:259-350.

——. "The Literary Heritage: Eddas and Sagas." In Icelandic Sagas, Eddas, and Art, pp. 9-25. New York: Pierpont Morgan Library, 1982.

——. "The Roots of the Sagas." In Sagnaskemmtun: Studies in Honour of Hermann Pálsson on his 65th Birthday, 26th May 1986, ed. Rudolf Simek, Jónas Kristjánsson, and Hans Bekker-Nielsen, pp.

183-200. *Philologica Germanica* 8. Vienna: Hermann Böhlaus Nachf., 1986.

Kristjánsson, Klemenz Kr. "Áhrif skógarskjóls á kornþunga." *Ársrit Skógræktarfélags Íslands*, 1976, pp. 23-26.

Kristjánsson, Lúðvík. "Grænlenzki landnemaflotinn og Breiðfirzki báturinn." *Árbók hins íslenzka fornleifafélags*, 1964, pp. 20-68.

Kristni saga. Ed. Guðni Jónsson. *Íslendinga sögur*, vol. 1, *Landssaga og Landnám*. [Akureyri]: Íslendingasagnaútgáfan, 1953.

Krogh, Knud J. *Erik den Rødes Grønland*. Copenhagen: Nationalmuseet, 1967.

Kuhn, Hans. *Das alte Island*. Düsseldorf: Diederichs, 1971.

————. "Das Schenken in unserem Altertum." *Zeitschrift für deutsches Altertum und deutsche Literatur* 109(1980):181-192.

Kulturhistoriskt lexikon för nordisk medeltid. 22 vol. Malmö: Allhems förlag, 1956-1978. Abbreviated *KLNM*.

Landnámabók. Ed. Jakob Benediktsson. *ÍF* 1. 1968.

Lárusson, Björn. *The Old Icelandic Land Registers*. Lund: C. W. K. Gleerup, 1967.

————. "Valuation and Distribution of Landed Property in Iceland." *Economy and History* 4(1961):34-64.

Lárusson, Magnús Már. "Á höfuðbólum landsins." *Saga* 9(1971):40-90.

————. "Fabrica: Island." In *KLNM* 4, cols. 120-122.

————. *Fróðleiksþættir og sögubrot*. Iceland: Skuggsjá, 1967.

————. "Hreppr." In *KLNM* 7, cols. 17-22.

————. "Íslenzkar mælieiningar." *Skírnir* 132(1958):208-245.

————. "Kloster: Island." In *KLNM* 8, cols. 544-546.

————. "Odelsrett: Island." In *KLNM* 12, cols. 499-502.

————. "On the So-Called 'Armenian' Bishops." *Íslenzk fræði (Studia Islandica)* 18(1960):23-38.

————. "Prístirnið á norðurlöndum." *Skírnir* 141(1967):28-33.

Lárusson, Magnús Már, and Hamre, Lars. "Handarband; handsal: Island." In *KLNM* 6, cols. 110-114.

Lárusson, Ólafur. *Byggð og saga*. Reykjavik: Ísafoldaprentsmiðja, 1944.

————. *Grágás og lögbækurnar*. Fylgir Árbók Háskóla Íslands, 1922. Reykjavik: Prentsmiðjan Gutenberg, 1923.

————. *Lög og saga*. Reykjavik: Hlaðbúð, 1958.

————. "On Grágás—the Oldest Icelandic Code of Law." *Proceedings of the Third Viking Congress, Reykjavik, 1956. Árbók hins íslenzka fornleifafélags*, 1958, pp. 77-89.

————. "Die Popularklage der Grágás." In *Festskrift för professorn, jur. utr. dr. Otto Hjalmar Granfelt*, pp. 87-101. Helsingfors: Ab. F. Tilgmann, 1934.

Laws of Early Iceland. See [*Grágás*].
Laxdæla saga. Ed. Einar Ól. Sveinsson. ÍF 5, pp. 1-248. 1934.
Laxness, Halldór Kiljan. *Atómstöðin.* Reykjavik: Helgafell, 1948. 2d
ed., 1961. English translation: *The Atom Station.* Trans. Magnus
Magnusson. Sag Harbor, N.Y.: Second Chance Press, 1982.
——. *Íslandsklukkan.* 2d ed. Reykjavik: Helgafell, 1957.
——. *Sjálfstætt fólk.* 2 vols. Reykjavik: E. P. Briem, 1934, 1935. 2d
ed., Helgafell, 1952. English translation: *Independent People.*
Trans. J. A. Thompson. New York: Alfred A. Knopf, 1946.
LeVine, Robert A. "The Internalization of Political Values in State-
less Societies." *Human Organization* 19(1960):51-58.
Lewellen, Ted C. *Political Anthropology: An Introduction.* South Had-
ley, Mass.: Bergin & Garvey, 1983.
The Life of Gudmund the Good, Bishop of Hólar. Trans. G. Turville-
Petre and E. S. Olszewska. Coventry: Viking Society for Northern
Research, 1942.
Líndal, Sigurður. "Early Democratic Traditions in the Nordic Coun-
tries." In *Nordic Democracy: Ideas, Issues, and Institutions in Politics,
Economy, Education, Social, and Cultural Affairs of Denmark, Finland,
Iceland, Norway, and Sweden,* ed. Erik Allardt et al., pp. 15-43.
Copenhagen: Det Danske Selskab, 1981.
——."Lög og lagasetning í íslenzka þjóðveldinu." *Skírnir*
158(1984):121-158.
——."Sendiför Úlfljóts: Ásamt nokkrum athugasemdum um
landnám Ingólfs Arnarsonar." *Skírnir* 143(1969):5-26.
——."Upphaf kristni og kirkju," in *Saga Íslands* 1:227-228.
——."Utanríkisstefna Íslendinga á 13. öld og aðdragandi sátt-
málans 1262-64." *Úlfljótur* 17(1964):5-36.
Líndal, Sigurður, ed. *Saga Íslands.* 3 vols. Reykjavik: Hið íslenzka
bókmenntafélag, Sögufélagið, 1974-1978.
Lipset, Seymour M. *The First New Nation: The United States in Historical and Comparative Perspective.* New York: Basic Books, 1963.
Ljósvetninga saga. Ed. Björn Sigfússon. ÍF 10, pp. 1-106. 1940.
Lönnroth, Erik. "Government in Medieval Scandinavia." In *Gou-
vernés et gouvernants.* III: *Bas moyen âge et temps modernes (I),* pp.
453-460. Recueils de la Société Jean Bodin pour l'histoire com-
parative des institutions 24. Brussels: Éditions de la Librairie En-
cyclopédique, 1966.
Lönnroth, Lars. *European Sources of Icelandic Saga-Writing: An Essay
Based on Previous Studies.* Stockholm: Boktryckeri Aktiebolaget
Thule, 1965.
——. *Njáls Saga: A Critical Introduction.* Berkeley, Los Angeles,
and London: University of California Press, 1976.
——."Tesen om de två kulturerna. Kritiska studier i den isländ-

ska sagaskrivningens sociala förutsättningar." *Scripta Islandica* 15(1964):1-97.

McTurk, Rory."Approaches to the Structure of Eyrbyggja saga." In *Sagnaskemmtun: Studies in Honour of Hermann Pálsson*, ed. Rudolf Simek, Jónas Kristjánsson, and Hans Bekker-Nielsen, pp. 223-237. Philologica Germanica 8. Vienna: Hermann Böhlaus Nachf., 1986.

Magerøy, Hallvard. "Kvar står sagaforskningen i dag?" *Nordisk Tidskrift för vetenskap, konst och industri* 54/3(1978):164-175.

————. *Norsk-islandske problem.* Omstridde spørsmål i Nordens historie 3. Foreningene Nordens historiske publikasjoner 4. Oslo: Universitetsforlaget, 1965.

Magnússon, Sigurður A. *Northern Sphinx: Iceland and the Icelanders from the Settlement to the Present.* Montreal: McGill-Queen's University Press, 1977.

Mann, Michael. *The Sources of Social Power: 1. A history of power from the beginning to A.D. 1760.* 2d ptg. Cambridge: Cambridge University Press, 1987.

Mannfjöldi, mannafli og tekjur. Reykjavik: Framkvæmdastofnun ríkisins, 1984.

Marcus, G. J."The Norse Traffic with Iceland." *Economic History Review*, 2d ser., 9(1957):408-419.

Maurer, Konrad. *Die Entstehung des isländischen Staats und seiner Verfassung.* Munich: Christian Kaiser, 1852.

————. *Island: von seiner ersten Entdeckung bis zum Untergange des Freistaats.* Munich: Christian Kaiser, 1874.

————. *Die Quellenzeugnisse über das erste Landrecht und über die Ordnung der Bezirksverfassung des isländischen Freistaates.* Abhandlungen der königlich–bayerischen Akademie der Wissenschaften, 1. Classe. Vol. 12, pt. 1. Munich: F. Straub, 1869.

Middleton, John, and Tait, David, eds. *Tribes without Rulers: Studies in African Segmentary Systems.* London: Routledge & Kegan Paul, 1958.

Miller, William Ian. "Avoiding Legal Judgment: The Submission of Disputes to Arbitration in Medieval Iceland." *American Journal of Legal History* 28(1984):95-134.

————."Choosing the Avenger: Some Aspects of the Bloodfeud in Medieval Iceland and England." *Law and History Review* 1(1983):159-204.

————."Gift, Sale, Payment, Raid: Case Studies in the Negotiation and Classification of Exchange in Medieval Iceland." *Speculum* 61(1986):18-50.

————."Justifying Skarphéðinn: Of Pretext and Politics in the Icelandic Bloodfeud." *Scandinavian Studies* 55(1983):314-344.

Mitteis, Heinrich. *The State in the Middle Ages*. Trans. H. F. Orton. Amsterdam: North-Holland, 1975.

Moberg, Ove. "Bröderna Weibull och den isländska traditionen." *Scripta Islandica* 25(1974):8-22.

Mundal, Else. "Íslendingabók, ættar tala og konunga ævi." In *Festskrift til Ludvig Holm-Olsen på hans 70-årsdag den 9. juni 1984*, ed. Bjarne Fidjestøl et al., pp. 255-271. Ø. Ervik: Alvheim & Eide, 1984.

————."Til debatten om islendingasogene." *Maal og Minne* (1975):105-126.

Mundal, Else, ed. *Sagadebatt*. Oslo, Bergen, and Tromsø: Universitetsforlaget, 1977.

Mundt, Marina. "Pleading the Cause of Hænsa-Þórir." In *Alþjóðlegt fornsagnaþing, Reykjavík, 1973*. Reykjavik: International Association for Scandinavian Studies, 1973.

Musset, Lucien. *Les peuples scandinaves au moyen âge*. Paris: Presses Universitaires de France, 1951.

Njáls saga (Brennu-Njáls saga). Ed. Einar Ól. Sveinsson. ÍF 12. 1954.

Njarðvík, Njörður P. *Birth of a Nation: The Story of the Icelandic Commonwealth*. Trans. John Porter. Iceland Review History Series. Reykjavik: Iceland Review, 1978.

Nordal, Jóhannes, and Kristinsson, Valdimar, eds. *Iceland 1966: Handbook Published by the Central Bank of Iceland*. Reykjavik: Ísafoldarprentsmiðja, 1967.

————. *Iceland 874-1974: Handbook Published by the Central Bank of Iceland on the Occasion of the Eleventh Centenary of the Settlement of Iceland*. Reykjavik: Ísafoldarprentsmiðja, 1975.

Nordal, Sigurður. *The Historical Element in the Icelandic Family Sagas*. W. P. Ker Memorial Lecture 15. Glasgow: Jackson, Son, and Co., 1957. Translated into Norwegian as "Det historiske element i islendinge sagaene." In *Rikssamling og kristendom*, vol. 1 of *Norske historikere i utvalg*, pp. 126-143. Oslo: Universitetsforlaget, 1967.

————. *Hrafnkels saga Freysgoða: A Study*. Trans. R. George Thomas. Cardiff: University of Wales Press, 1958.

————. *Íslenzk menning*. Reykjavik: Mál og menning, 1942.

————."Sagalitteraturen." In *Litteraturhistorie*, ed. Sigurður Nordal, pp. 180-273. Nordisk Kultur 8B. Stockholm: Albert Bonniers förlag, 1953.

————."Time and Vellum." *Bulletin of the Modern Humanities Research Association* 24(1952):15-26.

Norges gamle love indtil 1387. 5 vols. Vols. 1-3, ed. R. Keyser and P. A. Munch. Vol. 4, ed. Gustav Storm. Vol. 5, ed. Gustav Storm and Ebbe Herzberg. Christiania: Chr. Gröndahl, 1846-1895.

Ogilvie, A. E. J. "The Past Climate and the Sea-Ice Record from

Iceland: Part 1: Data to A.D. 1780." *Climatic Change* 6(1984):131-152.

[*Ólafs saga Tryggvasonar*] by Oddr Snorrason of Thingeyrar. *Olav Tryggvasons saga: etter AM 310 qv.* Ed. Anne Holtsmark. Oslo: Selskapet til utgivelse av gamle norske håndskrifter, 1974.

Ólafs saga Tryggvasonar en mesta. 2 vols. Ed. Ólafur Halldórsson. Editiones Arnamagnæanæ, ser. A 1-2. Copenhagen: Munksgaard, 1958-1961.

Ólason, Vésteinn. "Bókmenntarýni Sigurðar Nordals." *Tímarit Máls og menningar* 45(1984):174-189.

————. "Frásagnarlist í fornum sögum." *Skírnir* 152(1978):166-202.

————. "Íslensk sagnalist: Erlendur lærdómur." *Tímarit Máls og menningar* 45(1984):174-189.

————. "Nokkrar athugasemdir um Eyrbyggja sögu." *Skírnir* 145(1971):5-25.

————. *Sjálfstætt fólk.* Bókmenntakver Máls og menningar. Reykjavik: Mál og menning, 1983.

Olgeirsson, Einar. *Ættasamfélag og ríkisvald í Þjóðveldi Íslendinga.* Þriðji bókaflokkur Máls og menningar 5. Reykjavik: Heimskringla, 1954.

Ölkofra þáttr. Ed. Jón Jóhannesson. ÍF 11, pp. 81-94. 1950.

Olrik, Axel. "Epische Gesetze der Volksdichtung." *Zeitschrift für deutsches Altertum und deutsche Literatur* 51(1909):1-12.

Olsen, Olaf. *Hørg, hov og kirke: Historiske og arkæologiske vikingetidsstudier.* Copenhagen: Gad, 1966.

Ong, Walter J. *Orality and Literacy: The Technologizing of the Word.* New York: Methuen, 1982.

Páls biskups saga. Biskupa sögur, vol. 1, pp. 125-148.

Pálsson, Hermann. *Tólfta öldin: Þættir um menn og málefni.* Reykjavik: Prentsmiðja Jóns Helgasonar, 1970.

Peters, Emrys L. "Some Structural Aspects of the Feud among Camel-Herding Bedouin of Cyrenaica." *Africa* 37(1967):261-282.

Pétursson, Einar G. "Kirkjulegar ástæður fyrir ritun Landnámu." In *The Sixth International Saga Conference 1985*, vol. 1, pp. 279-297. Copenhagen: Det arnamagnæanske Institut, 1985.

Phillpotts, Bertha S. *Edda and Saga.* London: Thornton Butterworth, 1931.

————. *Kindred and Clan in the Middle Ages and After: A Study in the Sociology of the Teutonic Races.* Cambridge: The University Press, 1913.

Pospísil, Leopold. *Anthropology of Law: A Comparative Theory.* New Haven: Human Relations Area File Press, 1974.

Prestssaga Guðmundar góða. Sturl. 1, pp. 116-159.

Rader, Trout. *The Economics of Feudalism.* New York: Gordon and Breach, 1971.

Rafns saga. See *Hrafns saga Sveinbjarnarsonar.*

Rafnsson, Sveinbjörn. *"Grágás* og Digesta Iustiniani." In *Sjötíu ritgerðir helgaðar Jakobi Benediktssyni 20. júlí 1977,* ed. Einar G. Pétursson and Jónas Kristjánsson, pt. 2, pp. 720-732. Reykjavik: Stofnun Árna Magnússonar, 1977.

————. *Studier i Landnámabók: Kritiska bidrag till den isländska fristatstidens historia.* Bibliotheca historica Lundensis 31. Lund: C. W. K. Gleerup, 1974.

————. "Um Kristniboðsþættina." *Gripla* 2(1977):19-31.

Saga Íslands. See Líndal, Sigurður, ed.

Sahlins, Marshall D. "Culture and Environment: The Study of Cultural Ecology." In *Horizons of Anthropology,* ed. Sol Tax and Leslie G. Freeman, pp. 215-231. 2d ed. Chicago: Aldine Publishing Company, 1977.

Samsonarson, Jón Marinó. "Var Gissur Þorvaldsson jarl yfir öllu Íslandi?" *Saga* 2(1958):326-365.

Sawyer, P. H. *Kings and Vikings: Scandinavia and Europe, A.D. 700-1100.* London: Methuen, 1982.

Schach, Paul. *Icelandic Sagas.* Boston: Twayne Publishers, 1984.

Schier, Kurt. "Einige methodische Überlegungen zum Problem von mündlicher und literarischer Tradition im Norden." In *Oral Tradition—Literary Tradition: A Symposium,* ed. Hans Bekker-Nielsen, Peter Foote, Andreas Haarder, and Hans Frede Nielsen, pp. 98-115. Odense: Odense University Press, 1977.

————. "Iceland and the Rise of Literature in 'Terra Nova.' " *Gripla* 1(1975):168-181.

————. *Sagaliteratur.* Stuttgart: L. B. Metzler, 1970.

Schmid, Karl. "The Structure of the Nobility in the Earlier Middle Ages." In *The Medieval Nobility,* ed. Timothy Reuter, pp. 37-59. Amsterdam: North-Holland, 1979.

Scovazzi, Marco. *La saga di Hrafnkell e il problema delle saghe islandesi.* Arona: Paideia, 1960.

Searle, Eleanor. "Fact and Pattern in Heroic History: Dudo of Saint-Quentin." *Viator* 15(1984):119-137.

See, Klaus von. *Altnordische Rechtswörter: Philologische Studien zur Rechtsauffassung und Rechtsgesinnung der Germanen.* Hermaea, 2d ser., 16. Tübingen: Max Niemeyer Verlag, 1964.

Seggewiss, Hermann-Josef. *Goði und Höfðingi: Die literarische Darstellung und Funktion von Gode und Häuptling in den Isländersagas.* Europäische Hochschulschriften Reihe 1. Deutsche Literatur und Germanistik 259. Frankfurt am Main: Peter Lang, 1978.

Service, Elman R. *Origins of the State and Civilization: The Process of Cultural Evolution.* New York: W. W. Norton, 1975.

————. *Primitive Social Organization: An Evolutionary Perspective.* New York: Random House, 1962.

Sigfússon, Björn. "Full goðorð og forn og heimildir frá 12. öld." *Saga* 3(1960):48-75.

_____. "Gamli sáttmáli endursvarinn 1302." In *Sjötíu ritgerðir helgaðar Jakobi Benediktssyni 20. júlí 1977*, ed. Einar G. Pétursson and Jónas Kristjánsson, pt. 1, pp. 121-137. Reykjavik: Stofnun Árna Magnússonar, 1977.

_____. "Íslendingabók." *KLNM* 7, cols. 493-495.

_____. "Millilanda-samningur Íslendinga frá Ólafi digra til Hákonar gamla." *Saga* 4(1964):87-120.

_____. *Um Íslendingabók*. Reykjavik: Víkingsprent, 1944.

Sigurðardóttir, Anna. "Islandske kvinders økonomiske retslige stilling i middelalderen." In *Kvinnans ekonomiska ställning under nordisk medeltid*, ed. Hedda Gunneng and Birgit Strand, pp. 89-104. Lindome: Kompendiet, 1981.

Simpson, John. "Guðmundr Arason: A Clerical Challenge to Icelandic Society." In "Fyrirlestrar: Alþjóðlegt fornsagnaþing, Reykjavik, 2.-8. ágúst 1973" (mimeo), vol. 2.

Skúlason, Páll. "Hugleiðingar um heimspeki og frásagnir." *Skírnir* 155(1981):6-28.

Sørensen, Preben Meulengracht. "Sagan um Ingólf og Hjörleif: Athugasemdir um söguskoðun íslendinga á seinni hluta þjóðveldisaldar." *Skírnir* 148(1974):20-40.

_____. *Saga og samfund: En indføring i oldislandsk litteratur*. Copenhagen: Berlingske forlag, 1977.

_____. *The Unmanly Man: Concepts of Sexual Defamation in Early Norse Society*. Trans. Joan Turville-Petre. The Viking Collection: Studies in Northern Civilization 1. Odense: Odense University Press, 1983.

Steblin-Kamenskij, M. I. *The Saga Mind*. Trans. Kenneth H. Ober. Odense: Odense University Press, 1973.

Stefánsson, Magnús. "Frá goðakirkju til biskupskirkju." Trans. Sigurður Líndal. In *Saga Íslands* 3:111-257.

_____. "Kirkjuvald eflist." Trans. Björn Teitsson. In *Saga Íslands* 2:55-144.

Steinnes, Asgaut. "Mål, vekt og verderekning i Noreg i mellomalderen og ei tid etter." In *Mål och vikt*, ed. Svend Aakjær, pp. 84-154. Nordisk Kultur 30. Stockholm: Albert Bonniers förlag, 1936.

Stephensen, Magnús. *Brjef til Finns Magnússonar*. Ed. Hið íslenska fræðafjelag í Kaupmannahöfn. Safn fræðafjelagsins um Ísland og Íslendinga 4. Copenhagen: S. L. Möller, 1924.

Storm, Gustav, ed. *Islandske annalar indtil 1578*. Kristiania: Udgivne for det norske historiske kildeskriftfond, 1888.

Strayer, Joseph R. "Feudalism in Western Europe." In *Lordship and Community in Medieval Europe*, ed. Fredric L. Cheyette, pp. 12-21. New York: Holt, Rinehart, and Winston, 1968.

Strömbäck, Dag. *The Conversion of Iceland: A Survey.* Trans. and annotated by Peter Foote. London: Viking Society for Northern Research, 1975.

Sturlunga saga. Ed. Jón Jóhannesson, Magnús Finnbogason, and Kristján Eldjárn. 2 vols. Reykjavik: Sturlunguútgáfan, 1946. Abbreviated *Sturl.*

Sturlunga saga. Trans. Julia McGrew and R. George Thomas. 2 vols. American Scandinavian Foundation Library of Scandinavian Literature 9-10. New York: Twayne Publishers, 1970-1974.

Sturlu saga. Sturl. 1, pp. 63-114.

Stutz, Ulrich. *Geschichte des kirchlichen Benefizialwesens von seinen Anfängen bis auf die Zeit Alexanders III.* 1895. Repr. Aalen: Scientia, 1961.

Sveinsson, Einar Ól. *The Age of the Sturlungs: Icelandic Civilization in the Thirteenth Century.* Trans. Jóhann S. Hannesson. Islandica 36. Ithaca: Cornell University Press, 1953.

————."The Icelandic Family Sagas and the Period in Which Their Authors Lived." *Acta Philologica Scandinavica* 12(1937-38):71-90.

————."Íslendingasögur." *KLNM* 7, cols. 496-513.

————."Papar." *Skírnir* 119(1945):170-203.

————. *Ritunartími íslendingasagna: Rök og rannsóknaraðferð.* Reykjavik: Hið íslenzka bókmenntafélag, 1965.

Taylor, Paul Beekman. "Wielders and Wasters of Words: Bare Lies and Garnished Truths in *Njáls saga.*" In *Sagnaskemmtun: Studies in Honour of Hermann Pálsson,* ed. Rudolf Simek, Jónas Kristjánsson, and Hans Bekker-Nielsen, pp. 287-296. Philologica Germanica 8. Vienna: Hermann Böhlaus Nachf., 1986.

Thórarinsson, Sigurður. "Sambúð lands og lýðs í ellefu aldir." In *Saga Íslands* 1:27-97.

Þórðar saga kakala. Sturl. 2, pp. 1-86.

Thórðarson, Matthías. "Bólstaður við Álftafjörð: Skýrsla um rannsókn 1931." *Ársbók hins íslenzka fornleifafélags,* 1932, pp. 1-28.

Þorgils saga ok Hafliða. Sturl. 1, pp. 12-50.

Þorgils saga skarða. Sturl. 2, pp. 104-226.

Thorgilsson, Ari. See *Íslendingabók.*

Thorkelsson, Thorkell. "Alþingi árið 955." *Skírnir* 104(1930):49-67.

Þorláks biskups saga hin elzta. Biskupa sögur, vol. 1, pp. 87-124.

Þorláks biskups saga hin yngri. Biskupa sögur, vol. 1, pp. 261-332.

Thorláksson, Helgi. "Að vita sann á sögunum." *Ný saga* 1(1987).

————."Arbeidskvinnens, särlig veverskens, økonomiske stilling på Island i middelalderen." In *Kvinnans ekonomiska ställning under nordisk medeltid,* ed. Hedda Gunneng and Birgit Strand, pp. 50-65. Lindome: Kompendiet, 1981.

————."Kaupmenn í þjónustu konungs." *Mímir* 13(1968):5-12.

————."Miðstöðvar stærstu byggða: Um forstig þéttbýlismyndunar við Hvítá á hámiðöldum með samanburði við Eyrar, Gásar og erlendar hliðstæður." *Saga* 17(1979):125-164.

_____."Rómarvald og kirkjugoðar." *Skírnir* 156(1982):51-67.

_____."Snorri Sturluson og Oddaverjar." In *Snorri: Átta alda minning*, ed. Gunnar Karlsson and Helgi Thorláksson, pp. 53-88. Reykjavik: Sögufélag, 1979.

_____."Stóttir, auður og völd á 12. og 13. öld." *Saga* 20(1982):63-113.

_____."Stórbændur gegn goðum: Hugleiðingar um goðavald, konungsvald og sjálfræðishug bænda um miðbik 13. aldar." In *Söguslóðir: Afmælisrit helgað Ólafi Hanssyni sjötugum 18. september 1979*, ed. Bergsteinn Jónsson, Einar Laxness, and Heimir Thorleifsson, pp. 227-250. Reykjavik: Sögufélag, 1979.

_____."Urbaniseringstendenser på Island i middelalderen." In *Urbaniseringsprosessen i Norden: det XVII. Nordiske historikermøte, Trondheim, 1977*. Vol. 1: *Middelaldersteder*, ed. Grethe Authén Blom, pp. 161-188. Oslo: Universitetsforlaget, 1977.

Thorsteinsson, Björn. *Enska öldin í sögu Íslendinga*. Reykjavik: Mál og menning, 1970.

_____. *Enskar heimildir um sögu Íslendinga á 15. og 16. öld*. Reykjavik: Hið íslenzka bókmenntafélag, 1969.

_____."Handel: Island." In *KLNM* 6, cols. 118-119.

_____. *Helztu sáttmálar, tilskipanir og samþykktir konunga og Íslendinga um réttindi þeirra og stöðu Íslands innan norska og dansk-norska ríkisins 1020-1551*. Reykjavik: Hið íslenzka bókmenntafélag, 1972.

_____. *Island*. Politikens Danmarks Historie. Aarhus: Politikens Forlag, 1985.

_____. *Íslenska Þjóðveldið*. Annar bókaflokkar Máls og menningar 2. Reykjavik: Heimskringla, 1953.

_____. *Íslensk miðaldasaga*. Reykjavik: Sögufélag, 1978.

_____. *Ný Íslandssaga: Þjóðveldisöld*. Reykjavik: Heimskringla, 1966.

_____."Tollr." In *KLNM* 18, cols. 452-454.

Thorsteinsson, Björn, and Líndal, Sigurður. "Lögfesting konungsvalds." In *Saga Íslands* 3:17-108.

Tomasson, Richard F. *Iceland: The First New Society*. Minneapolis: University of Minnesota Press, 1980.

Tómasson, Sverrir. "Tækileg vitni." In *Afmælisrit Björns Sigfússonar*, ed. Björn Teitsson, Björn Thorsteinsson, and Sverrir Tómasson, pp. 251-287. Reykjavik: Sögufélag, 1975.

Turner, Victor W. "An Anthropological Approach to the Icelandic Saga." In *The Translation of Culture: Essays to E. E. Evans-Pritchard*, ed. T. O. Beidelman, pp. 349-374. London: Tavistock Publications, 1971.

Ullmann, Walter. *The Individual and Society in the Middle Ages*. Baltimore: Johns Hopkins University Press, 1966.

Ulset, Tor. *Det genetiske forholdet mellom Ágrip, Historia Norwegiæ og Historia de Antiquitate Regum Norwagiensium: En analyse med utgangspunkt i oversettelsesteknikk samt en diskusjon omkring begrepet "latinisme" i samband med norrøne tekster.* Oslo: Novus, 1983.

Vápnfirðinga saga. Ed. Jón Jóhannesson. ÍF 11, *Austfirðinga sögur,* pp. 21-65. 1950.

Walter, Ernst. *Studien zur Vápnfirðinga saga.* Saga: Untersuchungen zur nordischen Literatur- und Sprachgeschichte 1. Halle (Saale): Max Niemeyer Verlag, 1956.

Weber, Gerd Wolfgang. "Siðaskipti. Das religionsgeschichtliche Modell Snorri Sturlusons in Edda und Heimskringla." In *Sagnaskemmtun: Studies in Honour of Hermann Pálsson,* ed. Rudolf Simek, Jónas Kristjánsson, and Hans Bekker-Nielsen, pp. 309-329. Philologica Germanica 8. Vienna: Hermann Böhlaus Nachf., 1986.

Weibull, Lauritz. *Historisk-kritisk metod och nordisk medeltidsforskning.* Lund: C. W. K. Gleerup, 1913.

————. *Kritiska undersökningar i Nordens historia omkring år 1000.* Copenhagen: J. L. Lybeckers Forlag, 1911.

Wieland, Darryl. "Saga, Sacrament, and Struggle: The Concept of the Person in a Modern Icelandic Community." Ph.D. dissertation, University of Rochester, 1982.

Wilde-Stockmeyer, Marlis. *Sklaverei auf Island: Untersuchungen zur rechtlich-sozialen Situation und literarischen Darstellung der Sklaven im skandinavischen Mittelalter.* Skandinavistische Arbeiten 5. Heidelberg: Carl Winter Universitätsverlag, 1978.

Wimmer, Ludvig. *De danske runemindesmærker.* 4 vols. in 6. Copenhagen: Gyldendalske boghandels forlag, 1893-1908.

Wolfram, Herwig. "The Shaping of the Early Medieval Kingdom." *Viator* 1(1970):1-20.

Wood, Ian. "Kings, Kingdoms, and Consent." In *Early Medieval Kingship,* ed. P. H. Sawyer and I. N. Wood, pp. 6-29. Leeds: School of History, University of Leeds, 1977.

Wormald, Jenny. "Bloodfeud, Kindred, and Government in Early Modern Scotland." *Past and Present* 87(1980):54-97.

Wylie, Jonathan. *The Faroe Islands: Interpretations of History.* Lexington: University Press of Kentucky, 1987.

Index

Note: Icelandic names are alphabetized under first name.